The Lost Story of the *Ocean Monarch* – reviews

'With an expert eye for detail, Hoffs resurrects the dead in "The Lost Story of the *Ocean Monarch*" to retell a ghostly tale that will haunt you long after you've stopped reading it.'

Lindsey Fitzharris, bestselling author of *The Butchering Art*

'Using the widest range of contemporary accounts, Gill Hoffs has movingly reconstructed the distressing events of this grimmest of shipwrecks, investigated the causes, and followed the lives of those left scarred both literally and metaphorically by their unimaginable ordeal. But more than that, by carefully researching the circumstances that led so many poor and destitute people to risk an uncertain voyage in the hope of a better life, she has given the story an inescapable modern resonance. An engrossing and inspirational book: perfect holiday reading for anyone embarking on a cruise this summer.'

Jean Hood, author of *Come Hell and High Water*

'A thorough and fascinating retelling of the awful events of 1848, where, often fleeing famine and poverty, thousands of ordinary British men, women and children packed themselves onto ships and immigrated to the United States. Though many ships were not suitable for the journey, and several were poorly handled, the *Ocean Monarch* was a well manned modern ship. Then why did it never arrive at its destination? In retelling this tragic tale, Gill Hoffs recalls the frequent horrors of ocean travel in the nineteenth century, and shows that even the most ordinary ventures could end in tragedy. Weaving in the stories of many who travelled on this fateful journey, and utilising many contemporary sources, *"The Lost Story of the Ocean Monarch"* uncovers the human story of one of many nineteenth century maritime disasters.'

Dr Steven Gray, University of Portsmouth, author of *Steam Power and Sea Power*

'When the *Ocean Monarch* departed from Liverpool the morning of August 24, 1848, Captain Murdock anticipated a safe voyage to Boston, the ship's home port. Gill Hoffs adroitly engages the reader with backstories of many passengers and crew.

Using eyewitness testimony from survivors and those onboard rescue ships, Hoffs tells a suspense-filled story that builds as the fire spreads and engulfs the ship. She meticulously follows passengers as they seek escape from the burning vessel. Their struggles to survive are compelling, hopeful, and heartbreaking.

In addition to rescue efforts, Hoffs explores several lines of inquiry as to the cause of the fire. Extensive back matter includes newspaper accounts of the recovery of remains and lists of the names of passenger and crew—a treasure trove for historians and genealogists.

This riveting tale vividly brings to life a long-forgotten disaster. It's one that easily rivals stories told about the *Titanic*.'

Sally M. Walker, author of *Sinking the Sultana*

Reviews for *The Lost Story of the William & Mary*

'I loved the salty air of Gill Hoffs' book. A terrific, rollicking adventure that will stay long in the memory.'

Simon Garfield, author of *Timekeepers*, editor of *A Notable Woman: The Romantic Journals of Jean Lucey Pratt*

'Gill Hoffs has woven a story that is absorbing, well researched, and reads like a good adventure novel, only it's true. If you like reading tales of the sea, I can highly recommend this book!'

Deborah Patterson, Museum Curator, *Wyannie Malone Historical Museum*, Hope Town, Abaco, Bahamas

'The story is a pure sensory smorgasbord of life and death aboard an emigrant ship, complete with a cowardly, treacherous captain and crew, who leave the emigrants to die on a sinking ship.'

Dr Cathryn Pearce, author of *Cornish Wrecking, 1700–1860*

'This is a masterfully written micro-history which uncovers an obscure, forgotten story of betrayal at sea, told in a fast-paced narrative that also illuminates the harsh realities of transatlantic migration in the Victorian era.'

Dr William Kerrigan, Cole Distinguished professor of American History at Muskingum University

Reviews for *The Sinking of RMS Tayleur*

'… a gripping new book, *The Sinking Of RMS* Tayleur by Gill Hoffs, vividly tells the story of the *Tayleur*'s demise and reveals a compelling theory behind what caused this supposedly 'perfect' ship to sink.'

Daily Mail

'Book of the Month – A well-written and thoroughly researched account of this lesser-known tragedy.'

Sea Breezes Magazine

'A fascinating, well researched account of this memorable shipwreck … Highly recommended.'

Richard Larn OBE, author of *Lloyd's Shipwreck Index of Ireland and Great Britain*

'… a rare and unusual find … heartbreaking and humbling.'

Joe Jackson, author of *Atlantic Fever*

The Lost Story of the *Ocean Monarch*

For the people who talk to cats in gardens and dogs on walks, those who rescue worms from puddles and snails from pavements, and Mrs Prime and her elderly poodles, for consistently thinking I was marvellous (when I really, really wasn't).

The Lost Story of the *Ocean Monarch*: Fire, Family & Fidelity

Gill Hoffs

First published in Great Britain in 2018 by
Pen & Sword History
An imprint of
Pen & Sword Books Ltd
Yorkshire - Philadelphia

ISBN 978 1 52673 439 6

A CIP catalogue record for this book is available from the British Library.

Printed and bound in England
By TJ International Ltd.

Pen & Sword Books Ltd incorporates the Imprints of Pen & Sword Books Archaeology, Atlas, Aviation, Battleground, Discovery, Family History, History, Maritime, Military, Naval, Politics, Railways, Select, Transport, True Crime, Fiction, Frontline Books, Leo Cooper, Praetorian Press, Seaforth Publishing, Wharncliffe and White Owl.

For a complete list of Pen & Sword titles please contact

PEN & SWORD BOOKS LIMITED
47 Church Street, Barnsley, South Yorkshire, S70 2AS, England
E-mail: enquiries@pen-and-sword.co.uk
Website: www.pen-and-sword.co.uk

or

PEN AND SWORD BOOKS
1950 Lawrence Rd, Havertown, PA 19083, USA
E-mail: Uspen-and-sword@casematepublishers.com
Website: www.penandswordbooks.com

Contents

Of all situations in which human beings can be placed in this world, the most appalling is, we think, that of being on board a crowded ship on fire at sea. There, instead of either of the two elements which are usually regarded as the natural opposites of each other, affording the means of escape, both enter into awful combination to effect the destruction of every being and every thing exposed to their influence. So it has proved in the case of the Ocean Monarch, a splendid vessel, whose name might have been given her in bitter mockery…

(*Leeds Mercury*, 2 September 1848)

Preface

The people on the ill-fated *Ocean Monarch* were a mixed bunch of the penniless and the privileged, black and white, emigrants and tourists, families and friends. Many were seeking new lives in America, some were fleeing people and places, and others were returning home to the Boston area after an absence of months or years. In the months following the deservedly negative coverage of coffin ships sailing across the Atlantic, it was reasonable for the passengers on this newly built triple decker to hope for a safe passage on such a well-regarded vessel. Unfortunately this was not to be.

It may seem as if a fire at sea should be no big deal – after all, ships are *surrounded* by water. But this was a time when life boats were scarce, inadequate, and carelessly maintained, and there certainly weren't enough provided to carry all on board a wrecked passenger ship to safety. Fire extinguishers were rudimentary and not always carried. The massive *Ocean Monarch* had none at all, and only a dozen buckets and a faltering water pump on the upper deck to fill them. When fire broke out there was little that could be done and few places to go until help arrived hours later.

All was chaos and confusion, so it is understandable that the many survivor and witness accounts reflect the disorder of the fire and the exhaustive rescue efforts. Initial reports included the opinion that all on board would be rescued, and suggested a lightning strike as the cause of the inferno. Even 170 years later, the actual source of the fire and the person responsible is still somewhat unclear, although a couple of contenders have emerged from accounts of the time and subsequent memoirs of survivors. It is clear, however, that the blame initially and currently placed on smokers in steerage is unfair and inaccurate, and I am glad to be able to lay that theory to rest. These people were not the architects of their own misfortune, they were the victims of a dreadful accident and it was the travellers in steerage who were actually most likely to perish because of this, so it seems additionally unjust to have them take the blame for it.

This was a difficult story to research and write about in many ways. This wasn't because of a scarcity of information or, as with my second book, a language barrier. It was simply an emotionally gruelling experience, involving lots of tissues and phoning relatives to tell them about breakthroughs with birth certificates and similar distractions, including dire 'jokes' from the *Varieties* columns of the press. However I took heart from the many examples of courage, decency, and kindness I uncovered in the newspapers and memoirs I read, and was particularly struck by this sentence in one article about the tragedy: 'A consolation for terrible calamities lies in the striking acts of generosity and sympathy which they occasion', (*Hampshire Advertiser*, 9 September 1848). This sentiment thankfully still holds true today.

A porthole in Warrington Museum & Art Gallery – and a kindly curator – led me to the shipwreck at the heart of my first book, *The Sinking of RMS Tayleur: The Lost Story of the 'Victorian Titanic'* (Pen & Sword, 2014, 2015). Research into contemporary wrecks drew my attention to the strange plight of the people on board a wreck in the Bahamas, and their captain's attempt at mass murder, which became *The Lost Story of the William & Mary: The Cowardice of Captain Stinson* (Pen & Sword, 2016). A search for instances where women's clothing helped or hindered them at sea brought me to the awful story of the *Ocean Monarch*, which caught fire near Llandudno in 1848.

Before I wrote my first book I wondered why on earth people would willingly venture out to sea for months on end in search of a new life or an escape from the old when there were an average of about three vessels wrecked every day in British and Irish waters alone. Why put yourself and those you loved in that position? Why endure the misery of seasickness and the villainy of (some) captains and crew in addition to the disease, vermin, vile food and thick green water you could experience on dry land? I understand their plight a bit better now, having read so many awful accounts detailing the experiences of ordinary people from the time, for all of my books.

One of the things I find so interesting about people in the nineteenth century is discovering how similar and how different our attitudes, values, and beliefs are. There are only a few generations separating us and yet also clearly so much more. Reading Victorian newspapers, diaries, letters, and books helped to give me an illusion of immediacy when researching their world as they saw it and also assisted with stripping away some of the benefits and/or hindrances of hindsight. For someone who finds modern conventions and attitudes at times completely baffling, there is a certain satisfaction and sense of revelation that comes with reading about really quite restrictive societal mores from a previous era which influence how and who we are today. This was particularly interesting when researching what would be considered acceptable behaviour during an accident as awful and prolonged as the tragedy of the *Ocean Monarch*. Even in survival situations class, gender, and colour came into play in a more obvious fashion than today, and when the aristocracy was involved with a rescue this became all the more apparent. Members of the French and Brazilian royal families who happened to be nearby and assisted with the rescue were given greater recognition and praise than, for example, the black stewardess who died in her attempt to save the lives of her fellow travellers.

I also wondered whether the high rate of infant mortality and prevalence of large families meant the parents and other adults on board the *Ocean Monarch* would be comparatively cavalier about the loss of children, although I doubted it having read of contemporary bereavements and the utter devastation these losses wrought for my previous shipwreck books. It was heartening to read of the bravery and kindness displayed towards some of the children involved with these wrecks, even from complete strangers who could perhaps have been forgiven by their peers for putting themselves first in moments of extreme danger.

Then as now, there were some roles which altered expectations for the behaviour displayed in emergencies. Captains and their crews, whether from the ship directly affected by misfortune or on vessels nearby, were expected to behave with valour, chivalry, and clear-headed compassion despite there not being emergency protocols and procedures in place, nor the ability to fully evacuate vessels if necessary. Any perceived failure in their duties provoked outrage among the general public, even if there were excellent reasons or understandable errors involved.

My admiration for those who braved the unknown for a chance at something better – or at least different – and for the people who endeavoured to keep them safe as they took such a colossal risk, was already huge. I grew up in a fishing village on the Scottish coast where storms brought salt to the panes of my bedroom window, people sometimes went to sea and didn't come back, and the RNLI were – rightly – revered. My Aunt Jean and Uncle Jim told me about the local shipwrecks and my Papa's barometer, presented to him for his heroism at sea, was an object of intrigue that caught my eye whenever I walked past it in their hall. The stories I've read while writing my trilogy of shipwreck books means my respect for all those who assist others at sea has increased enormously.

A few of the men, women, and children I've written about received recognition of their brave acts and selflessness within their lifetimes, even if this was just a brief acknowledgment in a newspaper article. A few of them even received medals and money for their acts of valour. However, some of these heroes remained anonymous or their actions were besmirched with accusations of selfishness and cowardice. This is something I hope to correct wherever possible with the publication of this book.

Almost half of the approximately 400 people on board the *Ocean Monarch* died that day. Although many bodies were recovered, the majority of these were unidentifiable by the time they came ashore. From looking at newspaper reports, church records, and my compilation of names lists, I was pleased to be able to (tentatively) identify six sets of previously anonymous remains. I hope to be able to pass this knowledge to the descendants of the people involved, and encourage anyone with questions or information relating to this tragedy to get in touch. Even so, this book is unfortunately the only memorial many of the dead will have.

As with every wreck I write about, I hope to hear from descendants of those on board and to help people to rediscover their forgotten history. It was an honour to be able to tell the stories of those involved with the tragic events of Thursday 24 August 1848. Thanks to the assistance of many generous researchers (especially Maureen Thomas), archivists, and institutions, I have been able to uncover the fate of the *Ocean Monarch* and those on board.

Their stories are lost no more.

Gill Hoffs
29 October 2017, Warrington

NB – if you are of a sensitive disposition or particularly squeamish I strongly recommend you skip pages 158–60 and page 199. Avoiding this piece of information will not stop you following the events included in this book but it might help you sleep better at night.

Chapter One

Subjects of an empire, on whose territory and treasures it is boasted the sun never sets, are doomed without a crime, to prolong a miserable existence on the carrion flesh of asses, horses, and dogs – to linger under the maddening tortures of excruciating hunger, until they become living skeletons, breathing corpses – and worse sill [*sic*] *to behold, all that were dear to them – the wives of their bosoms, the children of their affections – their gray-haired old men, and helpless aged mothers – all stricken down around them, all drinking of the same bitter cup – all victims of wasting want – all suffering agony which no language can describe – and then, when exhausted nature can no longer bear up against the overwhelming load of accumulated miseries which presses it down – strewing the roadsides with their dead bodies, to be food for dogs – lying whole days unburied, or huddled promiscuously, without shroud or coffin, into a hole in the earth – an unconsecrated grave. All this tragedy of human woe is being enacted at this moment, almost under the eye of the British minister, and still there is not a farthing proffered in his financial statement to rescue the people from such a terrible fate!*

(*Galway Vindicator, and Connaught Advertiser*,
23 February 1848)

Early August 1848, getting ready to leave

The summer of 1848 was a time of superstition and science, desperation and disease. Happy reports of a gold rush in California vied with revolutions in countries around a world which seemed less stable than ever before. England's first public lending library was opened in Warrington, near the prosperous port of Liverpool. Newspapers carried excitable discussions of experiments with electric lights, and teeth removed painlessly using ether for anaesthetic, as well as accounts of 'A reputed old witch [from Fife, Scotland, who] enjoyed the perquisite of a fish from every fisherman who desire good fortune' and a fair amount of money besides (*Coleraine Chronicle*, 27 October 1849), a bigamist being tarred and feathered, and 'a peasant woman from Watton [who] begged a piece of the gallows, to cure her son of fits' (*John O'Groats Journal*, 29 September 1848). Folk medicine would often be the only kind of remedy available to many, even with the advent of various pills and potions advertised as curing everything under the sun, and the *Bolton Chronicle* (9 December 1848) reported an example the following autumn of, 'A rustic barbarian, in a village in Dorsetshire, about a fortnight back, [who] cut the cross out of a donkey's shoulders as a remedy for the [w]hooping cough, with which his child was afflicted. The poor animal died from the effects of the mutilation.'

That year, as with the three years before, starvation paired with disease to wreak devastation. For many people edible food and clean water were an impossible dream, and the only thing keeping them from a hideous death was a meagre measure of corn, or turnip stalks gleaned from a field. A bleak winter had been followed by the nightmarish return of the potato blight in Ireland, and the resulting exodus to England (and elsewhere) placed increasing pressure on an already failing support network for the impoverished and unlucky of Great Britain and Ireland. It was a deliberately harsh environment, and one many sought to escape through suicide, penal servitude, and emigration.

This was due in part to the attitudes of the assistant secretary to HM Treasury, Somerset-born Sir Charles Trevelyan, who was in charge of dispensing relief to those affected by the famine. He wrote to his friend, the generally humane Anglo-Irish landlord Lord Monteagle, 'Every system of poor relief must contain a penal and repulsive element, in order to prevent its leading to the disorganization of society' (9 October 1846), and that the famine was 'the judgement of God' and an 'effective mechanism for reducing surplus population'.

Some in the press, then as now, stirred resentment and ill feeling with every issue, making it all the easier to deny aid to the dying. *The Times* of 26 July 1848 said:

> *The English are very well aware that Ireland is a trouble, a vexation, and an expense to this country. We must pay to feed it, and pay to keep*

> *it in order ... we do not hesitate to say that every hard-working man in this country carries a whole Irish family on his shoulders. He does not receive what he ought for his labor, and the difference goes to maintain the said Irish family which is doing nothing but sitting idle at home, basking in the sun, telling stories, going to fairs, plotting, rebelling, wishing death to the Saxon ... The Irish, whom we have admitted to free competition with the English labourer, and whom we have welcomed to all the comforts of old England, are to reward our hospitality by burning our warehouses and ships and sacking our towns.*

Other journalists sought to visit the worst affected parts of Ireland to see for themselves the truth of the matter, despite the exposure to dropsy, dysentery, diarrhoea, and typhus this would entail. Newspapers filled with columns headed 'STARVATION DEATHS' such as the *Tuam Herald* of 22 April 1848, and included such melancholy details as, '... a poor man near this town, was suffering excruciating spasms from eating a part of the putrid liver of an ass! The wretched creature having since died, his remains were laid outside the workhouse door and the guardians, not liking his company, had him interred.'

Those lucky enough to have pets boiled and ate them, or devoured them raw. Many dogs escaped such a fate and wandered in packs, growing fat from gnawing corpses and, occasionally, the not-quite dead. In the same column on recent famine deaths, the *Tuam Herald* reported that, 'A poor man was found dead on the road near Westport, on Friday; in his mouth was a tuft of some grass and some earth which he was masticating when death released him from misery. In his hat were found some shell fish.'

These kinds of deaths were so common as to cause almost no reaction in a disheartened or uncaring readership. As *The Southern Reporter and Cork Commercial Courier* would later comment, 'So accustomed are we to death by famine, that spectacles which in other lands would be regarded with horror are by us passed unheeded by.' But that didn't stop journalists from trying to get the message through to an ambivalent public and those in charge who could – and should have – made a difference. *The Dublin Evening Post* included an account of a visit to the parish of Feakle, 'I saw the children, five in number; their little arms were not thicker than the pen I write with', (8 February 1848). 'Women died in the fields and the ditches, vomiting the grass they devoured in the agonies of hunger, and maddened mothers appeased their cannibal longings on the bodies of their dead children!', reported the *Dublin Evening Packet and Correspondent* of 19 August 1848, and 'now, with a scant harvest and rotting potato crop – with cholera sweeping rapidly hitherwards from the continental cities almost desolated by that awful plague – now Ireland is to be left to her own resources…'

The year known as 'Black '47' saw many who were able to leave Ireland doing so in a panic, abandoning boggy strips of green worked for generations by the same families who may not previously have strayed more than a few miles from their places of work and worship. Many were too weak or impoverished to carry on from Liverpool to the port they had hoped to reach, and were effectively trapped in the area near the docks. The *Derbyshire Advertiser and Journal* of 2 April 1847 included part of the Report of the Health of Towns Commission,

> *Speaking of the cellars in Liverpool, Dr Duncan says, 'At night the floor of these cellars – often the bare earth – is covered with straw, and there the lodgers – all who can afford to pay a penny for the accommodation – arrange themselves as best they may, until scarcely a single available inch of space is left unoccupied. In this way as many as thirty human beings or more are sometimes packed together underground, each inhaling the poison which his neighbour generates, and presenting a picture in miniature of the Black Hole of Calcutta.'*

Some escaped the squalor of the slums and boarded floating cesspits known as 'coffin ships' and many died on the voyage or shortly after reaching Canada, America, Australia, and the Cape Colony of what is now South Africa. Another crop of surviving seed potatoes – many had been eaten out of dire necessity – was planted in the spring of '48 only to be found rotting to an inedible grey sludge that June. With precious little aid forthcoming from the British government, landlords encouraged to clear people from their land, and corn still being exported by the shipload from Irish ports, it's hardly surprising that there was an attempt at a nationalist uprising. Two were killed in what was known as the Young Irelander Rebellion of 29 July 1848, in a prolonged gunfight in Ballingarry, South Tipperary.

The unrest wasn't limited to Ireland. A few weeks later, on the night of Monday 14 August, there was a riot in the Ashton-Under-Lyne area of Manchester. For a decade, ordinary people had repeatedly petitioned to have a People's Charter which would give the working class a role in running the country. Feelings ran so high as the date approached for the presentation of the third petition to parliament that public buildings were fortified and Queen Victoria and her family were sent to the safety of the Isle of Wight. Unfortunately for one policeman on duty that night, 33-year-old James Bright, some of the so-called Chartists were armed. His murder and the subsequent manhunt for those responsible for his death added to the turmoil of the time.

When it became clear that for many 1848 would be no improvement on the previous year, thousands more followed on from the exodus of 'Black '47', though in a slightly more organised manner. Some were aided in their passage to America or Australia by thrifty landlords and benevolent charitable organisations, with the twin aims of reducing pressure on the economy in Britain and Ireland and giving the unfortunate people a fresh start elsewhere. They would pay for transport and sometimes a meagre store of provisions and a few essential items of clothing for families or parties of young men or women, to enable them to leave the country and settle abroad. It was cheaper to do that than it was to feed, clothe, and house them at home. Many, however, were in no state to travel to the Unions for a meagre portion of soup, let alone the ports, and the roads and ditches were littered with corpses. Some would-be emigrants pawned their clothes to provide for the aged relatives they were forced to leave behind, ending up naked on board the ships regardless.

Due to the British government's requirement that postage on all letters to *and from* America should be paid for in Britain and Ireland, much of the money sent home to help friends and family improve their circumstances or join the successful émigré abroad, remained in the dead letter office. But enough reached those left behind to allow reunions in many cases, as with the Hill family from Rochdale and the Taylor family of Leeds, both of whom were preparing for new lives in America with their loved ones. Nothing set these families apart from the thousands of others leaving England in the mid-nineteenth century, nothing but their unfortunate fate.

Many accounts in papers exhorted people to brave the crossing and come to America, including extracts of letters home, like this one included in the *Sheffield Independent*, 16 September 1848,

> *America is one of the finest countries in the whole world. I can go in the prairie, and see twelve miles all of a level. There is plenty of work … The Yankees like to talk about the Queen and all her family. I can go out any time and fetch a couple of rabbits for dinner, without being made to pay £5* [a vast sum of money at the time]. *There is any quantity of game – wild ducks, wild geese, pheasants, prairie chickens, and deer; there is plenty of deer. … If I were in your place, I would sell all I had and come to America. The folks here are agreeable with you. If you are travelling, and call any where, they will ask you to have something to eat. They live on the best of food; everything is so cheap, that they can live for nothing, or nearly so. We can grow tobacco, and all kinds of fruit; of walnuts, hazle-nuts* [*sic*], *I can go out and gather four or five bushels in about three hours; and grapes there are plenty, and plums. I got hazle-nuts in May off the trees; they are so plentiful, they are never gathered.*

Others warned readers not to believe everything they read, such as a workman who emigrated from Bolton that summer then struggled with his health as well as with finding work, and said, 'The people must not expect to find America as it is represented in England', (*Bolton Chronicle*, 25 November 1848), but plenty of English families like the Hills and Taylors still decided to take their chances along with the Scottish, Welsh, and Irish travellers thronging the docks.

Many people were driven to extreme measures in their quest to emigrate, and ships were checked for stowaways before departure. Some would-be emigrants were more wily than others, and the *Stamford Mercury* reported one 'who wished to get to America without paying passage-money, was found at Liverpool, the other day, on board the West Point, sewed up in a feather-bed!', (6 June 1848). Others hid in barrels or the darkest, dankest corners of the hold, only to be found too late into the journey to turn back – or as limp corpses, nibbled by rats, having perished as they sought refuge in the foulest areas of the ship. The *Kentish Gazette* of 31 October 1848 reported, 'A female was lately found suffocated in a box, on board a vessel about to sail from Liverpool to America. It is supposed she secreted herself to avoid paying the fare.' As *The Welshman* of 3 November 1848 detailed, she was 18 and 'The box was only 3 feet long and 1½ deep and when opened on board the ship to let the girl out she was found to be lifeless. It is not known who 'packed' her.'

Some even committed crimes – or confessed to them – in order to be transported abroad as punishment, or given shelter and an extremely restricted diet on one of the rotting ships permanently moored as prison hulks near the shore. The *Cork Examiner* of 28 June 1848 reported on such a case involving the Mallow Union, and was directly critical of the workhouses and unions meant to support the poorest, most unfortunate members of society, titling their article: 'GUARDIAN-MADE STARVATION BOTH CRIME-CREATING AND EXPENSIVE'.

The journalists took the moral high ground, attempting to appeal to staunchly religious and/or practical readers, saying,

> *STARVATION is not only a positive evil in itself, but it is the cause and parent of many evils. It is a belly-pincher and a man-slayer; it is likewise a crime-producer and a community-debaser. … At this Sessions, children of the tenderest years, from seven to fourteen years of age, were charged with offences for which they were liable to transportation. – A highly intelligent and respectable gentleman of the Riding, who was in attendance at the Sessions, assured us that he never witnessed a more deplorable spectacle than that presented by the dock, full of emaciated little children, with the impress of starvation upon their drawn and haggard features. These wretched children, with scarce a single exception, pleaded 'guilty'; and the Policeman who arrested seven or eight of them, swore that these miserable little creatures came to him, and declared that they had stolen the articles merely to save themselves from starvation. … starvation is the parent of crime … starvation and therefore crime, are the necessary results of the pinch-belly policy so highly cherished and resolutely enforced by the great majority of Boards of Guardians in this hapless country.*

Workhouses were generally callous, cruel places where dignity was denied upon entry, families were separated, and children were farmed out as 'apprentices' with sometimes dire consequences. They were woefully ill-equipped for the crisis years of the Famine, with the likes of Skibereen workhouse, intended for the use of 800, instead crammed with 2,500 inmates in March 1848. Around that time the 130 workhouses in Ireland housed about 250,000, and the workhouses in Scotland and England were struggling, too. Some paupers only entered these grim buildings when they knew they were dying, in hopes of a decent burial in a coffin. Demand was such, however, that those bodies which were placed in a coffin for transportation to the (often shared) grave would be slipped out upon arrival, thanks to the coffin's hinged design enabling reuse.

Staff varied from kindly but overworked, to downright brutal, with some school masters and mistresses at the schools onsite keeping their young charges in line with whips. With so much power in their hands, and so many vulnerable individuals in their care, these were roles which brought out the best or worst in people. For example, John Thomas Walter, the schoolmaster to the boys of St Luke's workhouse, London, Middlesex, was spending his summer in the House of Correction serving a sentence of three months' hard labour for 'indecently exposing his Person to some Females residing in the house of corner of Eagle Street [and] Shepherdess Walk', where the workhouse was situated (workhouse records, June 1848). This area was well known to the likes of Charles Dickens, just off the City Road, in neither the best of locations nor the worst. Perhaps the most remarkable aspect of this case was that it reached the court at all. The *Morning Advertiser* of 9 June 1848 reported that Walter was 'charged with having grossly insulted several respectable women, by repeated acts of indecent exposure' and commented that the evidence heard in court 'was totally unfit for publication' – which given the content of many newspapers of the time suggests his actions were considered truly vile even then. He was classed as 'a rogue and a vagabond', but if his victims weren't regarded as 'respectable' this case may not even have made it to the attention of the authorities.

Workhouses were initially, in principle at least, meant for the able-bodied poor. The unfortunates who entered these forbidding buildings were set to work on such thankless tasks as crushing bones for fertiliser, breaking stones, and picking oakum (unravelling tarred rope) in an effort to deter anyone seeking an easy life at the expense of others. Some entered due to disease or disability leading to a change of circumstances, such as Deptford man Thomas Nicholls, 50, who became unemployed after losing three fingers on his right hand in an accident. He was set to picking oakum with his remaining fingers until his thumb 'festered'. The process of 'thinning out' meant any inmates who did not pay their way through working in the workhouse were made to leave. As Nicholls could no longer work for his keep, he was instead given a loaf of bread and a shilling once a week and made to fend for himself. The *Kentish Mercury* of 29 January 1848 reported on his post mortem after he was found dead, '…the stomach was exceedingly contracted, so as to resemble an intestine; and being laid open the mucus coat was found [to be] completely dissolved by the gastric juice'.

Andover workhouse was another example of an abuse of power by those in charge. An official inquiry in 1846 revealed such dire neglect of basic needs like food that when inmates were set to crushing bones, they would supplement their meagre diet with the marrow. If they found 'a fresh bone, one that appeared a little moist, [they] were almost ready to fight over it, and that the man who was fortunate to get it was obliged to hide it that he might eat it when he was alone.'

As the *Cork Examiner* of 14 June 1848 said,

> *Were a death's head and cross-bones placed over the entrance gate of the workhouse, it would not more effectually keep out the miserable poor, than does its fearful reputation. It is looked upon as the threshold to the grave – the entrance to the tomb. There, old age is extinguished – manly strength is withered up – female beauty is changed in ghastliness – childhood is blighted, as a flower by a harsh wind. And when a poor creature does leave its walls, with starting bones, hollow checks* [*sic*]*, the colour of the grave, and the appetite of a wolf – his very aspect speaks a dreadful warning to his brethern* [*sic*] *in poverty; so eloquently, that any intention they may have to quit their little rooms, and enter the workhouse, is at once given up; and they prefer waiting for the merciful stroke of death, in their miserable abodes, to entering that place which they look upon with unmitigated horror. This, reader, is not in the least over-stated or over-charged. Were it necessary, we could substantiate it by a number of authorities such as would bring conviction home to the most sceptical. … Is poverty that loathsome thing, that it must be starved off the face of the earth? Is there such contagion in an empty pocket, that it extinguishes the divine essence in GOD's noblest work, and degrades man to the level – not*

> *of the brute – but of vermin?… The feeling of too many is that of hatred; the solicitude of too many is for their own selfish interests. To save one farthing, they would experimentalise as cooly* [*sic*] *on the stomachs – nay, the lives – of paupers, as an enthusiastic naturalist would upon a frog.*

Small wonder then that so many of the able poor were keen to emigrate rather than subject themselves to such horrors, although unfortunately there were plenty of other hazards in store. Some families who had survived the Great Hunger which raged through the country since 1845, like the Sullivans of Mitchelstown, County Cork, in the south and the Donnellys of Loughgall, County Armagh, in the north, were preparing to sail for Liverpool and an uncertain fate. So were a Mrs Murphy and her daughter from Killarney, though they were leaving their home for very different reasons. This pair was sneaking out of the country using an alias to join the crooked Mr Murphy in America, and the many thousands of pounds he had purloined from Killarney Savings Bank. There wouldn't be a warm welcome for any of them in Liverpool unless they could pay for lodgings and a passage elsewhere, such as on the *Ocean Monarch* for the thriving city of Boston.

Renamed in 1630 from Trimountaine to Boston after the town in Lincolnshire, England, this was one of the oldest cities in the United States. Situated on the Shawmut Peninsula, 200 miles north of New York, this prosperous port was the site of many crucial events during the American Revolution such as the infamous Boston Tea Party in 1773. Boston had previously been involved with the transportation of slaves to southern ports, but abolition was becoming an increasingly popular cause in this American city.

Many major thinkers lived in Boston and the surrounding area, including the writers Nathaniel Hawthorne, William Ellery Channing, Ralph Waldo Emerson, Henry David Thoreau, the travelling transcendentalist Margaret Fuller, and 16-year-old Louisa May Alcott. This was a forward-thinking city focused on small trade, artisanship, and crafts, where neither agriculture nor industry had flourished until the sudden influx of Irish immigrants began in 1845, changing the makeup of the population forever and turning Boston into a 'labour reservoir'. Before that, the people moving into the area from overseas were mainly German and sympathetic to the society into which they sought to integrate, idealistic intellectuals who thrived among the craftworkers and tradespeople working in this waterlocked city. Boston was a community of readers, with superb libraries and over 120 periodicals with an aggregate circulation of more than half a million copies, along with societies keen to diffuse knowledge rather than guard it.

As a sermon from Ezra S. Garnett in Boston explained in 1840,

> *Every packetship* [brings] *the thought and feeling which prevail there, to be added to our stock of ideas and sentiments. We welcome each new contribution. We read and reprint foreign literature, we copy foreign manners, we adopt the ...rules of judgment which obtain abroad. This is natural. It is foolish to complain about it. Imitation is the habit of youth; we are a young people ... Hence we shall ... for a long time ... receive from Europe a considerable part of our intellectual persuasions and our moral tastes.*

This was a healthy, humane, educated and community-minded city, but the sudden influx of thousands of immigrants who had more in common with each other than with the people already living there led to the development of a somewhat insular community within the general population. In an area as cosmopolitan as Boston, where people generally valued fun and optimism, the fear and perceived pessimism of the Irish Catholic community trapped by tolls in the inner city stood out. The usual balls, picnics, clubs and parades held by and for different nationalities did not seem to help these impoverished families to integrate or explore their new surroundings, but as anti-Catholic prejudice and violence was on the increase this was not unsurprising. Despite this bigotry, many Irish immigrants in Boston found work in factories or as domestic servants.

In America, social structures and expectations meant free individuals who worked in other people's homes did not 'serve', they 'helped'. This distinction riled some of the well-to-do who wished to have loyal and deferential servants attending to their whims and needs without requiring respect or particularly humane treatment in return, so domestic staff accustomed to the British class system were in demand. Many of those on board the *Ocean Monarch* planned to take such jobs upon their arrival on the east coast.

It wasn't just new emigrants seeking safe passage who would book berths on this magnificent American barque for her second venture from Liverpool across the Atlantic. Alexander B. Dow, 29, a farmer who had previously emigrated from Scotland with his family and settled in Ryegate, Vermont, was now seeking a cabin passage with his new bride, Jane, 19, having married her on the scenic island of Cumbrae off the west coast of Scotland on 9 August, the day after the *Ocean Monarch* entered the loading dock. They weren't the only newlyweds planning to sail the Atlantic on the *Ocean Monarch*, either. George Jones, a 28-year-old saddler from Bilston, Wolverhampton, planned to marry local woman Leodosia, 29, in the beautiful whitewashed church of St Leonard's on 15 August before taking her north to Liverpool where they would wait to board the ship.

There were also a couple of esteemed Boston gentlemen in this northern port eager for a smooth voyage home. The celebrated miniaturist Nathaniel Southworth was returning home alone having made the initial crossing with friends almost a year before. James Knowlton Fellows had also booked passage on the *Ocean Monarch*. He had recently turned 39, towards the end of his trip abroad. A quiet, abstemious, generous man, he was a watchmaker and jeweller by trade having previously tried his hand at printing and typesetting, and was looking forward to seeing his wife and three children again. Fellows had spent the last four months travelling through Ireland, England, Scotland, and 'the continent', both to see the sights and – he hoped – improve his health.

Joining them on board would be Mr Thomas Henry, a crockery merchant born in Ireland in 1816, who was returning to his new home in Mobile, Alabama. He noticed James Murdock (also spelled 'Murdoch') listed as captain in the advert for 'TRAIN'S LINE OF BOSTON PACKETS' and resolved to remain in Liverpool for an extra fourteen days in order to cross the Atlantic with him. Henry had sailed with Captain Murdock two years prior, and later said he 'much admired his conduct, both as a seaman and a gentleman', enough to delay his journey home. He booked a berth in a first class cabin, confident in the captain's capabilities with this relatively new ship.

Some vessels were disease ridden, rotten, and unseaworthy. Some ships were decent enough but badly handled, with callous or incompetent captains and dastardly crews. It was worth spending extra time and money in Liverpool, if you had it, to ensure you were in safe hands on a safe ship. The newspapers were full of accounts of ships found dismasted and drifting with nothing but a mess of birds on board, or simply not reaching port. But there was only so much a person could do to protect themselves against this kind of eventuality. The *Ocean Monarch* was a fairly new ship with a competent captain and crew, and, like so many other vessels before and after her, she would not reach port either. This enormous triple-decker would barely leave Liverpool in the first place, as Thomas Henry and his unfortunate fellow travellers would soon find out.

Chapter Two

…servants are troublesome and expensive – the usual wages being double those given in England. The 'helps,' however, have one distinguishing virtue – they are scrupulously honest, and, fortunately, have no temptation to be otherwise. Poor relations are an unknown quantity in America. Every one earns enough and to spare; so that servants are not induced to purloin from their masters to give to their friends. … The manner of the servants is much more familiar than we are accustomed to here. They chat familiarly on your family affairs with the freedom of equals; and when their business is over go out without asking leave – a most heretical departure from the ancient usage of all civilised society. … 'I have heard,' says this lady, 'more words at one soiree at Boston than would be spoken in a year at Liverpool.' Of course she has; but, then, is the comparison at all fair between this classical Boston … and dull, opaque Liverpool, of whose inhabitants a distinguished oriental traveller lately remarks, describing the impression they made on him – 'Their talk was of cotton – I only wished to fill my ears with it.'

(*Dublin Weekly Nation*, 17 June 1848)

Monday 21 to Wednesday 23 August 1848 – Liverpool, preparing to sail

While crockery merchant Thomas Henry saw the sights and waited for notice of Captain Murdock's readiness for departure, and his fellow travellers attempted to avoid the runners and rogues that plagued the waterfront, many of the would-be emigrants who were to join him on board the *Ocean Monarch* were saying farewell to their loved ones. Irish families, such as the Donnellys of County Armagh and the Sullivans of Cork, travelled hundreds of miles past bare boggy fields and uncountable corpses just to reach Liverpool – *the* port of choice for merchants and emigrants alike.

This in itself was an unpleasant and difficult journey, and often proved the final straw for the starving hordes fleeing the famine. Cattle and other livestock took priority over the huddled humans crowding the decks of the ships that plied their trade between the Irish ports, Holyhead on the Welsh island of Anglesey, and Liverpool. If shelter was to be given against the harsh winds, rain, and cold on that journey, then it was the sheep, pigs, chickens, and cattle that received the benefit of it. There were financial consequences involved if the animals were damaged or harmed by the crossing, whereas the people paid upfront so it made no odds if they were drenched, feverish, or dead on arrival. Deaths were fairly common and rarely raised an eyebrow, except among their loved ones – if any were left.

The Dows, Scottish newlyweds excited about their new life together in America, were travelling 250 miles south towards the docks, breaking their journey with friends in Manchester who reluctantly let them go, while in London 30-year-old Whiston Bristow was saying his goodbyes. Born into a successful Anglo-Italian family, he had previously worked for W. Anderson, Senior & Co., as part of the East India Company, and had booked a second class cabin passage on the *Ocean Monarch* for the trans-Atlantic leg of his journey to Cincinnati, but first he had to travel 220 miles north. He wouldn't be the only Londoner travelling in style, but he may have been the only one to travel under his own name.

It is impossible to do more than estimate how many people came in and out of Liverpool as migrants seeking to move elsewhere or people in a state of destitution. From weekly reports from the *Manchester Guardian*, however, it seems over a quarter of a million Irish people arrived in Liverpool in 1848, and perhaps 94,000 of them were paupers. The London 'family' currently plotting an escape abroad via Liverpool were no paupers, but they had their own problems nevertheless.

The previous Thursday, James Smith Bacon, the workhouse master of St Luke's, London, had begun the week's leave he had agreed with the workhouse board at the end of July. He claimed he would be visiting Bangor, Wales, for his health, while his wife Emmeline and their five children stayed behind. James and Emmeline married while she was pregnant with their eldest daughter, also called Emmeline, who was now 16. He had an appetite for adventure and, six years prior, had travelled round America in pursuit of a vestry clerk who had stolen 3,628*l.* from workhouse funds, and sometimes disguised himself with a black wig and whiskers. Bacon succeeded despite such impediments and returned home with some of the money, much of it having already been spent by the fraudster and his family on extravagances and travel. This time, however, the 38-year-old was seeking something altogether different: a new life with new people abroad.

When John Thomas Walter, the schoolmaster at the workhouse, had been imprisoned for three months in June, his extremely beautiful wife, Mary Anne, was left to raise their two children herself while also working as schoolmistress. Their son, John, was almost 13, and of an age where he could almost fend for himself as an apprentice or worker if he had to leave school, but their daughter was only 9. It is unlikely that her father confined his sexually predatory behaviour to just the 'respectable women' who raised the complaints that led to his imprisonment. With Walter due for release in a few weeks' time, Bacon put together a plan with Mary Anne. Sadly, this would end in disaster.

On Saturday, Bacon arrived in Liverpool instead of Bangor, Wales. He took a room at the St George's Inn & Eagle Hotel on Fenwick Street then supposedly proceeded to Bangor the following day, saying he would return on Wednesday and asking James Giddings, the 'Boots' of the inn to post a letter to Mary Anne for him. Giddings, who was used to running errands for the inn's guests, remembered him well. Bacon returned a day earlier than planned and, while many of the steerage passengers trudged aboard the enormous *Ocean Monarch*, taking care not to slip on the wet stone and the wooden gangway, he spoke with the captain.

Captain Murdock later told Bacon's brothers-in-law that a man giving his name as James Andrews 'engaged a passage to America, for himself, his wife, and child for the sum of forty eight pounds as first cabin passengers'. The ship was originally advertised as sailing the previous Sunday but as bad weather had already delayed their departure, and £48 was a considerable amount of money, the captain was amenable to delaying the ship a further twenty-four hours. 'Andrews' aka Bacon booked their passage, 'subject to the arrival of his wife' and said he would 'send a telegraph dispatch to Manchester for her and that he expected her in Liverpool by 2 o'clock on Wednesday'.

Bacon then visited the Electric Telegraph Company's Office. His message to London, not Manchester, read:

Ship sails on Wednesday afternoon, – you must leave by ¼ past 6 train on Wednesday morning.
Signed, James Andrews.
London.
Mrs Walters,
Number 5 Upper Fountain Place
City Road.

His message sent, he returned to the inn on Fenwick Street with luggage described by the 'Boots' as 'a common box, painted red, the hinges on the top were about six inches from the back', ready to spend his last night in Liverpool.

******

That Tuesday the *Ocean Monarch*, a regular sight in Liverpool's Waterloo Dock since her launch into the Atlantic the previous year, dwarfed many of the American vessels moored beside her. American ships were generally larger than British ones but at 1,300 tons burthen she was one of the largest ships to come out of Boston, and, at little more than a year old, also one of the more glamorous.

Her builder, Donald McKay, was developing a reputation as one of the foremost shipbuilders in America. Born in Nova Scotia and, as his name suggested, a descendant of Scottish emigrants himself, he had a gift for shipbuilding and had skipped school as a child in order to build a fishing boat with his brother Lauchlan. The *Ocean Monarch* was his tenth ship and launched in July 1847 from his East Boston shipyard at the foot of Border Street. According to the *Boston Post* of 14 June 1847,

> *The Ocean Monarch, the object of universal admiration, beautiful as the dream of a mermaid, was also decked with flags and streamers. From her bowsprit end waved the American jack, at her fore the British red – the owners private signal (a red flag with a white diamond in the centre). All East* [B]*oston, and thousands from the city, assembled in and around Mr McKay's shipyard, to witness the advent of the Ocean Monarch into the deep and restless blue.*

The year before that, he had built the largest sailing ship in the world. This, the 1,400 ton *New World*, was now moored nearby and being made ready by First Mate Bragdon's friend, sailor Frederick Jerome. Both vessels were easily recognisable as members of the Train line by the large black 'T' in their fore top sails and renowned for their swift passages across the Atlantic.

Captain James Murdock, currently waiting out the weather on board the *Ocean Monarch*, was the ideal choice to command such a prestigious vessel. The heavyset 41-year-old, born in Cuba to a French mother and American father, had attended Phillips Exeter Academy with his brother before working his way up to captain. He had a reputation for competency and capability from his time in charge of the *Joshua Bates*, another well regarded ship from McKay though less than half the size of the vessel now waiting for the 'Andrews' family to arrive at the docks. Upon leaving Liverpool he could reasonably expect to reach the ship's home port of Boston in perhaps twenty-four days, depending on the winds they encountered on the way. It would be an enormous culture shock to many of the families on board.

Due in part to tolls hemming people into the area near the docks, which ensured the poorer passengers – like the famine Irish – could not leave for new lives elsewhere, Boston had 37,000 Irish immigrants living there in 1847. As the *Freeman's Journal* commented on 27 September 1847, Boston was 'the most Irish of any city in the United States, and particularly abounding in Cork and Kerry settlers'. A third of the city's population had come over from the Emerald Isle only to be effectively confined to an area known as Ward 8.

This previously prosperous area, now abandoned by those who could afford to move elsewhere, was full of elegant houses of beautiful design, now subdivided into verminous and mouldy tenements with rickety wooden additions tacked on to enable even more families and friends (and complete strangers) to be crammed in. Many who reached the shores of America were weak, ill, and unclothed, and had only the vaguest notion of what to expect in this alien environment.

In an effort to avoid being totally overwhelmed by the diseased and dying, a law was passed in Boston that year forcing captains of immigrant ships to post a bond of $2,000 for every ill passenger they landed. Common diseases such as cholera, dysentery, and typhus spread easily in the cramped confines of steerage, where captains rarely ventured and passengers squelched through their waste as it lay ankle-deep on the floor. This legislation meant that some ships had to then sail north to Quebec, Nova Scotia, and Halifax, with more passengers – and crew – sickening and dying as a result. The docks in many cities on both sides of the Atlantic were often busy workplaces, not usually picturesque areas by any means, and the filth and crime to be found there meant they were not generally places to visit for fun.

In stark contrast, the visitors' handbook, *Pictorial Liverpool* (1848), stated that 'The chief objects of attraction in Liverpool are, decidedly, the spacious Docks, that border the river line.' This beautiful albeit smoky city spread along the banks of the River Mersey as it reached the sea in a broad brown stretch of water, and boasted thirty-six miles of docks and mooring. The guide continued,

> *On the outside of the western wall is one of the longest marine parades in the kingdom; it is 750 yards in length, and eleven in breadth, having a parapet to prevent accidents. The view from it is very fine, the Cheshire woods are seen to the southward in the distance, and to the northward the Irish channel, Bootle Bay and Crosby on the Lancashire coast, and the Rock Perch Lighthouse and Fort; the eye takes in the whole line of the Cheshire coast, including the New Brighton, Egremont, Seacombe, Woodside, Birkenhead, Tranmere, Rock, New, and Eastham, Ferries. This view is extremely interesting. At high water the parade is lined with spectators.*

The view proved so interesting that 9-year-old Andrew Tait, who had been waiting to board the *Ocean Monarch* with his family decided to leave the docks and go exploring instead. Andrew was meant to be emigrating with his parents, two brothers, and little sister in an effort to escape the famine and cholera then raging in Dalbeattie, Scotland. Although this family were no doubt worried about their adventurous son, and presumably annoyed to miss boarding their ship, it would prove a relief in the long run.

The self-appointed 'chaperon' of the visitors' handbook went on to say of Waterloo Dock,

> *American liners may generally be found here in considerable numbers. The stranger is always welcome to inspect these beautiful vessels without hindrance, those in charge or authority on board being civil and attentive, and giving every information to inquirers. The beautiful woods, the costly fittings, the*

> *cleanliness of the linen, and the air of luxury and comfort prevalent in all these vessels, cannot fail to impress upon the mind of the visitor, that a sea voyage in one of them, must be deprived of some part of its horrors.*

One stranger in particular had done more than inspect the *Ocean Monarch*, he was hiding in it. Stowaways were very common, and holds were routinely inspected with lanterns and sharp-tipped sticks, but this was no ordinary stowaway. This man was wanted for murder.

A Chartist riot in Ashton-Under-Lyne the week before had ended with the shooting of Police Constable James Bright. One of the men involved, wheelwright Joseph Ratcliffe, knew his older brother, James, was due to sail on the *Ocean Monarch* on 22 August. He duly made his way to Liverpool and sneaked on board, leaving his wife in Manchester. Unfortunately for him, the ship's departure was delayed – and the police harboured strong suspicions that he and the other suspects had hidden themselves among the ships currently moored at the docks. Posters bearing his description were attached to placards round the docks and someone tipped off the police about where Ratcliffe and his fellow suspects might be. A search ensued as the rain lashed down and a westerly wind gusted through the masts bristling between the warehouses and storage sheds crowding round the port.

As Matthew Maiden, police inspector, later recounted in court, 'in consequence of information I received I went to examine some vessels which were detained at Liverpool in consequence of the unfavourable state of the weather' (*Manchester Courier and Lancashire General Advertiser*, 23 September 1848). When Ratcliffe saw the little boat pulling alongside the great ship with the inspector and one of the Liverpool officers on it he sneaked into one of the darkest corners of the ship and hid among the cargo. The men began a systematic search of the vessel and eventually entered the hold, where Inspector Maiden 'saw a man concealed among the timber; he was nearly covered with coal and hay'. The lamps the searchers carried had illuminated more than just the cargo. It was common for working men's footwear to be studded with hobnails, and these proved to be Ratcliffe's undoing. 'I saw his shoes, the nails were bright; I said, what are you doing there? I said, come out; he did so, with a little assistance.'

Ratcliffe initially claimed to be called 'Jones' and to know nothing of Ashton-Under-Lyne, but upon further questioning – and the production of his brother from his quarters above – his identity became clear. He was removed from the *Ocean Monarch* and his brother James was once again left to listen to the rain and prepare for the perilous journey alone.

*****

The *Ocean Monarch* was to carry goods worth upwards of £20,000 (equivalent to almost £3 million today) as well as about 400 people and some livestock to supplement the usual menu of dried or otherwise preserved foodstuffs. The hold was packed with 96 tons of salt, 220 crates of earthenware stuffed with straw to minimise damage from movement in heavy seas, about 600 tons of iron and 'dead weight', and 200 bales and cases of fine goods which included items purchased by Ralph Waldo Emerson. The renowned American author had returned home from Liverpool the previous month having toured Scotland, England, and Ireland. His friend, Thoreau, reminded him in a letter of Emerson's son's desire for a rocking horse so one was duly bought in London for 4-year-old Edward and packed with two busts and a figure into the *Ocean Monarch*'s hold along with some of Emerson's books.

The last of the cargo was stored below decks while the rain lashed down, chilling the dock workers and crew as well as the cows, sheep, and pigs currently penned above, pattering on the wooden deck and cabin skylights as hundreds of emigrants settled into their berths below. It had been wet and windy for the last day or so, typical for Liverpool, or so the American jeweller James K. Fellows believed from his time there. Some of the crew recognised old shipmates from previous voyages or excursions to the inns that often crowded around dock areas, and First Mate Jotham Bragdon was pleased to see the well regarded Fred Jerome on a nearby American packet, the *New World*.

Jerome, originally from Portsmouth on the south coast of England, had worked on ships for ten years as a merchant sailor, having swum ashore from a naval schooner after realising a naval apprenticeship wasn't for him. He was now based out of America where he attracted attention two years prior for his heroic rescue of the passengers and his fellow crewmen on the *Henry Gray*. This ship had been bound for the busy port of New York when it ran aground at Barnegat, New Jersey, and despite the awful weather and cold water Jerome managed to swim for shore with a rope around his waist then rescue all on board. If someone was in peril, they could count on him for help.

Jerome was an example of what was considered a successful emigrant, someone who had settled in his new home and was regularly employed in a job he enjoyed while also managing to contribute to society. Although there were obvious issues with paupers being shipped abroad with poor health and no clothes, provisions, or idea of what to do when they got there, many immigrants were welcomed. As the *Dublin Weekly Nation* put it on 17 June 1848,

> *The Americans know well the value of this sinew, muscle, and brain, that we export so recklessly. One of their eminent men, noticing the arrival of 6,000 emigrants in the first three days of one week, says this is just equal to an increase of six millions of dollars in the wealth of the nation; and affirms that it is questionable whether the great works of internal improvement could have been carried on without this addition to the muscular strength of the country.*

In an attempt to avoid a repeat of the horrors of the coffin ships of 'Black '47', the American Passenger Act of 1848 had recently been passed. This was an attempt to 'legislate against the recurrence of the evils complained of during the past year' (HC Deb 11 February 1848, Vol 96, cc536–41), including a lack of food, water, and space below deck, and a mortality rate of approximately seventeen per cent. Unfortunately for prospective passengers, this decrease in the number of fares paid per vessel meant the price of a passage went up.

When Bacon booked his 'wife' and 'daughter' a first class cabin passage for £48 he actually had a bargain. Fares for the *Ocean Monarch*'s most luxurious and comfortable accommodation were advertised at £20 per person, and a child's ticket would likely have been half that, meaning he saved £2. Second class tickets went for £12 each, with the profits going straight to the captain's own pocket, a state room cost £5, the first deck of steerage was £4 a person, and the cheapest berths were £3 10s. for the second deck of steerage, closest to the stinking bilge water in the hold and furthest from the fresh air of the top deck.

By choosing an American ship like the *Ocean Monarch*, the passengers were more likely to arrive at their destination alive and perhaps even well. Under American law each child counted as a 'full' passenger with the same space allotted to them as an adult and more rations than they could expect on a British or Irish ship. British law instead classified anyone under 14 years old as entitled to only half an adult passenger's space and provisions, which were meagre enough to begin with. If you were choosing to make the hazardous journey across the Atlantic to America, this was the ship you would want to sail with, and many of the passengers were excited about the weeks ahead.

The steerage passengers clattered about below deck in their hobnailed boots, those with bare feet being careful to avoid being trampled, finding their berths along the sides of the hull. Each bunk was about 6ft square and divided into four, allowing each adult a strip 18-20 inches wide. People travelling alone or in pairs usually came to know their bunkmates well during a voyage. Often people would fall ill with something worse than seasickness, which, for all its unpleasantness, wasn't catching, although it could kill through dehydration and general weakness leaving them susceptible to other diseases.

Many ships sailed without a ship's surgeon on board but the *Ocean Monarch* had offered free cabin passage to Boston for the right man, and William Ellis, MRCS, from Belfast in the north of Ireland, had been engaged for the journey. Passengers were supposedly inspected before boarding by medical officers, who were meant to examine them for signs of illness such as rashes, pustules, and fevers, but in such a busy port as Liverpool a quick glance at their tongues and perhaps a query as to whether they considered themselves well was often deemed quite sufficient and doomed many passengers and crewmen to burial at sea.

Dysentery, cholera, and typhus spread easily in the confines of a ship, sometimes killing off dozens of travellers in a single voyage, and leading despairing doctors to order the chamber pots and slop buckets used below deck to be gathered up and flung overboard in an attempt to prevent further fatalities. Some of the more callous crewmen on these unlucky ships would hose down passengers with cold seawater with little or no warning, and no easy way of drying their clothes – or anything to keep them warm while they waited for their shirts and skirts to be donned again. Surgeon Ellis would be available in case any of the pregnant passengers on board the *Ocean Monarch* went into labour, or the usual seasickness and malaise experienced when first going to sea gave way to something more sinister.

As letters home to relatives often reported, food on ships was frequently an issue, too. Each adult passenger was legally entitled to 7lb per week of bread, rice, oatmeal, flour, rice, or ship's biscuits. These were hard as brick and required breaking into chunks then soaked until they turned to mush, and boiled or baked again till the maggots and weevils writhing within them had cooked. There was an expectation that passengers would bring their own provisions to supplement this stingy allotment of rations, including spices and sauces to alleviate the bland food and render it more palatable, especially as the 'fresh' water carried in barrels and tanks grew ever less potable the longer they were at sea. While cabin passengers would receive larger rations and a better quality and range of food, and transport their own favourites too, this was often beyond the means of steerage passengers. Marmalade and cayenne pepper were recommended for those suffering with seasickness or keen to stave the first queasy feelings of nausea off.

The *Ocean Monarch* was run by the well regarded Enoch Train & Co., operating as the White Diamond Line. Train's main competition was Samuel Cunard, who prioritised the wellbeing of everyone who used his ships and was renowned for safety and the quality of the food they served. Cunard ships kept live animals on board to ensure a source of fresh milk and meat was available to supplement the dried and bottled provisions common at sea. This helped his customers and crew avoid the awful discomfort of malnourishment, and aided young children who were particularly vulnerable on these journeys.

This ship was a huge triple-decker, 178ft long, and 40ft wide with a depth of 26ft, which was registered as 1,300 tons. Many British ships of the time were a fraction of that, averaging approximately 500 tons burthen. Consequently there was more than just a single cow on board, and passengers noticed cows, sheep, and pigs in pens on the upper deck, near the paddle-box. The sweet smell of hay would perhaps staunch the homesickness felt by many of the passengers who were unused to the dank, salty aroma of the sea, and helped settle the animals after the upset of being hoisted aboard.

It was common for rural families – and sometimes city-based people, too – to share their home with farm animals if they could afford them, as well as the usual cats and dogs kept to keep down vermin. Pigs would sometimes vie with carriages for space on the streets of busy cities, their droppings collected by urchins and sold for fertiliser or fuel, and cows grazed on common areas of grass while washing dried on the bushes around them, guarded by their owners. Thirty years prior the *Northampton Mercury* of 8 February 1817 gave sensible advice on how to get the best out of your cow, saying,

> *Cows on board a ship are always curried and brushed like a horse, which is found to contribute much to their health and good condition. In Ireland, too, the cottager's cow is housed of a night, which is highly beneficial, and keeps them longer in milk – besides their yielding a larger quantity.*

So although the animals on deck were in completely unnatural surroundings they could look forward to plentiful attention before they were slaughtered for meat and butchered for the benefit of the passengers and crew.

*****

Back in London, Mary Anne Walter had received Bacon's letter. She approached his wife, the unsuspecting Emmeline, and applied to the matron for a leave of absence. Mary Anne claimed her mother was dying in Mansfield, near Nottingham – though nothing could be further from the truth. Permission was granted for this unexpected time away from her duties as schoolmistress, and she readied herself and her daughter for an early start in the morning. Meanwhile she told John, her son, that she had been 'advised [a] change of air and she determined to visit some relatives in New York America'. The 12-year-old asked her for a book she had won as a prize when at school herself in Miss Woods's Seminary in Mansfield, called *Catalogue of Books and Fancy Articles.* His thirteenth birthday was less than two weeks away. She gave him this treasured possession and on Wednesday at 6.15 am she and Mary left London on the train for Liverpool.

Bacon met them both in the beautiful environs of Lime Street Station, having wisely continued with his subterfuge at the inn. He lied about his plans when asking the gossipy 'Boots' to hail him a cab as he was 'going by rail to London', clearly aware that there would be some kind of investigation into his continued absence from the workhouse at some point. Months spent as a manhunter himself while on the trail of the thieving clerk had given Bacon the experience he needed to help him buy some time and make his escape to America. In his pocket, ironically, he carried a warrant offering a reward for 'the apprehension of a man who had deserted his wife' (*Bristol Mercury*, 30 September 1848).

Afterwards, the nosy dogsbody talked to the cab driver who told him '[Bacon] took up a lady and child at the station, also a great deal of luggage, and that he conveyed the Gentleman with the lady and child on board the *Ocean Monarch*.' The threesome known as the 'Andrews family' were the last to venture onto the ship in Liverpool, joining almost 400 other travellers that afternoon as the rain continued to pelt down around them. In the evening Bacon played whist with another cabin passenger, George Gregg of Salem, Massachusetts, and prepared himself for the start of a new adventure, while the livestock swayed in their pens and munched their feed. Tomorrow it would all begin. Tomorrow they would be off.

*****

Among the people looking forward to the ship setting sail was 42-year-old Nathaniel Southworth. This gifted Boston artist, born in Scituate in 1806, was respected for his beautifully rendered miniature portraits and liked for his quiet and amiable personality. Southworth was homeward bound with almost a year's work having studied in France, Italy, and England with the artists Joseph and Sarah Fisher Ames since late 1847. His father had been a sea captain, drowning near New Orleans when Nathaniel was 13, so it made sense for him to choose as safe a ship as possible for his return home, especially since some of his artist friends had recently escaped wrecks themselves.

As a wooden ship surrounded by a forest of masts and rigging, stuffed with barrels of spirits and other combustibles or loaded with coals, and lit below decks by lamps and candles, the *Ocean Monarch* was still a risky place to be.

The visitors' handbook, *Pictorial Liverpool* (1848), warned, 'All lights or fires are interdicted [forbidden] in the docks, and penalties are enforced most rigorously for any infringment [*sic*] of this rule.' Liverpool was an exceedingly popular port for emigrants and merchants, but many sailors grew to dislike it due to rules prohibiting them from cooking or warming through their food while docked, or even seeing their way to their berth. Spending time and money on land quickly whittled away their wages, as did the numerous rogues that preyed on anyone not as wily – or violent – as they were.

Naked flames were, in theory, strictly forbidden after a costly warehouse blaze at the docks many years prior, but in practice these rules were impractical, difficult to enforce, and regularly broken, including on the *Ocean Monarch*. According to the *Chester Chronicle* of 8 September 1848, at least three workmen in the lower hold of the ship had used two or three naked candles at a time, held on candle sticks against stanchions, and admitted as such at a quarter meeting of the Dock Labour Association on 31 August in the Portico-room, Newington.

Captain Murdock lectured the passengers and crew repeatedly on the importance of safety, uttering dire warnings of tragedy and fire. Smoking was restricted to the upper deck or the shelter of the smoking room there, matches and fires were banned totally below decks, and First Mate Bragdon took the time to talk to people in every area of the ship, checking they were settling in alright and understood that if they were caught with a naked flame or a pipe below deck they would have their water stopped for the day or worse. It was raining heavily and the ship itself was surrounded by thousands of tons of water so to many of the passengers he and the captain would have seemed overly cautious – but they were right to be wary.

The press was full of reports of shipwrecks – at the time there were an average of two or three vessels lost daily in British and Irish waters alone – and among the usual storms and collisions were also accounts of fires consuming ships with many dying as a result. Just the month before, it was reported that a ship, the *General William Nott*, was a total loss from fire. 'The fire had been burning several hours [when rescuers arrived]. The crew were found clinging to the wreck in momentary expectation of death, the boats being damaged, and all escape cut off, when they were rescued; shortly after they were taken off, their vessel blew up with a terrific explosion', (*Belfast Protestant Journal*, 8 July 1848). The crew were then landed at Liverpool and quite possibly mingled with the crew of the *Ocean Monarch* among the inns and hostelries around the docks when the ship arrived from Boston on 28 July.

Even if there had been no smokers on board and only lamps used below deck rather than candles, the *Ocean Monarch* was still at risk of fire because along with fancy goods and paintings it also carried coal, the dark dust of which would still be covering the clothes of the Chartist now locked up in the nearby Bridewell.

One ship, the barque *Henry*, of London, was on its way to Bombay with a cargo of coal when this caught fire, as sometimes happened. Being at sea and unable to reach the lowest level of the coal, where the blaze raged, the men 'worked day and night turning over the coals [to cool them and prevent the upper layers catching, too] but they were unable to withstand the sulphurous vapour for any lengthened time. Some hundreds of tons of water were thrown on to the cargo; the pumps being at work the whole time.' On their arrival at the Cape of Good Hope, they discovered that most of their cargo of coal had been consumed and the bottom of the vessel was 'nearly burned through' (*Morning Advertiser*, 2 February 1848). If their pumps had clogged or failed, or more coals had caught light, all would likely have been lost.

Captain Murdock did his best, checking for fire risks and even removing several of the passengers' pipes when they continued to smoke below deck regardless. But he was only one man, tasked with the care of hundreds, many of whom simply would not listen. As the *Westmorland Gazette* of 26 August 1848 said in their reports of the Chartist removed from the hold, 'The police, probably, did this fellow a friendly office in detecting him, for he escaped the melancholy fate that befel [*sic*] many better men than himself…' Captain Murdock's best would, unfortunately, not prove good enough.

Chapter Three

It was Thursday morning, at four o'clock (not Friday, of bad omen, as thought by sailors), that we were taken in tow by a steam-tug and dragged twenty miles, against wind and tide, down the river and into the English Channel [*sic*], *leaving us to continue our voyage alone, at eight o'clock, and giving us hearty cheers at parting. All were full of hope and satisfaction, now that the ship was so far on her course, with the prospect of a speedy voyage to the port of Boston. The passengers gazed upon the lovely scenery at the right and left of the river, and the beautiful features of the land which we were leaving. Behind us lay the city of Liverpool, half-hidden in the mist; the red-painted buoys, which pointed out the channel, and light-houses on the chalky bluffs; at a distance were seen the farm-houses and fine, cultivated lands. Thus all was excitement…*

(James K. Fellows, cabin passenger)

Leaving Liverpool, morning of 24 August 1848

Many vessels had been waiting for the tide to be right for leaving port. As the men of the *Ocean Monarch* heaved sodden ropes from the edge of the dock, amusing the passengers awake for the occasion, the steam boat puffed its way through the dock gates. The people crowding the deck and waving goodbye with hats and handkerchiefs stood high above the water lapping at the roman numerals carved into the grey stone wall of the dock. There was a party atmosphere aided by the pennants 'gaily fluttering' in the forest of masts around them. As the visitors' guide, 'Pictorial Liverpool' (1848), said,

In some of the docks may be observed small strongly built sloops painted white, with a green stripe, having generally a number flying at the mast head, or painted on the sails. These are the Pilot Boats belonging to the

> *port, which buffet through many a 'fearful night, and encounter many a storm.' There are twelve of these tight little vessels, manned by crews of brave, intelligent and hardy fellows, who 'take turn and turn about' in the channel, to conduct either in or out the various vessels frequenting the port. As soon as a pilot is taken on board the master has no longer control over his ship, the pilot being responsible for her safety.*

Clouds of smoke swirled away in the fresh breeze as the pilot boat guided the mighty *Ocean Monarch* into the muddy brown river. This would have been a thrilling novelty to many of the passengers, some of whom would only have seen the city from land. To the likes of Charles Thompson, a 32-year-old mariner from Liverpool travelling with his wife and niece, the only thrill would have been in knowing this was probably the last time he would see his workplace and home, whereas his fellow Liverpudlian, John Coombes, would have seen a completely different view of his home and perhaps craned his neck hoping for a view of his father's shoe shop nearby.

There was a chill in the air, the temperature being noticeably lower as they moved away from the city, and one passenger was feeling decidedly fragile in his cabin. Henry Powell, 26, a merchant who gave his address as 52 Portman-place, Maida-hill, London, later told an inquiry of his 'delicate state of health' and said he had 'long been an invalid'. He wore his thickest, heaviest boots in an effort to protect his feet from the damp of the deck and keep warm.

As the city's windmills and warehouses grew smaller, and gulls swooped and squawked beside the ships taking advantage of the tide, Powell couldn't help but overhear the other passengers chattering as they settled into their temporary home, and their interactions with the crew. There were some notoriously contemptible characters to be found at sea, as well as charmers whose civility disappeared as soon as land was out of sight. The brutality of some captains and crew was legendary and to be feared, so the kindness and courtesy generally displayed on the *Ocean Monarch* was a relief. Powell was particularly impressed by the generosity of First Mate Jotham Bragdon.

> [His] *Kind and gentlemanly conduct won the esteem of every one for the few days we were on board the vessel. When it was found, after we had sailed, that many of the steerage passengers had come on board without*

> *providing themselves with provisions, he immediately distributed bags of biscuits amongst them, and had a word of comfort and pity for all the poor creatures. Although the law compels vessels to take out a certain quantity of bread for the steerage passengers, and there may not appear to be any merit in his doing this, I certainly took particular notice of his sympathizing with them in their poor and destitute condition. It was his manner, not the act.*

The role of the first mate was a difficult one. He was, for many, the face of discipline on a ship. An extension of the captain, an intermediary between him and the passengers and crew, and sometimes a sounding board, too. He would sometimes work his way up to being captain of his own vessel, or step into the role with little or no notice if the captain fell ill, died, or was otherwise incapacitated while their ship was at sea. For some men, this power brought out the worst in them. With 35-year-old Jotham Bragdon it is clear he took his position as a guardian of the vulnerable extremely seriously, and that if he was able to do someone a good turn, he did. It may have been Captain Murdock's name on the adverts for the *Ocean Monarch*, but it was Bragdon who made the passengers feel safe, comfortable, cared for, and at ease – though it should be noted that the first mate was only able to behave as he did with the approval and, perhaps, encouragement of his captain. With a brute for a boss it would have been a different story, or Bragdon would have found himself punished and demoted.

At 7 am they passed one of a series of 'Floating Lights' stationed as warnings to river traffic. Formby lightship was described in the guidebook as being,

> *at the entrance of the Formby channel … distant about six miles from the town, exhibiting one light by night, and a red ball by day. … In the summer time steamers frequently make trips to these vessels, and are generally crowded with passengers. Besides these friendly beacons to the mariners there are several lighthouses on the Cheshire and Lancashire coasts.*

Jellyfish, tangles of seaweed, and the usual debris that lingered near a busy port would have been spotted by those looking out to sea but some may have been watching for other, more exotic creatures. The newspapers had recently included reports of an enormous sea serpent off the east coast of America, and with no previous experience of the sheer enormity of the ocean they hoped to cross, it was impossible for many of those on board the *Ocean Monarch* to gauge just how far away that was. According to the *Staffordshire Advertiser* of 12 August 1848, a Captain Samuel Thomas of the schooner *Elizabeth* had

> *discovered a huge snake, which appeared to be about one hundred and fifty feet long, as near as he could judge, swimming slowly along a short distance from his vessel. The ocean was perfectly calm at the time, and nearly the whole of the animal could be plainly seen. The hands on board the vessel concur in the statement of the captain, all of them having seen the serpent for some time without the aid of a glass. The head was as large as a fifteen-gallon cask, and the body about the size of a common flour barrel in circumference. It was black, and distinctly seen for the space of half an hour.*

An hour later, as they passed the Bell buoy, the pilot boat disengaged from the *Ocean Monarch* and began its return to Liverpool. The mood was celebratory, and the American jeweller, Fellows, was not immune,

> [T]*he thought that I was bound homeward, after four months' journeying … had its full effect upon my spirits. It was a happy time of one's life! … the steam tug parted with us at eight o'clock. The sails were immediately set, and the ship put in the best of trim, flags and pennants flying. No ship probably ever floated down the British Channel* [*sic*] *making a finer display.*

Children clattered up and down the stairs as the crew busied themselves with the sails. Neptune brandished his trident on the figurehead, and spray spattered the gilt-painted crown as the massive ship tacked across the sea. Below deck, the steerage passengers accustomed themselves to life on the open wave. Many were feeling awful, the motion of the waves affecting them dreadfully, and Surgeon Ellis recommended they take to their berths for a while to rest.

A lot of the ships crossing the Atlantic with a cargo of emigrants carried a surgeon in name only, fraudulent men with the barest bones of medical knowledge gained from pamphlets and reading the labels of the bottles and boxes in the medicine chest. Some ships didn't even have that, leaving passengers to dose themselves with all sorts or allowing the mates to in effect experiment with them. William Ellis, however, was the real deal, and the travellers on the *Ocean Monarch* were lucky to have him to hand. As the vomiting passengers clutched their buckets and bowls, and pregnant women clutched their extra layers of waistcoats about them to fend off the usual chill of sea travel, one of the sailors, Edward Jenkins, was seen entering the lazarette below the cabin, a lit candle in his hand.

Lazarettes were storage areas situated in the stern of a ship. As the name suggests, they were originally used to store the bodies of people of note, or whose corpses would need to be taken back to shore rather than buried overboard, as would usually happen if someone died at sea. This spacious locker was at the rear of the ship to help keep the stench of decay to a minimum, the air passing over the vessel ensuring the gases released during decomposition would be blown away from the decks instead of through them.

Jenkins reappeared twenty minutes later without the candle. When asked about it he claimed to have used it to grease his boots, waxing them in an effort to keep out the damp then putting the remaining stub in his pocket. Several people remembered this later, though no one thought it worth checking to see if this was the case at the time. The *Ocean Monarch*'s lazarette didn't contain any bodies, but it did hold combustibles such as wine, spirits, and straw. Jenkins should have kept naked flames well away.

*****

The stretch of water north of Wales was a heavily trafficked area of sea. Pleasure boats, yachts, fishing vessels, steamers, ferries, and packet ships like the *Ocean Monarch* and the *New World* criss-crossed paths, and collisions were a definite risk, especially in bad weather and poor visibility. Today, however, there was enough wind to fill sails without splitting them, and cottagers along the Welsh coast could see the people on deck and the White Diamond Company's red pennant snapping in the breeze.

Also visible was the *Orion* on her way from Beaumaris, on the Welsh island of Anglesey. Thick clouds of smoke billowed from the ship as she steamed eastwards. Meanwhile in the historic town of Beaumaris, named after the 'beautiful marshes' or 'beaux marais' on which Norman builders had partially constructed a low grey castle, the *Orion*'s opposition boat was preparing to leave port. Captain John Hunter of the *Cambria* was keen to be away but first he had to help another ship, the *Medina*, by giving all his spare coal to the steamer. He retained just enough fuel to make Liverpool but no more, and as the decks were overcrowded with passengers and livestock he was keen to make haste for his destination.

About thirty miles to the east, the cook was making breakfast on the *Ocean Monarch*. American ships were renowned for their superior cuisine, and although Train's ships could not compete with the Cunard Line's feasts the food served was certainly an improvement on that of many British and Irish ships. Captain Murdock had arranged for a decadent feast to be served at 10 am and the delicious smells of cooking and hot coffee mixed with the odours of vomit in steerage and manure on deck. The cows had been milked, the sails were set, and all was ready for a wonderful voyage. It would prove an adventure for many.

There was an atmosphere of celebration as the cabin passengers settled to their meal. As James Fellows later recalled in his memoir,

> [We] *sat down to a sumptuous breakfast, Captain Murdock at the head of the table. A variety of liquors were ordered from the store-room; brandy was freely mixed with hot coffee by the captain and many of the passengers, c*[h]*ampagne bottles reported like pistols on every hand, and all went merrily at the festive board for an hour and a half.*

Stewards and stewardesses, black and white, attended to their every need, and when supplies of alcohol ran low, Captain Murdock sent boys running below into the darkness for more.

First Mate Bragdon had sent a keg of whiskey and a cask of brandy aboard the day before, to be stowed in the dark storeroom, away from the passengers and crew. The Custom-house seals were removed and the booze flowed freely. While the captain and more fortunate passengers indulged in delicious food and beverages, the *Ocean Monarch* zigzagged through the water, tacking across the path of the *New World* and attracting admiring (and envious) glances from other sailors.

In Liverpool another very different vessel was preparing for a day out. The Brazilian vice-consul of Liverpool, Mr J. R. Froes, was on board the Brazilian steam-frigate *Afonso* with a host of other dignitaries as the ship departed port for testing. The newly built *Dom Afonso*, often also spelled '*Affonso*' or '*Alphonso*' in the press, was 180ft long with 300 horsepower engines, a powerful ship with the ability to sail with the wind or manoeuvre regardless of weather conditions using its steam engines. While the sea trial was expected to provide members of the Brazilian Navy on board with valuable information regarding the handling of the vessel, including Admiral John Pascoe Grenfell, a father of eight who lost his right arm in the Cisplatine War of 1826, it was also an occasion for celebration and an opportunity to show off the might of the newest addition to the Brazilian fleet. Also on board were exiled French royalty including the artistic Prince de Joinville, his wife Francisca, daughter of the Emperor of Brazil, and their children, and local dignitaries and hoteliers such as the Lynns of Liverpool who were responsible for the lavish spread of delicacies laid on for the grand day out. Here, too, there was a party atmosphere, and the pleasure cruise looked set to be a great success. However, this wouldn't be the kind of trial any of them were expecting.

Over to the west, Thomas Littledale Esq. was returning to Liverpool with friends after an enjoyable few days in Wales. The 30-year-old commodore of the Royal Mersey Yacht Club had competed in the Beaumaris Regatta on Tuesday and was now bringing his friends home on his yacht, *Queen of the Ocean*. The *Cambria* overtook them on her way out of Bangor and ten minutes later, at 10.35 am, they passed Puffin Island which was covered with fledglings and surrounded by birds diving for their dinner; the cries of kittiwakes and acrid ammonia stench of the guano reached anyone sailing past. The men discussed the steamer's speed and attempted to compare their rates of knots as they sailed against the tide.

Back on the *Ocean Monarch*, seasickness was proving more than many of the passengers could easily cope with. Sarah Summersgill, 16, was travelling to America with her cousins and widowed aunt following the death of her father, who had fallen down a cutting at Godley-lane near Halifax. She and her cousin Jane Neesom, 17, were manufacturers of artificial flowers, while her other cousin, 19-year-old Edward of Marsh-lane, Leeds, intended to continue working as a stuff presser like his late father before him. 'Stuff' was a term which could be used for any woven textile, but usually referred to worsted and other woollen cloths that didn't have a pile or nap. Stuff pressers had the often dangerous job of laying the cloth between sheets of special paper then passing it through a hot press, which gave the fabric its finish. It was easy to burn or crush fingers while doing so, and there were few effective treatments for such injuries, but Edward intended to carry on with this work nonetheless.

Sarah and her aunt, the feisty Mrs Blamire, had spent the morning on deck, watching the men work and the coast go by. The fresh air and visibility of the horizon would have helped alleviate some of the symptoms of seasickness, but not enough. At about 11 am Sarah felt too ill to remain above and instead retired to the berth she shared with Jane. The two slept in their clothes as others groaned with misery around them.

Mary Ann Taylor was one of them. She, like several other mothers in steerage, was travelling alone with her young children. Some were widows seeking a better life abroad, meeting friends and relatives already settled round Massachusetts or moving country for a new job, but Mary Ann was joining her husband. There were rumours that he had been pressured to join the navy and fled to America to avoid such a fate, but according to the *Leeds Mercury* of 2 September 1848,

> *James Taylor* [had been] *an overlooker of power looms. … he having formerly been in the employment of Messrs. Clapham and Co., stuff manufacturers, of Dyer-street* [and] *having been for three months out of employment, determined to try his fortune in America, where he has now resided for nearly ten months. After breaking up a comfortable home, his wife went to reside with her mother, Mrs Gibson, a widow, at No. 1, Victoria-place, Buslingthorpe-lane, Leeds … It appears that the emigrant is getting on comfortably in America, and being anxious to have the society of his wife and two children, arrangements were made for joining him in America. They accordingly left Leeds and took berths in the Ocean Monarch … Mrs Taylor is a young woman only twenty-four years of age, her husband being ten months older*

Their children, Sarah Ann, age 3 years 9 months, and George, who was two months shy of his second birthday, were beside her on the prickly straw mattress. Too unwell, cold, or uncomfortable to undress, she later recalled that 'we were all in bed in the berth assigned to us. I had been very sick, and, as recommended, had gone to lie down.' There were over seventy children under the age of 14 on board, and many of them were also lying in the berths or perhaps playing at, or under, the table that ran along the middle of the room, listening to the hubbub of strange voices, creaks, splashes, and moans.

Some of the more seasoned passengers were too busy enjoying themselves to allow the misery in the berths below to put them off their fun. Three friends from the Nottingham area, Elisha Bannister, John Freckleton, and James Walker, all 22, described themselves as 'in high spirits and in good health', and they were making the most of it. Some of their high spirits may have rubbed off on fellow traveller Henry Powell, or perhaps the boozy breakfast helped, as he decided to change his thick, heavy boots for lighter versions. He would be grateful that he did.

*****

Yet another ship named after royalty was in the area that day – the *Prince of Wales* steamer was leaving the Mersey for Bangor. As with many of the vessels plying their trade in the area, her decks were crammed with passengers looking out to sea or at the men and boys clambering skilfully through the rigging as the ships weaved their way across the waves. Among those taking the air on the *Ocean Monarch* were the 'Andrews' family, who stood out to their fellow cabin passenger Whiston Bristow. Mrs 'Andrews' was a woman often noticed for her beauty and was described in such glowing terms as 'a genteel and remarkably good looking woman' (*The Welshman*, 15 September 1848) and 'striking' by staff at the workhouse where she worked. Her 'husband' was 38, 5ft 11in, and stout with a fair complexion, light hair, and 'rather large whiskers', set off nicely by his black linen suit, but 9-year-old Mary barely merited a mention, along with the other little girl in cabin class.

Mr 'Andrews', also known as James Smith Bacon, was struggling with his health and was noticeable for another reason. He had recently sought treatment for an unspecified complaint and was bearing the marks of cupping on the back of his neck. Two of the key procedures carried out for general health issues at this time were bleeding – often involving leeches - and cupping, where a glass cup was heated on the inside then pressed against the naked skin. Cooling led to contraction, and the suction of the patient's flesh upwards into the cup was regarded as beneficial to the complainant. Sometimes a pump was used to extract the air from inside the cup instead. This often resulted in rings of bruising, like a circular love bite, and Bacon's bruises were obvious to those travelling with him.

Back in London, the cat was out of the bag. Mary Anne's widowed mother, supposedly dying near Nottingham, arrived at the workhouse on a visit from Devonshire. She was demonstrably not dead, and hoping to see her daughter and grandchildren. Elizabeth Gudgeon, 72, could not have had worse timing. Emmeline Bacon, matron of St Luke's, and currently missing her husband and the extremely attractive school mistress, contacted her brothers-in-law. They were successful men, married to Bacon's sisters and used to respect. Baker was a surgeon and Fontaine ran tallow factories nearby; they were men with many connections. The hunt was on.

Emmeline had married Bacon in Hornsey, Middlesex, in 1832 while pregnant with their first child, Emmeline Mary Ann. Good with his hands, her husband worked as a yeoman, joiner, builder, and carpenter when not in charge of St Luke's workhouse or chasing thieves in America. They went on to have a further three daughters and three sons. Unfortunately two of their youngest daughters, Alice and Clara, died a few months apart in 1841. Mortality was high, particularly for children, but their deaths from convulsions and 'water on the brain' would still have been a terrible blow. Their youngest son died four years later.

Bacon seems to have been an adventurous and generally decent man. Over his years as Master he stuck up for children apprenticed to what turned out to be brutal employers and there was not a whiff of the scandal currently attached to his paramour's husband, John Thomas Walter. Rightly or wrongly, Bacon had even given the sex-pest schoolmaster a glowing character reference in court a few months earlier. The workhouse board began looking into the accounts, no doubt fearing a repeat of the clerk's massive theft of their finances a few years prior, but found them correct. They formally stated,

> *their unanimous feeling that, but for the late affair, Mr Bacon's conduct during the whole of the time he was Master of this Workhouse, was most exemplary, his ability great, his perseverance most enduring, and his*

> *anxiety for the welfare of his trust most praiseworthy, and that a more perfect Master of a Workhouse never existed. They feel that though highly culpable for* [his and Mary Anne's] *affair he has left the house, as well as his accounts, in thorough order, – they deplore the fall of such a man, and can only suppose that his recent illness had affected his intellects.*

Divorce was expensive, rare, and difficult, and usually led to women losing custody of their children to the ex-husband – sometimes with disastrous consequences including neglect, rape, and murder – which was exactly what Mary Anne was seeking to avoid. The Walters were appointed to their positions in St Luke's in 1842, a fresh start after much mourning in Chippenham, Wiltshire, where her husband had worked at the National School. Like the Bacons, Mary Anne and John Thomas Walter married while expecting a child, and their son, John, was born less than two months later. Mary, currently taking the sea air on deck beside her mother, was born four years later, another 'Moonraker', as Wiltshire natives were sometimes called. She was followed by George, Ann, and William, all three dying very young before the end of 1842. This adventure in America would be yet another new beginning for the mother and daughter.

The Jacksons of Sheffield were also seeking a new beginning, although their quarters in steerage were nowhere near as luxurious as the cabin of the 'Andrews family', and their circumstances were considerably more straightforward. William Jackson, formerly a pawnbroker on Pinstone-street, had recently turned 31 and was heading for Boston with his wife Esther and their three 'little lambs', as he called them. William was on deck near the captain, watching the world go by as his wife took care of their children, 5-year-old Elizabeth, Willy, 4, and baby Richard, the youngest at only 19 months, in their berth below.

Many of the people in steerage were from the manufacturing districts of the north of England, such as 24-year-old John Sheard, a handloom weaver from Huddersfield; one of the two Samuel Fieldings on board, a widowed fustian weaver in his mid-sixties from Glossop, Derbyshire, who was planning to join his children in America; and the Hills. Rebecca Hill, 36, looked young for her age. She was short with light auburn hair, and dressed all in black with just a wedding ring for jewellery. Mrs Hill was a woollen weaver like her husband, George, who had gained a position in Massachusetts and waited there for the arrival of his family. She was bringing with her their children, Sophia, 9½, and Sarah Ann, 8½, from Rochdale in Greater Manchester, where her parents still lived. Like others on board, she carried letters of introduction in her pockets, in order to assist her when she reached this utterly foreign country, along with purses of money. She would need it in order to leave Boston and find her husband.

Others were lying in their berths wearing nothing but a light shift or their blankets, sick being easier to clean from bare skin or a single layer than an outfit of coarse cloth, especially if that was the only set of clothes they had available for the voyage. It was also easier to vomit without stays or a corset constricting the torso. Surgeon Ellis had done what he could to reassure the poorly passengers and retreated to the cabin to read, where 'Mrs Andrews' was also sitting reading on the sofa. Thomas Henry, their fellow cabin passenger, was in the smoking room with another passenger. Situated on the upper deck aft, the men puffed away at their leisure while playing backgammon and listening to the hustle and bustle at the rear of the ship.

In slightly less comfort in first steerage, the Tobin sisters perched on some boxes as the ship repeated the last leg of their previous journey in reverse. Johanna, 26, and Mary, 38, had sailed from Ireland to Liverpool in order to reach Boston. They were two of many Irish on board, some of whom only spoke Gaelic and may have had little idea of the size of the ocean they were hoping to cross – if a river or lough was the only body of water they had previously seen it was difficult to imagine something so utterly enormous. Elsewhere below deck, the ship's first carpenter, William James Moore, was working. It wasn't easy to hammer, saw, or chisel wood on a moving vessel, especially one moving at speed, but he managed well enough to be the head carpenter on board a prestigious packet like the *Ocean Monarch*.

As they sailed further away from Liverpool, Captain John Hunter on the *Cambria* was growing ever closer to his destination. He could see the splendid ship standing in towards the shore, then saw her tack and stand to the north. Every manoeuvre required many hands on ropes and rigging, shouts, and sails tautened or furled, an impressive sight even if it was a familiar one. Murdock's ship had made two tacks already, and was about to make a third. At a little before twelve, the captain was on the larboard side of the quarter deck calling orders to the crew on duty, while other sailors including William Roberts asked for their rations of tobacco and waited for the mate to dole it out. Londoner Whiston Bristow stood on the starboard side of the ship, across from the captain and steerage passenger William Jackson, fascinated by the goings-on. The yards were being hauled, a little east of the limestone headland known as the Great Orme's Head people were watching from their doorways, and all seemed well.

Seaman Roberts later recalled that the mate 'went down and gave [my ration] to me, and I, with others, went below with the tobacco, put it into my chest, and came on deck again' (*Liverpool Mail*, 29 August 1848). Passenger Joshua Wilson watched as the mate went down the stairs to put away the rest of the tobacco, and two men rushed up past him. First Mate Bragdon was on his way forward to tack ship when the steward ran over to the captain and the cook approached the crew. The first wisps of smoke started to curl out of one of the aft ventilators, unnoticed by many of the busy crewmen currently engaged in manipulating the many ropes and sails on board. These looked a little like chimneys, and were fashioned of sheet metal (although on some ships they were constructed with wood) and stretched all the way down to the third deck. There were two at the front of the ship and two at the rear, providing fresh air to passengers and crew on every level and allowing the gases and odours that soon built up to dissipate safely. They were usually ignored, and the passengers currently watching smoke seep out were unaware of its significance.

According to the *Manchester Courier and Lancashire General Advertiser* (26 August 1848), John Bell, a machine maker from Manchester, saw smoke seeping from the captain's cabin but before he had the chance to do anything more than watch in horror, 'up rushed two dark coloured men, one of whom came to two sailors with whom [he] was standing, and said "The ship is on fire"'. It was the worst possible news.

Chapter Four

At about twelve o'clock, M. one of the passengers discovered the Ocean Monarch several miles on our larboard quarter, apparently enveloped in smoke, and the awful thought occurred to his mind that she might be on fire! Happening to be standing by the side of this gentleman at the time, he directed my attention to it; expressing his fears that she might be on fire. I looked, and though I could see the vessel and her stern enveloped in smoke, yet supposing such a catastrophe almost impossible, concluded as she was several miles off, that there must be a steamer near her, the smoke of which we saw, and accordingly, I dismissed it from my mind, and thought no more of it, until some half an hour afterwards, when my attention was again directed to the smoke, by seeing Capt. Knight and his officers, scrutinizing it through the glass. It was then that I began seriously to fear that the suspicions of my friend, who had first directed my attention to it, were too well founded. A few moments more and the question was settled. To my inquiry, is the Ocean Monarch on fire? 'It is nothing else!'

(Rev. S. Remington, passenger on the *New World*)

Catching fire, near the Welsh coast, noon, 24 August 1848

James K. Fellows, jeweller and philanthropist, had enjoyed a magnificent breakfast with the captain and his fellow cabin passengers, and was looking forward to going home to Boston. As he later told the *Glasgow Herald* (28 August 1848), he was also apparently the first to discover the fire:

> [I] *was at the time lying on one of the sofas, perceived a strong smell of smoke and fire, and on more minute examination, found that it proceeded from the scuttle* [a small hatch with a movable lid], *down which the stores had been conveyed, and which is under a part of the first-class passengers' cabin.*

He told the steward to raise the alarm, then went into his nearby state room, and 'packed from my trunks many hundred dollars of value (of small bulk) into a carpet-bag'. Surgeon Ellis was reading in the first class cabin with Mrs 'Andrews' when they realised what was happening. Mary Ann Walter immediately – and quite understandably – panicked, and went in search of her daughter.

Many of the steerage passengers were lying prone in their berths, feeling wretched and completely unaware of the peril they were in. Some were on deck, watching the crew wrestle with the sails while others began pumping water into buckets and disappearing downstairs.

First Mate Jotham Bragdon was forward, at the front of the ship, when the first alarm was given. The captain carried on giving orders to tack ship, having sent a couple of his men below decks to extinguish the fire and retrieve the culprit. Bragdon later told the inquiry (*Morning Advertiser*, 1 September 1848), he initially 'understood it to have been one of the passengers on fire'. He immediately ran down into the second cabin to assist but 'Before [he] got there several of the men passed [him], running forward with buckets, and finding no fire in the second cabin, [he] went to the first cabin.' He saw very little smoke in the area but near the larboard wall of the state room he 'discovered at the side of the ventilator some appearances of fire'. Passenger Whiston Bristow, the first mate, and a few others, according to the *Liverpool Mail* of 2 September 1848 'tore away the cabin table, and lifted up the scuttle, and then discovered the ship was on fire'. Where there should have been darkness, they could clearly see the bright glow of flames. It was deeper than they feared: there was fire below the cabin deck, towards the rear of the ship – somewhere very difficult to reach.

Meanwhile the second mate, William Perry Gibbs, returned to the deck to find a very concerned captain, who told him to go below deck with the steward to see 'what the fire was'. He hadn't noticed any signs of it himself while putting away the tobacco mere minutes earlier, but when he went into the lower between decks aft, 'All [he] could see was a thick smoke'. He proceeded into the first cabin, 'where [he] found the chief mate and several of the hands of the ship passing water as fast as they could'. James Chiene was one of the hands working the deck watch, and was sent below with Second Mate Gibbs to help extinguish the fire. Having worked at sea for ten years, Chiene had unfortunately already been shipwrecked twice in the last twelve months.

The sound of the men exerting themselves and clattering up and down the stairs with buckets alerted some of the seasick passengers to the drama unfolding elsewhere on the ship. Mary Ann Taylor later told the *Leeds Mercury* (2 September 1848) that,

> [at] *about noon I was alarmed by cries of 'fire,' and having my clothes on, I instantly ran on deck to see what was the matter. I met one of the sailors near the hatchway, and inquired if there was any danger. He said 'no, not the least.' I thought there was great danger from what I saw, as the smoke was coming thickly from the store-room, by the steerage wheel. I immediately returned for my children, but could scarcely get them out for the smoke, which had very much increased, and was become so dense as almost to suffocate us.*

Mrs Taylor, her little girl Sarah Ann, and toddler George had made it to the deck together, but in the confusion, many others didn't. The screams of stranded children and sickly adults would have been punctuated with coughing fits as they fought to breathe, and knocked into boxes and other belongings as they tried to find a way out.

The first mate described some of the conditions adding to the lethality of the steerage accommodation at the inquiry. There was 'a temporary bulkhead made of boxes piled up between the passengers and the crates of goods. The passengers had straw to sleep on – they supplied themselves with their own straw. The straw [was] on both decks, either sewed up in bed sacks, or on the loose boards of the berths,' (*Morning Advertiser*, 1 September 1848). Accounts of the fire later given to the *Hull Advertiser and Exchange Gazette* of 25 August 1848 stated that: 'The ship was almost instantly in flames, in consequence of a quantity of bedding, chaff, &c., lying along the lower deck.' Given the speed with which the fire took over the *Ocean Monarch*, it's amazing that so many people made it to the upper deck.

Ordering his men to keep filling the buckets with water, there only being twelve available, the captain carried on shouting orders to the men handling the ship. Some of the crew arrived in the state room with water and started throwing it down the scuttle, others including American seaman Charles Daniel Locke formed a human chain to pass along the buckets, but Whiston Bristow quickly grew frustrated. As a cabin passenger he had more influence with the captain than many of those on board, and he used it to full effect, declaring himself dissatisfied with the volume of water being brought to the scuttle, and the speed with which it was delivered. Captain Murdock accompanied Bristow down the stairs to see just what was happening. The steward had initially told him he thought a passenger in steerage had made a fire in one of the ventilators, mistaking it for a chimney, and that this had caught light, but as there were only metal ventilators on the *Ocean Monarch* this was impossible. There had to be another cause, and another location.

The men in the state room were struggling but soldiered on, and the captain joined them, urging haste among the water-passers. First Mate Bragdon later told the inquiry (*Morning Advertiser*, 1 September 1848),

> *I continued throwing water for two or three minutes; went out to take breath, and then returned to throw water, until I could stand it no longer. I closed the scuttle down, knowing the fire was forward of me, and asked the captain's permission to cut a hole through the deck, in order to come more directly at the fire. The Captain, who had been before superintending the use of the water, gave me liberty to cut a hole through the deck, which I did, with the assistance of one of the cabin passengers.*

Luckily William Moore, first carpenter for the ship, had been working nearby and brought two axes over. He and the first mate hacked at the sturdy wooden floor but the smoke billowed out and made it difficult to see or breathe. Exhausted, Moore handed his axe to a willing Whiston Bristow. He, Bragdon, and Second Mate Gibbs took turns to chop at the floor and take brief breaks for clean air outside the cabin. As soon as the hole was broad enough the men poured water down as fast as they could. They may as well have spat on it, and, unfortunately, creating a hole in the deck actually increased their problems as the buckets of water dumped on the fire meant great gusts of steam wafted up into the room, and the hole allowed more air to reach the flames, increasing its ferocity.

Captain Murdock sent the second mate and others, including William Roberts, to raise the alarm among the steerage passengers still below decks, while he went above. Many, like the Taylors, had heard the commotion and removed themselves from the immediate danger presented by the smoke, but others were deeply asleep or so unwell they couldn't bear to move unless they knew for sure they had to.

Sarah Somersgill, 17, told the *Leeds Mercury* (2 September 1848),

> *'I and Jane Neesom* [her cousin] *were asleep in our berth, when one of the sailors came and awoke us, telling us to get up and go on deck as the ship was on fire. Being dressed we got up at once, Jane going before me, and I never saw her after. I went to my aunt (Mrs Blamire),who had been on deck all the morning. She was nearly in the centre of the ship, and going to her she said 'Stick to me, for there is only one thing for us, death, either by fire or water.'*

Meanwhile, cabin passenger Thomas Henry realised his earlier attitude of calm had been misplaced. After putting away the backgammon board in the smoking room, he had gone on the top deck out of curiosity more than anything else. Now the smoke was increasing, pouring from below decks, and he could see the small pump aft struggling to cope with the demand of so many people at once. As he later said in the inquiry,

> *Seeing the danger was eminent, I went down to the cabin for a life preserver. On returning on deck the confusion was very great. The flames at this time was* [*sic*] *rushing out of the cabin-windows aft. The first thing I did, on coming on deck, was to go aft. When I put on the life-preserver I came about midships. Saw the captain there trying to keep the people quiet. They were making a great noise, and the scene was horrible. The captain appeared to be doing all he could to soothe and encourage the passengers, pointing out the different ships that were around from which they might expect relief.*

From the first sniff of smoke to the fire raging through the passengers' sleeping quarters and flooding the between-decks with thick black toxins took perhaps fifteen minutes at most. Fellows, the cabin passenger who initially raised the alarm and had then gone to his state-room to pack his carpetbag with a small fortune in goods, was in trouble. As he later wrote in his memoir,

> *On my return to the saloon,* [I found] *all had been driven on deck by the suffocating smoke and vapor. The stewardess, however, ran past me, saying she must get out the 'magazine'; but she never found her way back. The long table had been swung around, cutting off my escape by the companion-way, and the darkness from the smoke was so great, scarcely anything was to be seen. I made my way forward into the ladies' cabin, mounted a table directly under a large sky-light, and soon made myself heard by the crowd I could see and hear on the bow of the ship. The sky-light was speedily broken through, and by standing on my toes, two of the crew succeeded in reaching my hand and drawing me on deck, nearly suffocated and exhausted. But what a scene! All was consternation.*

The fire fighters were eventually forced to leave the area when the fire suddenly gained in force, running above deck but leaving their axes behind in the confusion, unable to see where the tools were or that the other men did not have them in hand. They had taken a tremendous risk staying for as long as they did, and were nearly suffocated by the time they reached the deck.

One of the two stewardesses on board had joined the men in passing water along in an attempt to douse the flames raging below. The other woman happened to overhear the captain mention the 25lbs of gunpowder stored below in the magazine, and realised their awful situation could become far, far worse if the fire reached it. If the kegs caught light the whole ship would blow to pieces. The smoke was thick and toxic, causing barking coughs, making eyes stream and blinding anyone setting foot on the stairs, but nonetheless this incredible woman descended into darkness in order to protect her fellow travellers. On her way she passed Whiston Bristow. He heard her desperate pleas to God and cries of 'I *must* get out the powder!', and realising her plan, joined her. But unfortunately they were soon separated in the lethal fumes.

The smoke proved too dense to breathe. Bristow appears to have managed to return to the upper deck only to try again. Captain Murdock passed Bristow a line to make fast over the broken skylight, as the flames were now coming up through the hatchways, cutting off the other entrances. He seems to have let himself down using the line, then clambered back up by balancing on an overturned bench. The stewardess made it back up the stairs only to collapse on the deck. She was dead. Somehow this passenger and the plucky stewardess managed to not only reach the kegs, but to move them from the small space of the after hatchway in such a way as to relieve the potentially lethal compression of the powder. When confined, gunpowder explodes when ignited, as in a gun, whereas if dispersed, it will burn with just a flash – scary but much safer – greatly reducing the potential for damage. By spreading the explosive out, this pair of heroes had removed much of its deadly power. As the American newspaper *The Sumter Banner* commented on 20 September 1848,

> *The self-devotion and heroism of the stewardess are worthy of a more enduring memento, than it will be likely to receive. …* [S]*he perished in the noble attempt to save the lives of many others. She was a young and beautiful grisette; and in thus making herself a martyr, she deserves to be ranked among the Grace Darlings of the race.*

A *grisette* was originally a young working-class Frenchwoman, but this had soon come to mean a flirtatious young working woman. There is no indication that she was French, or flirtatious, or of her age, or indeed many details at all regarding this woman in the accounts that would soon be published. She was black, perhaps American, and possibly married to one of the stewards. She died a heroine and no one seems to have acknowledged her name.

Some of the passengers and crew continued to pour water on the blaze from the upper deck, the passengers grabbing any utensils they could find and filling their assorted vessels along with the buckets at the pump. But the captain and crew were dismayed to find 'very great confusion indeed upon deck, among the passengers. They were shouting, screaming, and crying from midships forward to such a degree that scarcely anything could be heard.' As the First Mate later recalled,

> *The smoke was so thick that I could not see the Captain at this time, but heard him aft. Heard him give orders to brace the crotchet-yard, and bring her head to the wind. … I let go the crotchet-braces myself.* [The captain and I] *assisted in clearing away water casks and rolling them off to the scuttle. Then* [I] *made an ineffectual attempt to go below again, the smoke was so overpowering,*
>
> *(Morning Advertiser, 1 September 1848).*

The cows and sheep could smell the smoke and were starting to panic too, shifting uneasily in their pens as passengers ran past, stomping on their straw and adding their noise to the din. One of the cows thudded against the planks keeping it in place, mooing with terror. Elisha Bannister, travelling with two friends from Nottingham and sometimes prone to exaggeration and hyperbole, told the *Nottingham Review and General Advertiser for the Midland Counties* (8 September 1848) that:

> *The noise and confusion on board the vessel was indescribable, but above all, at one time, the horrible sound emitted by a cow, which literally shrieked, was perhaps the most awful. The Irish on board were busy invoking the assistance of saints, and the scene altogether was such as to beggar description.*

His friend, Freckleton, had been among the last to leave steerage, and told the paper,

> *I had been rather troubled with sea-sickness, and had gone to bed, and was there when the first alarm of fire was given. I got up, went on deck, and saw the state of things; and myself and another young man went down into the cabin, and got our boxes on deck. When we got there, we found it impossible to get them away further, the smoke and fire were so near upon us, and we had to leave them.*

Many others had done the same, and the decks were strewn with items pulled haphazardly from boxes in a search for valuables and mementoes. Silver and gold speckled the top deck, the slip hazard adding to the danger for the passengers and crew, but it wouldn't be long before the deck was inaccessible to all.

Whiston Bristow was still endeavouring to help as many people as possible. As the Londoner told the *Liverpool Mail* of 2 September 1848, he,

> *tore up some benches near the skylight, and hove them up into the wing or side of the ship, in order that they might be ready for any person to take hold of, and almost in a moment the flames burst out of the main hatchway, and suddenly the midship part of the ship ignited.*

In the panic, the wrong flag was initially hoisted in an attempt to signal distress to surrounding vessels, but as soon as it was noticed that the pilot flag (requesting a pilot ship's guidance) was up instead of the distress flag, this was corrected. The jack now flew at half-mast signalling their desperate plea for assistance.

As *Gore's Liverpool General Advertiser* reported on 31 August 1848, 'In the meantime all was terror or despair on board the ill-fated vessel. While the greater part of the ship was a perfect volcano, the small quantity of gunpowder below exploded.' Thanks to Whiston Bristow and the anonymous stewardess's exertions, although the powder went off with a boom like that of a cannon, it did not blow the *Ocean Monarch* apart.

The captain ordered the ship turned but barely a soul could hear him over the shrieks and prayers. In his report, he would later explain that, 'We put the ship before the wind in order to lessen the draft, but were obliged to bring her to again.' The fire had taken the after-sails and even the weather was against them.

> *Finding that nothing could be done with the yards, I caused both of the anchors to be let go, that the ship's head might be to wind, and the fire kept as abaft as possible. The passengers crowded in numbers to the bowsprit to avoid the heat of the flames. Many in alarm and despair leaped overboard, and although spars and all loose materials lying about deck were thrown for them to cling to, a great majority were drowned. In spite of all that could be done, the flames increased. I gave orders to get the boats out. Two of them were got out, but before the lashings of the others could be cut, they were enveloped in flames.*

Passenger Edward Sherne spoke to the cook who initially helped raise the alarm, and according to the *Carnarvon and Denbigh Herald and North and South Wales Independent* of 2 September 1848, when he 'Asked the cook was there danger or not, [he] said "It is all up with us". The cook then spoke to the captain who gave directions to launch the boats.' Lifeboats were seen by many as dangerous, an unnecessary expense which would give people a false sense of security and encourage carelessness, as well as cluttering up ships and providing a hazard for seamen as they went about their work. The *Ocean Monarch* was certainly not alone or to be condemned for only carrying enough boats to allow about a third of those aboard to escape under better conditions. As Second Mate Gibbs later told the inquiry, on the *Ocean Monarch* they,

> *did not keep any quarter boats – all we had were housed on board. We had four boats altogether. The launch, or long boat would carry about thirty people, the other two boats would carry about twenty each, and the other I went in about seventeen. Had the four boats belonging to the ship been launched we could not have taken more than 120 people altogether.*

The axes had been left behind in the chaos of the state room as the men escaped the inferno there. Gibbs had managed to cut the lashings of the boat using his knife at about 12.30 pm. At that point,

> *There was no one left on the poop* [the roof of a cabin at the rear of the ship]. *They were all forward on the forecastle* [at the very front of the vessel]. *It is my opinion that the fire might have originated in the locality where the crates were stowed. The crates were stowed up to the decks, but there was a passage left to the store room. Before I left the ship I don't think I could have got forward. I would have rather jumped overboard, the smoke was so thick.*

Among the passengers clustering near the bowsprit at the very front of the ship stood George Gregg and his fellow cabin passengers, the 'Andrews' family. The Bacon/Walter trio had gathered there out of sheer desperation. As another of the cabin passengers, the invalid Henry Powell, later told the *Carnarvon and Denbigh Herald and North and South Wales Independent* of 2 September 1848:

> *When the sailors were in the act of shoving the boat in which I escaped across the vessel, for the purpose of throwing her outwards, one of the cabin passengers threw his little girl into her, in the hope that the child would glide over the sides of the vessel with the boat, and thus be saved. The men standing by immediately snatched hold of the little creature, and threw it upon the deck.*

But they hadn't lost all hope of living, despite the speed of the flames now consuming the *Ocean Monarch*. Weeks or even months of planning their illicit adventure, and enduring the stress of living with such an enormous secret, surely could not terminate like this, with such an awful result. James Smith Bacon was a resourceful individual, a brave and canny manhunter with a tenacious streak, but there was only so much he could do in such terrible circumstances. As Gregg told the abandoned Emmeline's brothers-in-law, during their hunt for her errant husband:

> *I was at the bows of the vessel, Mr Andrews and the child stood between myself and Mrs Andrews; Mr Andrews said to me, 'Are we in a safe place, Gregg?' I replied 'I know not where a safer place is to be found just now'; at this moment the mast fell, and Mr Andrews, Mrs Andrews, the child and many others were knocked overboard; they clung to a rope, and Mr Andrews called out aloud, 'For God's sake save my wife and child', I stripped and leaped overboard for the purpose of attempting a rescue, but so many persons laid hold of me, that I was obliged to release myself from them by diving into deep water, to save me from perishing; I then swam to another part of the vessel, and by means of a rope got on the deck again. On looking over I saw the child sink first, and then the Lady, but I do not know whether Mr Andrews was lost or saved; he was at this time suspended by a rope and only his hands and head above water. The ship was from 8 to 10 miles from land and no boat near.*

As the situation grew ever more dangerous, people looked for ways to remove themselves from the immediate danger of the fire by securing ropes to anything that seemed solid, probably including cleats, deck rails, and fittings, and used those ropes to help them climb overboard and away from the conflagration. According to Joshua Wilson, a letter-press printer from Manchester, (*Manchester Courier and Lancashire General Advertiser*, 26 August 1848),

> *The fire soon seized hold of the masts, one of them fell, and killed several people on the forecastle; but it afterwards served to save many lives, for persons threw themselves overboard, swam to it, and there clung. The falling of the other masts did not, I think, do any harm as they went*

> *aft. The masts and rigging were used by many as a means of floating. Many people held on to different parts of the vessel until their hands were burnt, and then they dropped into the sea. The scene on board the blazing ship was awful. There was the crackling of the flames, the roaring of the cow, the noise of the sheep, the screaming and prayers of the distracted men and women, all anxious to save themselves and their families, if they could, but with little hope that they should effect it, having only the fire on the one hand and the water on the other. …* [After the bowsprit collapsed, killing many] *I saw a small boat coming from a steamer; I tied my child to my wife and went overboard, and she was to have followed me, but whether she was thrown over or fell I know not, but she came upon my neck when I was in the water: a wave came and separated me from her; I tried all I could to reach and save her, but I could not. Both wife and child were drowned.*

Walker, travelling with friends from Nottingham, had watched in terror as the masts toppled, but he spotted a vestige of hope across the waves, according to the *Nottingham Review and General Advertiser for the Midland Counties* (8 September 1848),

> *When I got upon the forecastle, I remained there a short time, looking out for other assistance. The Affonso shortly attracted my attention in the distance, and while she was making for us, one mast after another kept giving way. At last, the fore-mast was the only one standing, and that we watched with great anxiety indeed, for she swayed backwards and forwards, and we did not know which way she might fall. If the mast had fallen on the bowsprit, it would have killed a many. When the fore-mast fell, it tore away the jib with about thirty persons upon it.*

His friend John Freckleton told the paper,

> *I saw* [the fore-mast] *fall, and five minutes after the Affonso steamer got near us, and lowered her boats, and one of them made for the side of the vessel towards the forecastle, and the captain motioned for me to descend. I did so, by aid of a rope … then I was carried off by a wave into the water, and was there a few minutes. I could not swim, without*

> *fatiguing myself very much, and I got much water in me. At last I was thrown by a strong wave, upon the foremast, which had fallen a few minutes before. The part of the mast I got upon was very much under water, and every wave that came went over me. Every time a wave receded, I made a little progress to the top end, where a young man was sitting, but the water then was up to my waist. The boat then rowed up to me, and I was taken on board. On our way to the ship we picked up a little child which the mother had thrown overboard; and a woman that had been very kind to the passengers before the fire. We were particularly glad that she was saved. She was a Lancashire woman.*

Cabin passenger James K. Fellows later wrote in his memoir of his own lucky escape, and the awful sights he witnessed while trapped on board, saying,

> *At length the fore-mast crashed over the bow, striking not a yard from where I was standing, carrying over several from the bow, and snapping the fastenings of the jib-boom, which, with its load of human beings, dropped into the water, amidst the most heart-rending screams, both from those on board and from those who were falling into the foam below. The scene directly under and in front of me was terrible to behold. There might have been fifty men, women, and children struggling for life and supplicating for help; and many that were dead lay floating on the surface.*

Elsewhere on the burning ship the First Mate was about to make a decision that led to accusations of cowardice from some survivors and many commentators, but his reasons were pure. As he explained at the inquiry:

> *There was a great rush when the boat was launched. Seeing no one in the boat to take charge of her, and that if she was not got out of the way, the number of passengers who would get in, would have been so great, she would have been swamped, I jumped in myself, rather jumped overboard, and swam to her. The passengers had hold of the line and were pulling her under the gangway for the purpose of getting in the boat. Immediately on reaching the boat I ordered the line cut. There were 12, with myself, in the boat; eight of the 12 were passengers.*

Among the crewmen he took on board the sinking vessel was William Roberts, whose testimony at the inquiry was, like Bragdon's, included in the *Liverpool Mail*, 29 August 1848:

> [I] *have seen as bad as this before, and expected to get on a raft or piece of wood to save myself. The lashings of the boat from the main hatch were cut, and the boat launched. About twenty or thirty of the seamen and passengers jumped for her. I got on to the swinging boom, and one of the seamen advised me not to go in, as she was full of water, and plenty of people in. I was going to get back again to the ship, when one of the women who was on the boom got hold of me round the neck, and we went over together. I was picked up by the mate, and taken into the boat; but the woman was drowned. We drifted away from the ship and tried to bail the boat out with our boots.*

This vessel was the ship's waistboat, about 21ft long, and able – in better circumstances – to carry about twenty people. As Bragdon told the inquiry:

> *When the line of the boat was cut we were without oars. The crowd being so great I could not, in the urgency of the moment, get oars. With the assistance of bits of boards, which I picked up, we tried to keep the boat's head to the sea. There was a heavy short sea. The force of the water striking the boat when launched drove the plug out, and she was nearly full of water when I got in her.* [One of the men had to strip his stockings off and stuff them in a ball into the hole as a temporary and imperfect plug.] *I set two or three to assist in bailing out with hats, boots, or anything we could get; gave my own hat for that purpose. The boat could not, with safety, hold any more than we had in her; the boat was half baled out when we picked up the last passenger; in doing so nearly filled her again. The anchors were lowered from the ship after I was clear of her, which immediately brought her head to the wind. We continued to drift leeward, keeping the boat's head to the sea. It required all our exertions to keep her from filling. We drifted in this way perhaps some four miles…*

The ailing cabin passenger Henry Powell was among those rescued by First Mate Bragdon. As the Londoner told the inquiry later, his 'own escape was most providential'. Having moved away from the flames toward the crowd of people huddled at the forecastle, he waited for an opportunity to leave the ship for a boat. At the forefront of his mind was the likelihood of any approaching vessel being swamped by the crush of people who would no doubt surge onto it in hopes of safety, so he decided to remove himself from the crowd and returned to the centre of the vessel. This placed him nearer to the flames but, he reasoned, made it more likely he would make it off the ship alive. As he recalled:

> *fortunately, in a few minutes some of the crew threw the boat near to where I stood into the water. Another ten minutes it would have been too late … I then threw off my great coat and jumped overboard. As I fell I caught hold of the rope that attached the boat to the ship, and sunk into the water. On rising, an Irishman, who had also fallen in, immediately grappled hold of me, exclaiming, 'Let me hould on to ye, let me hould on to ye,' and I began to sink under his weight. This was a fearful moment, and the only one that I gave up all hope – for I had so frequently heard of persons losing their lives by being clung to in the water, the recollection of which flashed across my imagination, that I never expected to rise again.*
>
> *However, he fortunately let go his hold, and I rose to the surface and caught hold of the rope a second time, and had approached within a few inches of the boat when I heard the mate give order to 'cut away the ropes.' This was done, and I once more sank with the other end of the rope in my hand. I rose for the third time, and caught hold of some person's legs, who was clinging to the sides; I managed to climb up his back, and tumbled myself head foremost into the boat. Considering that I am no swimmer it seems almost a miracle that I accomplished it. I now felt, comparatively speaking, safe but the danger was not yet over.*
>
> *The sea was so rough, and the boat so full that we expected every moment to be swamped with every wave that we shipped. We had no oars to guide us this, so far, was a fortunate circumstance for me. Had the men been able to strike off when the mate ordered the ropes to be cut away, she would have been beyond my reach when I rose after having sunk with the rope end in my hand. Surely Providence has watched over me in a wonderful and merciful manner. I cannot be too thankful. …*

> *I had changed* [my very thick, heavy boots] *for a light pair only an hour or two before the fire broke out, and I have thought since that had I jumped overboard with the thick pair on, the probability is I should have sunk for ever.*

One of those picked up in the little boat was American cabin passenger Thomas Henry, who was fleeing the flames with the aid of technology not available to many on board the *Ocean Monarch*. He also gave evidence, saying he

> *went overboard by the main chains, having inflated my life-preserver. I was picked up by Mr Bragdon, the chief mate. Cannot tell how long I was in the water,* [I] *cannot swim much* [and] *owe the preservation of my life entirely to the life-preserver, under Providence. It is quite easy to inflate the life-preserver – and it kept me perfectly buoyant, although I could not swim.*

Aware of the criticism his rescuer was facing, the fortunate merchant added that,

> *I would here observe that the main object and desire of Mr Bragdon, chief mate, seemed to be to get us on board the pilot-boat as soon as possible, in order that he might more quickly get back to render assistance to the ship. I think the safety of the boat we were in is to be attributed to Mr Bragdon, as the sea was running very high, and we were without oars. Indeed, I did not consider my position in the boat much better than when in the water.*

Sarah Somersgill, her aunt, and other passengers including Mary Ann Taylor and her children were still on board, huddling as far from the fire as they could safely get. The animals were trapped in their pens and frantically attempting to escape. One of the cows managed to bash its way out, its hide on fire, making a sound as if it were screaming. The poor creature dashed overboard to its death, crushing a woman as it did so. As Mary Ann later recalled, 'The cattle and sheep, which were roasted to death, made a dreadful noise; the gravy ran out of the ship just like it does from a joint when roasting before the fire.' Their juices mingled with those of people burning in the crush, the deck running with what Mrs Taylor described as their 'gravy' as the fire feasted on their hair, clothes, and fats. One woman ran past, slitting her own throat with a straight razor before leaping overboard. Shawls caught light and feet blistered and stuck to the deck, cooking against the burning wood.

Mrs Taylor later recalled of her time on the forecastle that:

> *we stood till my feet began to feel hot from the fire underneath. About this time I saw the Captain outside the ship, and heard him say 'obey my orders.' The fire was now at least half-way over the ship, and as my feet were getting hotter, I began to think what I was to do. I looked around and found a piece of thick rope, which I first fastened round my little boy, then round my little girl, and tied the other end round my waist. We were thus all fastened together, and in order to make the knot secure I fastened it with a piece of a handkerchief which I picked up.*
>
> *In this position I got over the side of the ship, and let myself and children down into the water by a rope, suspending myself by it with one hand, whilst with the other I held my youngest child to prevent it falling. In a short time I was enabled to get on the wreck of the mast which was floating in the water. This mast was completely covered with human beings, some dead and some alive.*
>
> *I clung to it, but unfortunately my two children were very soon suffocated with the water, and the weight of their bodies became unsupportable. The rope by which I had tied them together and fastened to my waist, had by the weight of the burthen slipped down nearly to my knees, rendering me perfectly helpless. An Irishman spoke to me and said – 'Mistress, you must try to help yourself.' I said – 'I cannot, for the rope is round my legs.' He then attempted and succeeded in slipping the rope down over my feet and my two children, already dead, dropped into the sea (...)*
>
> *(Leeds Mercury, 2 September 1848)*

They were soon joined by many more, but thankfully the plight of the survivors had not gone unnoticed.

Chapter Five

Under any circumstances, the sacrifice of human life, on a large scale, presents a picture revolting to the principles and feelings of our nature; but not even the carnage of battle, nor the stealthy march of the pestilence, can equal in horror the agony of beholding a multitude of men, women, and babes, within sight of their own cottage doors, on the eve of an expected departure for a new world of adventure and hope, struggling between the two fiercest elements of creation, and in the endeavour to avoid one kind of horrible death forced to risk another almost as horrible. It has been the theme of the poet's fiction and of the painter's dream of terror; but what narrative or what pourtrayal [*sic*] *can equal the dread reality?*

(*Belfast News-Letter*, 29 August 1848)

A ship alight, Welsh coast, Liverpool, and at sea, 12.30pm, 24 August 1848

While terrified travellers made the awful choice of whether to die by fire or water, or had the decision made for them, there were hopes on the nearby land that all would be saved. This area of the Welsh coast was deemed particularly beautiful by a journalist writing for the *Liverpool Mercury* of 24 July 1849, who said, 'We predict that Llandudno and five miles round, will before long employ the skill of many pencils. We know not any district richer in the materials of the sublime and beautiful.' They singled out the path leading to the highest point of the Ormes-head for particular praise, saying it 'command[s] a splendid panoramic view of the ocean, (and occasionally of the Isle of Man)'. They also mentioned the practical purpose the height of this prominent headland had been used for, describing for their readers how,

Close to the summit is the telegraph station, w[h]*ere the very intelligent master affords ready information to inquirers, and who, at convenient*

> *moments, permits them to watch his operations in passing signals. ... It was from this station that the master reported to Liverpool the burning of the Ocean Monarch, and all the melancholy and thrilling events of that sad catastrophe, which was visible through his window and his telescope from first to last. The accuracy of his report was much commended ... May his abilities never have such another distressing trial! The stranger notices with pleasure the neatness, comfort, and extreme cleanliness of his abode, and also the unmistakeable strength of the building thus placed on an eminence 750 feet above the sea, from which the ascent to his front seems practicable only by sea-gulls and other bipeds which are feathered.*

A telegraph had been installed over twenty years prior along the North Wales coast and while the *Ocean Monarch* burned at sea, a group of men including the chairman of the Dock Committee and the Marine Surveyor were making their annual inspection of the many local telegraphs and lighthouses. They were checking Llysfaen-station and observing the many vessels dancing across the waves in Liverpool Bay when they noticed the trouble this triple-decker emigrant ship was in. As the *Carnarvon and Denbigh Herald and North and South Wales Independent* of 2 September 1848 reported, the group were,

> *in full view of the melancholy scene, but without the ability to render the slightest assistance, as not a boat could be had anywhere in the vicinity, the lifeboat station being at the Point of Ayr. All they could do was to transmit the intelligence to Liverpool, which they did as quickly as possible.*

Based on their reports, newspapers like the *John O'Groat Journal* of 1 September 1848 were initially full of misplaced optimism regarding the people on board, saying,

> *Liverpool, Thursday Evening. A considerable degree of excitement prevailed here on 'Change to-day, in consequence of a report having reached Liverpool by the old telegraph, that a large ship was on fire at sea, about 35 miles from this port, and off the Welsh coast. On proceeding to the Telegraph Office, we were handed the following notice:- 'A ship is on fire with the letter T., outward bound, No. per chart, 163. A steamer*

> *is bearing down towards her. Her main and mizen [sic] masts are gone.' On further inquiry we ascertained that she had some cabin passengers, together with 346 in the steerage, and a crew of 30. She is a ship of 1,224 tons register burthen, and stands at A 1 at Lloyds'. It is gratifying to be able to state that, according to the last reports, there is cause to hope that no lives will be lost, although the noble ship and her cargo will in all probability be totally consumed.*

As with almost any human disaster, one of the key issues was not pricking sympathy among the aware and able but marrying their desire to improve the situation with practical ways of doing so. Many onlookers were desperate to help but time and distance were issues, ones the would-be rescuers fought hard to overcome. However help was still some way off and in the meantime dozens were dying. They may have seemed utterly alone in their misery but there were many strangers watching and wishing them well. As local man Thomas Rowlands wrote several decades later in his *Adgofion am Llandudno* (Recollections of Llandudno, 1893),

> *One afternoon news reached the village that a large ship was on fire outside Llandudno Bay. Everyone abandoned their pleasures and their duties and raced to the Fach (the Happy Valley), on arrival we saw, about fifteen miles out to sea, the large emigrant ship, The Ocean Monarch, with flames running up the rigging and the masts. There were hundreds of emigrants on board when the fire broke out. They had just left the port of Liverpool and were full of high hopes of reaching America, and thought, as they left the old country, that they were bidding goodbye to oppression. But no, within a few hours the two most destructive elements had turned against them, the fire and the water and threatened not only their comforts but their lives.*

Dozens of people on shore were rooting for the vessels in sight to make haste for the stricken triple-decker, but some of the more obvious contenders continued their journeys without diverting nearer to the disaster or even slowing to send boats to assist those struggling in the water. One, the *Cambria*, hoisted a flag to alert other vessels in the area to a ship in distress nearby, but that was it. This decision may have cost hundreds of lives.

Luckily Thomas Littledale, 30, a wealthy cotton broker on his way home to Liverpool from the Beaumaris Regatta, was nearing the *Ocean Monarch* on his yacht. Also on board were his friends John Aspinall Tobin, Mr Aufrere of Windermere, Sir Thomas Hesketh (the high sheriff), and a chaplain. As *Gore's Liverpool General Advertiser* reported on 31 August 1848, as the yacht approached the ship 'the flames showed themselves several feet above the deck. The cries of distress reached them at a considerable distance, and the poor wretches on the wreck swarmed like bees about the head of the vessel.' The *Queen of the Ocean* was described as 'a fine stout yacht, and was provided with a capacious boat'. Littledale and Tobin 'directed all hands to lower the boat, and pull off to the rescue, they themselves managing the yacht in the meantime'. As the paper explained, 'The sea was too rough for her to attempt boarding the burning ship.'

Back on the *Ocean Monarch*, Whiston Bristow was in an awful situation. As the *Morning Advertiser* of 2 September 1848 reported him saying at the subsequent inquest, after he had torn up benches for other people to use as flotation devices he,

> *saw the flames form a junction, as it were, and all communication was cut off between the aft and fore part of the ship. At this moment, I saw the captain aft of me apparently employed in throwing overboard light loose spars for those overboard to save themselves upon. … I got outside the weather side of the vessel. Took my position on the bowsprit shroud. Many of the passengers whom I had known on board appealed to me to save them. Just at this moment I saw a sail, which at first I took for a Government cutter, but afterwards proved to be Mr Littledale's yacht. After a time I pulled off my boots and trousers and jumped overboard, and swam toward the yacht. I was the first man picked up by her.*

William James Moore, first carpenter of the *Ocean Monarch*, who had worked so hard to contain the fire, was now attempting to save as many lives as possible by throwing large pieces of wood overboard. Having returned from the smoke-filled cabin, he

> *assisted the captain* [in] *launching the top-gallant yard overboard, and then saved myself by jumping into the water and getting on it, as I could*

> *not get forward for the fire. When I jumped overboard I saw the captain standing on the top of the rail near the main hatch. …* [T]*he fire had cut off all communication* [between Captain Murdock and the people at the front of the ship]. *The house on deck and all the places about it were in flames. I saw the captain jump overboard a short time after me,*
> *(Morning Advertiser, 2 September 1848).*

In his statement later, Captain Murdock explained that, 'finding the flames approaching so rapidly that I could not get forward nor aft, I was obliged to heave myself overboard, and cling to the spar for a short time but finding that there were too many already clinging to it, I swam to a board which fortunately floated near us….'

Captain Murdock was, along with many others, desperately trying to keep his head above water and away from solid objects. He floated near his ship for perhaps half an hour as the waves collided and dashed water over his face. It was cold and exhausting and if he hadn't had the board to cling to he would have soon sunk beneath the surface. People near him screamed, shouted, pleaded and prayed, then fell silent as the waves battered over their heads, leaving them unable to draw breath, and they drifted deeper, away. Help was coming but for many it was too little, too late.

Edward Brimscome, the mate from the *Queen of the Ocean*, had left the yacht's owner and friend in charge while he and three of his men rowed the gig through the treacherous wreckage towards the ship. If this boat was holed by any of the spars or planks being thrust about by the waves they would be in no position to help the people screaming on the burning wreck. Over the following hour or so they pulled three women, including cabin passenger Anna Roper, from the water, along with almost thirty men. She had jumped into the water with her eldest daughter, Jane, in her arms, only to lose her in the waves. The men returned to the yacht twice to deposit the survivors aboard, including more than half of the crew. On their final trip the last person they retrieved from the water was Captain Murdock himself. He was in a state near death and unable to help himself. It would have taken some amount of effort to pull his 200lb frame into the boat without capsizing it, but they managed.

At first, with all the excitement and the rush to help the men in the gig to unload the lucky survivors, Thomas Littledale didn't realise they had managed to salvage someone as prestigious as the captain. Murdock was in no condition to make his presence felt. As the master of the yacht, Thomas Wills later told the inquiry, Captain Murdock,

> *was so far gone, I did not think he would recover. He was taken down and put into a berth in the ladies' cabin. One lady who came had broken her foot. When the captain was brought on board the yacht it was impossible for him to render any assistance. After taking him out of the boat he fell on the deck and lay there until assisted.*

Aside from saving lives by removing people from the water, they also helped by throwing life preservers out to those they could not reach, in an effort to help them stay afloat until other rescuers could get to them.

Meanwhile First Mate Bragdon was about four miles away from the inferno, rowing with the current for the nearest boat, the *Pilot Queen of Chester*. The men on board, John Bennion and Thomas Bithell, transferred nine of the passengers on board their vessel with the aid of their boy, John Foulkes. They were cold, wet, traumatised, and in some cases suffering from the effects of inhaling smoke and seawater. Bragdon was desperate to return to the sea surrounding the *Ocean Monarch*, and the people he knew to be clinging on to wood and ropes as the waves surged against the burning ship. He called for assistance, shouting, 'Boys, are there any of you will volunteer to go back with me to the relief of the ship?', and ended up with three of his shipmates agreeing to act as crew. His natural authority as a first mate worked to elicit four oars from Bithell and Bennion, and once he knew – or rather, trusted – that his passengers were safe with the pilots, he 'pulled with all energy for the ship'. If he had known what was to follow he may well have chosen differently.

As he later explained to the inquiry, he had a further stroke of luck and 'After proceeding about a mile the *Prince of Wales* steamer for Bangor came alongside and took us in tow, and steered for the *Ocean Monarch*.' This gave the exhausted men the opportunity to rest and recover a little from their arduous escape, but their pluck and courage were soon called upon again. 'Within about a mile of the ship we saw a passenger holding on to a lifebuoy. I picked him up and put him on board the steamer. I do not know his name.'

The lucky survivor was James Ratcliffe from Salford, Manchester, older brother of Joseph, currently in the custody of the Liverpudlian police after being found in the *Ocean Monarch*'s hold. Captain George Dani, who held medals for his actions at Copenhagen, the Nile, and Trafalgar and was one of the few crewmen still alive to have served under Lord Nelson, gave orders for the young traveller to be made welcome on board. Dani and his wife were following their usual passage from Liverpool to Bangor when, despite objections from some of their passengers, they diverted from their course in order to save as many as they could from the turbulent water. Upon seeing the conflagration, he had immediately ordered one of their boats to be readied and soon noticed Bragdon and his men rowing across the waves.

As one of their more supportive passengers, who was looking out on the forecastle later told the *Belfast Newsletter* (29 August 1848), 'a child floated past … floating cabbages and pieces of wreck came next, and then – horrible sight – bodies of men and women, just under the surface of the water, all the way to the burning ship, which was at anchor'.

There was a lot of wreckage in the water, which was both a good and a bad thing. It gave people something to cling to, to keep them afloat and allow even the stronger swimmers a necessary rest, and was considerably easier for rescuers to spot than a wet head bobbing among the cabbages in the water. However, the swell of the waves meant there was also a chance people in the water would be battered or skewered by it, or grow tangled in the ropes, sink, and drown. The closer they were to the wreck, the greater this danger became.

Captain Dani sent his mate, James Batty, out with three hands in one of the steamer's boats to see if they could retrieve any survivors from the water. As Batty entered the boat, he spotted a little girl bobbing beside it. He immediately pulled her from the sea. She blinked her eyes, looking not at him but as if at something far away, and died as he passed her to the second mate aboard the steamer. Her name was probably Jane Roper, and she was only 5.

They carried on towards the *Ocean Monarch*, picking people from the sea on their way but leaving the corpses of those beyond help to float and, with luck, wash ashore. There were far too many to pull aboard and still have room for the living, and it would take more minutes than the people clutching at kegs, boxes, and luggage had to spare. As a passenger on the *Prince of Wales* steamer continued in the *Belfast Newsletter* of 29 August 1848,

> *On coming up on her larboard bow, to our horror, it was crowded with poor wretches – men, women, and children – clinging to ropes, spars, and the wreck of the foremast, crying most piteously to be saved from their frightful position, the awful element fire literally chasing them into the equally destructive one, water, which was very rough, causing the vessel to surge ten or twelve feet at every heave, continually immersing those who had slid down the hanging wreck of ropes and sails on the chance of being taken off by the boats, which unfortunately, dare not approach, for fear of being swamped. Then came a sight, sickening and never to be forgotten: they, one by one, dropped off into the water, unable to hold on any longer, either from the heat or from exhaustion. We and the boats looked on unable to render help further than picking up those who were bold enough to jump.*

Another passenger explained of their approach to the *Ocean Monarch*, that the ship had,

> *both anchors down, with a strong wind and heavy sea running, which accounts for so many being on the fore part; indeed it was the only part they could retain, for when we first saw her no other part was tenable. A female, in the early part of the disaster, had let herself down with a rope, and had got, I believe, on or very near a piece of wreck alongside, but no sooner had she descended than the heading of the troubled sea, and pieces of the wreck that were around her, twisted her twofold, as it were. Her lifeless body was fast fixed to some rigging ropes that had wrapped round it, and at every rise and fall of the billows there was this woeful spectacle presented to our eyes. The living we had to secure, and could not risk our lives to save her poor remains. We also observed a female form, with a child clasped firmly in her arms, floating away, but life perfectly extinct.*

A little while earlier, at around 2 pm, the Brazilian steam frigate *Afonso* had neared the *Ocean Monarch*, and, with thirty-two survivors already on board the *Queen of the Ocean* and requiring much attention, Thomas Wills continued collecting people from the water but transferred them to the boats of the *Afonso* instead. Mary Ann Taylor, her children dead and dangling from her waist as she floated in the water beside the ship, had watched as the Brazilian steam frigate grew from the size of a cricket ball to that of her outstretched hand, then let down their boats, unfortunately far too late for little George and Sarah Ann. This bereaved mother still had a long time to wait before help arrived, but at least she had hope, which was more than could be said for many of her fellow travellers. She was not alone in enduring terrible trauma.

The American jeweller James K. Fellows was horrified to see the fate of one of the men who helped him raise the alarm only an hour before.

> *The steward (a large, heavy, colored man) had managed to slide down from the bow of the ship on a burned-off stay, to which he clung after he reached the water. The ship drifting and pitching, he was at one moment suspended in the water out of sight. Thus he sustained himself for nearly an hour. A large water-cask had been thrown over, and became entangled in the rigging that lay in the water. The man let go his hold on the rope and mounted the cask; but no sooner was he on than off, as the cask was constantly in motion and was frequently dashed violently against the bow of the ship. For more than two hours the poor man struggled for life – on the cask for a moment, and then off and out of sight; again and again rising to the surface and mounting the cask, only to repeat the same experience. No man ever labored harder for life, for two or three hours, than did this powerful man. But finally he became exhausted and helpless as a child. I can never forget the expression of his face as he disappeared the last time beneath the white foam.*

With the loss of this steward, a member of staff who had ensured Fellows's comfort while he settled into his cabin and then later at breakfast with the captain, the food of which was still filling his stomach, Fellows grew despondent and resigned himself to what he was sure would be a similarly unhappy fate.

> *I had become gradually reconciled to my lot, as there now seemed not to be the least hope or chance of my escape. My whole life was before me; incidents that had been forgotten for years were rapidly passing through my mind. The thought that my friends, and those most dear to me, could*

> *never know my feelings, and the way in which my days were ended, was intensely distressing. I felt sure, at that moment, it was 'not all of death to die,' nor the whole of life to live; and what matter if then, or a few short years later, I surrendered existence?*

He endured this despair for a few long and desolate hours then saw the *Afonso* which, as he put it, gave him 'hope of relief, with increased desire for life and safety'. He watched with interest and a lightened heart as the steam frigate anchored to windward, two or three hundred yards from the *Ocean Monarch*, noticing the uniforms of the Brazilian marines and their struggles to communicate in English. Fellows was delighted to see four boats being speedily lowered and manned, and even happier to see 'a heavy cable taken in tow and made fast to the wreck'. As he watched,

> *the large paddle-box of iron was taken, also, from over the wheel, and by connecting with the stretched cable they were enabled to go backward and forward with facility, carrying fifteen or twenty at a time. The heat was now insupportable, even to those on board of the boats around the ship.*

The dark and dashing Prince de Joinville, who had been enjoying the war ship's sea trial with his brother and their families until smoke was spotted across the water, assisted the *Afonso*'s remaining crew in hauling the ropes, moving the paddle-box boat between the steam frigate and the stricken emigrant ship as quickly as possible. A vice admiral in the French navy, this exiled prince was keen to save as many lives as he could and worked hard to help the boat reach the stricken vessel, but it still took time, more than many of the emigrants had left. Mary Ann Taylor, her children lost in the water beneath her, watched as they approached across the waves.

Fellows also wrote of his own attempts to help his fellow passengers, and subsequent lucky escape,

> *By my watch, I had occupied my position under the bow four hours, it being now four o'clock. I had saved one woman, who was sustaining herself by a stay* [rope], *which was suddenly burned off. Another, near by, was compelled by exhaustion to relax her hold upon her infant; she*

looked up imploringly and said she must save her child, and plunged into the surging foam. I caught hold of her dress, which gave way, leaving a large portion in my hand.

By making my way to the rope attached to the bowsprit and the foremast, lying near where the iron boat came up, I went down hand over hand, and was hauled into the boat by Admiral Grenfell, who acted a brave part in rescuing those who were floating at the mercy of the waves. Considerable time was unavoidably spent in gathering a boat-load from the water and those clinging to the ship. The crowded boat was slid along by the side of the frigate Alfonzo [*sic*], *and all were drawn on board by ropes thrown over and tied around their waists. One passenger, a lady, holding to the rail of the iron boat, lost three fingers by its dashing against the side of the ship.*

One survivor almost lost a lot more than that. The *Armagh Guardian* of 4 September 1848 included a letter one of the survivors, Patrick Donnelly, wrote home to Loughgall, Ireland,

A man took his wife and children and threw them into the sea, they were lost; he was preparing to follow them, when he missed his foot and fell back into the flames and was burned. By this time the steamboat had reached us, which was a frigate, whose name was Affonso … [T]*he heir of France, Louis Phillippe's eldest son,* [gave orders on] *how to save us all; they were not going according to his orders, being so terror-struck. He then threw off his coat and acted manfully till all was saved that life was in.*

We remained on the bowsprit till a small boat was sent out to take in all that was in greatest danger. We bid my father [Arthur Donnelly, 50] *go down as he could swim, and save himself, as by this time all hopes were gone of us being saved, as none of* [the rest of] *us could swim. He went down, and after great perseverance and hardship, being several times down out of sight, he at length reached the small boat.*

They called on me to do the same, but the feelings I had for a tender and affectionate mother prevented me leaving her, and [I] *told them I would not leave her till death, and that I would share the same fate with her. I got down a cable and prepared a place for her* [Betty, 40] *and*

> *sister. I went down till I came to the water, and got them after me, and held them as well as I could till the same boat came to our aid. They threw me a rope which I gave to my sister Catherine* [age 16], *and she got in with ease; my mother made a grasp at it and missed her grip, and fell into the water.*
>
> *I got into the boat with great difficulty, and fortunately got a hold on my mother, and strove to get her into the boat, but in vain – still I held her fast, while the boatmen were pressing on me to let her go, saying I would upset the boat, and took a sword to cut off the arm that held her. But I kept a deaf ear to all – dragging her through the waves till we got to the steamer, and thank God we were all saved. … The goodness and bravery of the Frenchmen was more than I can express; they gave us rum, cakes, and coffee, and everything we could take in the way of food.*

Fellows and the other survivors on board the ships anchored near the blazing hulk were certainly faring better than those deposited on board the *Pilot Queen of Chester* several miles away. According to an account given by J. R. Froes, the Brazilian vice consul of Liverpool and published in *The Welshman* of 1 September 1848,

> *The boats brought the survivors alongside of us, and one by one were hauled on deck – all of them more dead than alive. We did all we could for them. The women and children received every attention. The children, particularly, were carefully looked after by the Princess Joinville, and the Duchess d'Aumale. The two princes, elsewhere, gave every assistance in their power, and used every possible exertion in seconding the captain in his arduous exertions. The whole party on board the Affonso gave up nearly all their wearing apparel to the poor passengers; many of them, for the relief of others, divested themselves almost completely of clothing.*

Daniel Leary, 12, from Tralee, Ireland, had been brought on board naked along with his sister, Catherine, who was about 7. Many adults were also in dire need of some form of clothing so this generosity was much appreciated.

Mary Ann Taylor, whose children had joined so many others in the waters around the wreck, was still clinging to the spar along with her fellow travellers. She had been in the water for over an hour. The bereaved mother had her teeth knocked out at some point and her mouth was now a bloody, jagged mess. When all seemed lost, the paddle-box boat came near and she was pulled from the water. She told the *Leeds Intelligencer* of 2 September 1848, 'The Prince de Joinville was in the boat when I was taken in from the wreck. The people on the *Afonso* distributed their linen from out of their portmanteaus and gave us hot brandy to drink.' The heat would have been sorely needed after the shock of the fire and the death of her little children, and the alcohol would hopefully have numbed her physical pain, too.

Sarah Somersgill, 17, also had a lucky escape from the *Ocean Monarch*. As she told the *Leeds Mercury* of 2 September 1848, having escaped steerage with her cousin, Jane Neesom, she lost sight of her companion but managed to join her aunt in the centre of the upper deck. There Mrs Blamire told her 'Stick to me, for there is only one thing for us, death, either by fire or water.' The pair had then moved to the forecastle, near the bowsprit, and after waiting there for what seemed like ages Jane recalled that her aunt,

> *after telling me to follow her, walked over the side of the ship to let herself down. She got hold of a rope, which, being partially burnt, snapped in two as she was descending by it, and she fell into the water. I watched her for a long time, till I lost sight of her, and then I began to look out for myself. A sail had fallen down from the bowsprit, and, getting hold of the top rings of it, I intended letting myself down by passing myself from ring to ring, the sail end being in the water. A sudden gust of wind prevented me by at once wrapping the sail round me, and in this state I remained a long time till the wind released me again. As soon as I could get to the side of the deck I seized hold of a rope which had been fastened both to the ship and to a boat at a distance, along which I endeavoured to pass, but was prevented by an Irishman, who obstructed my passage, and who would neither go backwards or forwards. Some of the sailors made several attempts to get me into the boat, but could not get me past the Irishman.*
>
> *Besides the rope I at first caught hold of, another was thrown me out of the boat, which I seized, when, aided by the sailors, who got hold of my dress, I was pulled into the boat belonging to the Brazilian frigate. As soon as I had recovered from my exhaustion, I found my aunt was*

> *safe, and in the same boat with me. Whilst on the deck my aunt and I held a child for a woman till she could get over the side, and when suspended on the rope I gave it to her, but when she reached the boat the child had disappeared. This woman and her husband were the first persons I recognised on being placed on board the Affonso. The woman was fretting for her child, and her husband was consoling her by stating that the child would be sure to be happy, whether dead or alive.*

The ropes were a lifeline for many, but they were a perilous place to be – better than being amid the flames but still dangerous. Mary Ann Taylor had witnessed the demise of a fellow passenger there before she herself escaped. As she later described it in the *Leeds Mercury* of 2 September 1848,

> *Several others with whom I had become acquainted were drowned or narrowly escaped drowning. There was one John Bell, a brass-turner, and his wife Emma, from Manchester. This man, before leaving the burning ship, gave his wife £80 in money and tied his watch round her neck, telling her at the same time, that if she was saved it would do her good. Having done this, Bell let his wife down the rope, intending to follow her; but three other women, to save themselves, caught hold of her clothes, and as Mrs Bell could not sustain her hold of the rope, all four fell into the water, and were drowned in the presence of the poor man who had just supplied his wife with all the property he had in the world.*

Another Manchester man was even more unfortunate. As Mary Ann recalled, 41-year-old iron founder, James Hiley,

> *who left a wife and five children behind him* [at home], *perished about the same time. John Bell, who was saved, remained two hours suspended by the rope before he was taken off. He lost everything except his shirt, trousers, and cap, having thrown off his other clothes in order that he might be less encumbered in the water. Another man, named Joshua Wilson, a copper-plate printer, from Lancashire, having tied his child fast to his wife as a precaution, went down the rope, intending his wife to follow him, he was saved, but his wife and child were drowned. He had*

gone down first, thinking he could best sustain the weight of his wife and child, but he had scarcely reached the bottom of the rope, when the two fell upon his neck and into the water. It is supposed they had slipped, or had been pushed over in the confusion.

However Sarah Somersgill's cousin, 19-year-old Edwin Neesom, was more fortunate. He followed another chap who had successfully slithered down a rope into a boat below and managed to escape the *Ocean Monarch* without injury or even wetting his clothes. He was very, very lucky.

Chapter Six

[The people on the ship] *were so frightened that, except for wild and almost gibbering gestures to us, they might have passed for statues; their faces were of a greenish pale colour, and their eyes looked large and hollow. They clung to the wreck, and refused (by utter non-compliance) every endeavor to induce them to jump for the boats. At this time – will it be believed? some passengers and the captain (probably suggested by the latter) urged that we could do no more good, and that we had better proceed on our voyage! I shall ever feel gratified that human nature redeemed herself – the proposition was received with horror.*

(Witness account from passenger on *New World*, *Anti-Slavery Bugle*, 6 October 1848)

Rescues and ramifications, near the coast of North Wales, afternoon, Thursday 24 August 1848

The steamers *Cambria* and *Orion* may have had valid reasons for not rushing to the aid of the stricken *Ocean Monarch*, including a lack of coals and already overcrowded decks crammed with cattle and travellers with no room for more. But several accounts from passengers on other ships in the area relate a general reluctance among the captains and many of the passengers to render assistance to the people burning to death or drowning nearby.

Captain Knight of the *New World* initially displayed what may charitably be described as a misplaced sense of optimism, according to one of his passengers. An account published in the *Anti-Slavery Bugle* of 6 October 1848 states that this passenger openly disagreed with the captain – generally an unwise and dangerous course of action, but worth the risk in this case.

I spoke but a few words: 'When we saw this ship first, the captain said, all who were on board must either have perished or been taken off, and

> *therefore he did not wish to bear down; we came, and have saved at least ten. I say let us stay by her, no matter how long it may be, so* [long as] *there is a living thing aboard her. Look at that little child clinging to the boon – will you leave it?' A groan and 'never!' was answered from all save two or three.*
>
> *The captain appeared vexed. He turned our boat, ran astern, picked up his boats, and ordered the helmsman to 'run us close alongside.' He had refused to do this three or four hours before, when there was little or no danger; now it was expected that the whole head of the burning ship would fall, and the experiment be really dangerous. Some who had advocated it before now demurred; but the more bold declared they would run the risk, and the voice of fear was stifled. I give our captain credit here, it was a trying time, my heart fluttered, for I was afraid; but still I could not look at that child which for hours we had seen hanging with mute determination of despair, without resolving every risk rather than no rescue.*

The Reverend S. Remington was also a passenger on the *New World*, and as he later recalled in *The Sailor's Magazine and Naval Journal* (1848),

> *The captain turned upon his heel, and took his position on the quarter-deck. We being some five miles from the burning ship upon our larboard tack, and steering directly away from her, it was necessary to bout ship, in order to go to the relief of the sufferers. Instantly the captain shouted; 'Stations for stays?' In a moment the officer forward answered: 'All ready forward, Sir!' 'Put your helm down!' Which was answered by the man at the wheel, 'Helms a'lee, Sir!' The next moment – 'Tacks and sheets – Main-sail haul – Stand by your head braces – Fore bowline – Let go and haul – Shift your helm, and brace sharp up,' and we stood for the burning wreck.*
>
> *The wind was blowing more than half a gale with a heavy sea on, and it appeared as though we should not reach the burning ship, till it would be too late to rescue her horror stricken passengers from their perilous position. The lives of hundreds seemed pending upon our speed, and that of other vessels, who, like us were bearing down upon this scene of horror, and every moment was fraught with the preciousness of human life.*

> *Never, while memory endures, can I forget that awful hour! As our ship neared the burning vessel we could distinctly see the flames approaching the bow, and crowding the horrified passengers forward, until they were huddled together in heaps like sheep for the slaughter, and were literally strung upon the fore rigging and bowsprit.*

For once, there was a stroke of luck for the people still alive on or near the *Ocean Monarch*. As Reverend Remington was happy to relate, 'Singular as it may appear, though we had been out but a few hours, yet the captain but an hour before had had the boats put in perfect order for use.' If only Captain Murdock had ordered the men on the *Ocean Monarch* to do similar, perhaps the fearless First Mate Jotham Bragdon would have been spared the frustrations of attempting a rescue in a leaky rowboat.

> *The oars were all placed in the boats and fastened; the India rubber buoys of the life-boat freshly inflated, and thus every thing put in complete readiness for immediate use. When I saw them thus preparing the boats, I confess that I thought strangely of it, and a kind of presentiment came over me that they might possibly be called for before we reached our desired haven. The captain afterwards remarked that he scarcely knew how it was, that he came to attend to that business so soon after leaving port.*

The *New World* drew closer, dwarfing the blazing triple decker and other vessels nearby, until the people on board became visible to the naked eye and distinguished themselves as men, women, and children instead of a more easily ignored anonymous group of emigrants. As the Reverend recalled with horror,

> *the extreme bow, the bow sprit, and the figure-head were the only places of refuge for the poor sufferers, from the devouring element, and from our ship's deck we could distinctly see them strung out upon the bow sprit and rigging, like bunches of grapes … so intense was the heat, that the huge iron-cable was heated nearly red-hot* [almost 700 degrees celsius] *for some feet, and there being a heavy sea on at the time, it was rendered extremely dangerous for boats to go under her bow in order to take the people off, as the ship by the action of the waves would rise and fall some*

> *ten or fifteen feet at a time. In this case it was exceedingly hazardous to venture near the bow, lest the boat should be caught between the bow of the ship and the chain cable, and thus as the wreck plunged and rose, be cut in two by the chain.*

The majority of the *Ocean Monarch*'s crew had escaped the ship and were either assisting with the rescue attempts, recovering on nearby vessels, or awaiting their own salvation from the waves. Unfortunately, at least two perished while moments from safety. According to the Reverend on the *New World*,

> *Mr Baalham, the third mate informed me that he saw two sailors floating upon a spar near the burning wreck, when one of them cried, 'shipmate, for God Almighty's sake save us.' The next moment a wave struck them, rolled the spar over by which their hold was broken, and these sons of the ocean sunk to rise no more.*

And as the Reverend Remington noted, 'the destruction of life among the passengers was appalling'. He recounted some particularly gruesome deaths he witnessed for the hopefully hardened readers of *The Sailor's Magazine and Naval Journal* (1848), who may well have seen similar situations in their time at sea,

> *Many there were, who, in order to avoid the devouring element with which they were threatened, fastened themselves to a rope, one end of which being made fast to the wreck, and thus strung, they voluntarily precipitated themselves into the sea, the action of which destroyed the most of them in the most shocking manner. Some were cut in two, others were washed to death against the bow of the ship, by which means her bow and figure head were literally covered with blood.*

Others had a less gory but perhaps more distressing death after the ship's masts toppled, crushing many and knocking others into the sea. The reverend was close enough now for a clear view of the disaster.

> *We could distinctly see them fall into the ocean, with the masts like apples from the limb of a tree when shaken the most of whom probably*

> *perished. At this moment a great number jumped into the belly of the jib* [the large triangular sail at the very front of the ship] *as it lay upon the surface of the sea, where they seemed to be perfectly safe. Others on seeing their apparent safety jumped also upon the sail in such great numbers that their weight caused it to sink beneath them, closing it upon them like a bag, and awful to relate they were all buried in this sack to rise no more. Such was the progress of the flames, that others who stood upon the forecastle were suddenly precipitated into the burning mass beneath them, and consumed.*

One of the *Ocean Monarch*'s more fortunate crewmen, William Roberts, had assisted First Mate Bragdon in rowing between their ship and the vessels nearby since the mate had pulled him from the water over three and a half hours earlier. Every time they paused beside a vessel to transfer survivors on board, they were thrown bottles of drinks to help them keep going, but not always the kind that would refresh their parched mouths and quench their raging thirst. As *The Sailor's Magazine and Naval Journal* (1848) stated, this greatly disappointed the volunteers in a boat from the *New World*, with Third Mate William Baalham in command.

> *The men in this boat, as well as in all the rest, toiled nobly and severely during the seven hours they were engaged in plucking the brands out of the fire. As they came along side the anchored Brazilian steamer* [the *Afonso*] *to put on board the saved, they several times asked for water, and at first half a dozen bottles of liquor were thrown into the boat for them. The liquor was instantly thrown overboard, the noble seamen indignantly demanding, 'What kind of refreshment is that for such men on such an occasion? Water! water is what we want'.*

The magazine continued, with approval for the temperance displayed by the thirsty rescuers, 'In every instance afterwards water was given them.'

Even with these brief breaks for refreshment they were growing increasingly exhausted. At around 4 pm Roberts could take no more. As he explained at the inquest, 'I got terribly fagged, and went at last on board the *Affonso*,' (*The Tablet*, 2 September 1848). Having saved dozens of lives, he agreed to swap places with another volunteer, allowing Bragdon to carry on with his mission to save even more.

It wasn't just their exertions that made them so thirsty, it was the heat, too. Although the day was cold, wet, and windy, the rescuers were spending a lot of time near the fiery bulk of the *Ocean Monarch*. As the *North Wales Chronicle and Advertiser for the Principality* of 29 August 1848 pointed out,

> *The heat was very intense, and even to those on board the boats alongside was very oppressive. What it must have been to those who were crowding on the poop and bowsprit of the vessel, none can tell but those who experienced it. It was sufficient, however, to make them jump into the water, seeking succour from one element, by taking shelter in another equally as destructive, but far less agonizing in its effect. From the crowd of human beings in the water clinging to the spars, &c., the boats were unable to get as close to the vessel as they otherwise would have done, and, of course, considerable time was unavoidably consumed in rescuing the poor unfortunates.*

The heat was so intense that the survivors still clutching to the wreck or ropes in the water beside the ship faced an additional hazard, as did their plucky rescuers. The fire burned so ferociously that the pitch applied to the wood to keep it watertight was dripping off the ship. According to the *San Francisco Call* of 16 August 1895, 'The boats on their third attempt found it impossible to go near the burning vessel on account of the great heat. So fierce was the fire at this time that the lead of the melting scuppers ran down the ship's side like water.' Small wonder that, as the paper continued, 'Now and then an unhappy wretch with a burning death behind and a watery grave in front of him, plunged into the angry sea to be seen no more.'

It was incredibly difficult for the rescuers attempting to approach the cluster of survivors crowded round the bowsprit. As Jotham Bragdon, 34, later told the inquest,

> *I endeavoured to get under the bows, but utterly failed in my exertions to persuade the passengers to come down. All but two, a man and a woman, refused. These two I saved. After putting them on board the Affonso I*

> *took from her life-boat* [a] *sailor belonging to the New World. His name was Frederick Jerome.*
>
> *(Belfast Commercial Chronicle, 30 August 1848).*

This sailor would prove an incredible asset and make all the difference to the survivors remaining on the blazing ship.

Having departed from Liverpool in a race with the *Ocean Monarch* for Boston that morning, the enormous American *New World* was now engaged in the rescue of dozens of her fellow ship's passengers, many of whom had drifted far from the ships anchored near the inferno. All the vessels involved in the removal of the living from the wreck and the water were taking on board whoever they could, swapping exhausted rowers for fresh hands, and supplying the crews in the rowboats with bottles of water and porter. No distinctions were made regarding age, ranks, or nationalities – something that particularly impressed journalists later. The men were united in their desire to save lives despite the terrible risk to their own.

Bragdon was relieved to have Jerome with him, knowing of his fellow sailor's stamina and daring. He seemed to know no fear. As the *San Francisco Call* of 16 August 1895 noted, 'Jerome acted on this occasion with that promptitude which brave men display in a great crisis.' Bragdon later recounted at the inquest that they 'then went to the *Prince of Wales*, which had anchored to the windward, and had a line from her to slack away under bows. Jerome took a small line from the boats, and having divested himself entirely of his clothes, climbed on into the head of the *Ocean Monarch*.'

Two years earlier, when Jerome had saved hundreds on the *Henry Clay* – including Jotham Bragdon – by swimming for over two hours for shore, he had done so with a similar rope tied round his chest and ended up 'bruised, bleeding, and insensible' on the beach with deep cuts to his breast and shoulder as a result. Although doing so again with a hauling line would no doubt have aggravated his scars and perhaps awakened unpleasant memories, he still pressed on.

As passengers on the *Prince of Wales* watched, a naked Jerome began to remove the few left alive on board the ship. This was approximately an hour after the rest of the survivors to be removed from the wreck had been rescued, a man and a woman who were persuaded to leave their precarious perch and leap for the boats. One witness was quoted in the *Examiner* of 16 September 1848 as saying,

> *a cluster of our fellow-creatures crowded on the only one part of the vessel which remained, so far, beyond the reach of the raging element, but under momentary expectation of its invasion, the heaving ocean beneath threatening destruction in another form. Their stretched-out arms and wailing cries for relief reached us from time to time through the lull of the wind and waves, completing a scene the most appalling and heart-rending that can be well conceived.*
>
> *At the time we approached her nearly the whole who are known to have perished had already gone to their great account, some by fire, and others meeting a watery grave in their endeavours to escape a death so horrible. We shared in the means of relieving these poor remaining sufferers for more than two hours, until at length only about sixteen or seventeen remained upon the wreck. These were an aged man and several women and children – their every faculty seemed to have been paralysed with terror, and they could by no means be persuaded to make any endeavour to lower themselves down and trust to being picked up by the boats plying underneath. One or two men made an attempt to reach them, but without success.*
>
> … [Jerome] *plunged into the vortex caused by the surging of the ship and the formidable wreck of spars, ropes, chains, and torn sails hanging from her bows. In truth this continuous pitching and these attaching impediments gave rise to the difficulty and danger of relieving the sufferers throughout the whole disastrous period. With less of this there would have been comparatively little difficulty, and with a degree more of storm many more must have perished.*
>
> *To return to Jerome – taking a rope in his hand, he attained the site of the forlorn occupiers of the small space still spared from the fire, and his progress to this point was a splendid display of muscular power, requiring a strength of arm which but few thorough-bred sailors possess. Now it was when the harrowing spectacle we had been witnessing so long assumed an aspect more pleasurable and more hopeful, and we crowded to the side of the steamer like the spectators of a drama.*

A witness on the *New World*, who had urged the captain to assist the survivors on the *Ocean Monarch*, was quoted in the *Anti-Slavery Bugle* of 6 October 1848 as saying that Frederick Jerome 'declared he would not leave [the *Ocean Monarch*] until he had saved them all'. This passenger was impressed by the risks the rescuers were taking in their efforts to save all on board, and recalled that Jerome,

> *swam under her bows, caught by the hanging rigging, and, by climbing and shinning, got up to the head. The loose sticks, the risk of being struck by which was imminent, and remember that we all looked momentarily for the falling away of the head, bowsprit, passengers and all, and you may conceive the noble spirit, the only one out of the hundreds around, that dared venture his life for the salvation of his fellow-creatures. I weep at the recollection.*

The *New World*'s lifeboat was commanded by Thomas Forbes, a native of Gayhead, Massachusetts, who usually acted as boatswain. His expertise proved essential in this situation. Reverend Remington, who was also travelling on this massive emigrant ship, was full of praise for him, saying,

> *famous as the vicinity of Cape Cod has been, and is, for her daring seamen, she never produced a stouter, or nobler heart, than the one that throbs in the breast of Thomas Forbes …* [He had] *refused to leave* [the last few survivors on the *Ocean Monarch*] *hoping that when the tide should slack something might be done for them. And as it turned out, as the tide slacked at about 7 o'clock, the sea became much more smooth.*

When the tide is about to change direction there is a period of time when the water grows less rough and, having swapped some of the men about – including Frederick Jerome – they were now in a much better position to conclude the rescue operation successfully.

The reverend also recounted a rescue using the other boat, captained by Third Mate William Baalham, an hour or so before the naked Jerome clambered up the figurehead to remove the final passengers from the ship. Mary Crook had been en route to Providence, Rhode Island, with her younger sister Rachel and brother-in-law Peter Coxe. The couple were sailing with their young family and persuaded Mary to travel from Dukinfield, Manchester, to assist them with their children on the journey. Mary and her 3-year-old niece Mary Anna were sitting in the bow of the ship beside the beautifully carved Neptune and his trident, clinging to its feet. A few minutes prior, the little girl's parents had taken her infant brother and let themselves down from the braces (ropes) into the water but the baby was washed from his mother's arms and drowned. The flames were now so close they were scorching Mary's clothes.

According to a passenger on the *New World*, when Baalham threw his rope among the cluster of survivors, Mary Crook 'caught it, but as she sat still, he gave it a sudden jerk which caused her to fall into the water. She quickly floated astern, and was picked up by him just under the ship's quarter'. But it hadn't been as easy as that. In a later testimonial, her near-nakedness on recovery was explained as apparently she,

> *sank and disappeared for some time, and, was in and under the water nearly five minutes … and was at last with difficulty caught by the boat-hook (for the dress she had on was literally torn to rags by it,) and was taken into the boat perfectly insensible, and remained so for two hours.*

In the meantime, the reverend recalled,

> *the little girl was told to jump. The distance from where she was to the water was about 15 feet. As might be expected, she was at first too timid to make the attempt; but the mate held out his arms and said, 'jump little girl, I'll catch you.' This inspired her with confidence and she let go her hold – fell into the sea from which she was immediately snatched unhurt, and Mr Baalham, the mate, brought her in his bosom to the New World in the same boat with her Aunt, who seemed more dead than alive when the boat came along side* [our] *ship. … When I saw this poor woman, who looked pale and ghastly lifted into the ship, and the poor little motherless child, who had been snatched from the destructive elements … I could weep – before all was horror – now all sympathy and tenderness – the terrible and awful gave place to the free scope and exercise of the tenderest emotions of my heart.*

Baalham clearly inspired confidence, as another witness described little Mary Anna hearing his entreaty to jump and 'roll[ing] into the water as if she was falling on a bed of feathers'. They also praised her aunt's 'perfect coolness and self-possession … While others scarcely knew where they were or what they were about, she seemed conscious of her awful situation, and yet perfectly self-possessed and collected in the time of her greatest danger.' The witness was careful to note this brave woman 'had delicacy and a nervous temperament like most other females', and to point out that 'There are some occasions, however, in which female shrinking and diffidence can be overcome. When it is in her power in a becoming manner to express her gratitude for protection and help, woman was never backward to acknowledge her obligations.' Despite watching her sister and nephew die, Mary Crook managed to keep her niece calm and safe for several hours even with the heat, smoke, and danger. She was just as much a hero as the men in the boat who pulled them aboard.

Meanwhile, Frederick Jerome and Jotham Bragdon were still labouring at what was left of the *Ocean Monarch*, collecting the final survivors from the wreck. The spectator on the nearby steamer *Prince of Wales* continued in their account of Jerome's heroics for the *Examiner*,

> *One after another he lowered the women and children by passing a rope round them, letting them gently down until within reach – that is, until a man could fasten a long boat-hook to their clothes, by which they were drawn to the boat.*
>
> *As one after another they were placed in safety, a round of clapping of hands was given. I had for two hours watched the very aged man lying with a child in his arms, and he was the last to be saved. The scene, which had become more and more exciting, now attained an interest the most thrilling. The child was secured in the boat, and Jerome proceeded to pass the rope round the old man. Senseless from long exposure in such circumstances, he seemed to resist, and either could not or would not unclasp his rigid grasp. Some violence on the part of the gallant sailor was necessary to cause him to quit his hold. This was at last effected, and he also was lowered in safety.*
>
> *Three hearty cheers on our part announced this, and three more – energetic and heartfelt – greeted Jerome when he himself attained the*

> *boat. Were I a painter, I would try to depict Jerome, the old man, and the child; the Athlete, in Grecian nakedness, feeble age, and innocent childhood in a group; the ship's head – a bearded Neptune of hug*[e] *dimensions under them, and lower still the dashing waves – over them and behind, for fifty yards, a raging furnace.*

The naked hero 'looked down into the *Ocean Monarch*'s hold, and could see the rail road iron, and that she was all burnt out to a mere shell. … the fire had burnt off all the wood work about the fore-chains, so that you could see the irons standing upright, red hot, by themselves.'

Jerome's hands and arms had been badly burned and the smoke would no doubt have affected his lungs, eyes, and throat too, but he didn't falter. This was at around six or seven o'clock, when all the vessels involved should either have been back in port or, in the case of the *New World* and the unfortunate *Ocean Monarch*, well on their way past Wales and Ireland. But, apart from the yacht *Queen of the Ocean*, which had sailed for Liverpool with thirty-two survivors once her owner, master, and mate agreed there was nothing more to be done, the rest of the ships remained anchored near the blazing wreck. As Jotham Bragdon recalled at the inquest,

> *The whole of the upper deck was all burnt off, and the fire was bursting through the sides down to the water's edge. Jerome having lowered down the last person, a man, he descended, and we put him on board the Prince of Wales, as well as the remainder of the passengers. I went on board the Affonso, where I experienced congratulations and every kindness. The Prince de Joinville, the commander, and the other persons on board gathered around us. There were 139 persons saved from the wreck on board; many of these were women and children, partially naked. I saw all busy in clothing, and comforting them; but among the most zealous, kind, and active were Mr and Mrs Lynn, of the Waterloo Hotel, who were on board. Mrs Lynn went over to the poor children, seized them in her arms as they came on board, dried them, caressed them, and covered them in the best way she could. Mr Lynn supplied the fainting with brandy and wine, and the less helpless with hot soups, meats, &c.*

The little girl, an extremely pretty 3-year-old with big blue eyes, gave her name as 'Lissy'. She was the reason an anonymous and assertive passenger on the *New World* had urged the captain and crew to come to the rescue, her eyes connecting with his – or so it had seemed – across a nightmarish sea filled with corpses and wreckage while the *Ocean Monarch* consumed itself with fire around her.

When Lissy's mother disappeared into the sea with her sister she had clung to the grey-haired old man and he, in his turn, took care of her until hours later they were rescued from their little space beside the figurehead. Samuel Fielding's hands were severely burned but still he had kept his charge safe on the ship, putting her wellbeing ahead of his own. The kindly old man had been emigrating from Glossop to be with his children in America. A fustian weaver by trade, his raw, blackened hands would be unusable for some time to come.

Also saved from the bowsprit by Bragdon and Jerome were the Hill sisters, Sarah Ann and Sophia from Rochdale, the hair singed off the little girls' heads, their mother lost in the wreck. Another orphan was being fussed over with them, a 3-year-old who gave her name as 'Kate' and could speak only Irish. This was probably Catherine Sullivan of Mitchelstown, Ireland, sole survivor of a family of six. Johanna Ronayne, 28, from the Manchester/Rochdale area of England, could sympathise with the little girl. She watched the other five members of her party take a rope and descend from the ship only to plunge to their deaths beneath the waves. Johanna had been about to take her chances and follow them anyway when a stranger grabbed the rope from her hands, also died, and somehow cut her off from that almost certainly fatal route. Instead Johanna was rescued by Frederick Jerome and the crew of the boat beneath the bowsprit.

They were joined in this by men from the *Prince of Wales*, which had arrived at the wreck soon after the *Afonso*. Despite protestations from some of the passengers, the coasting steamer had diverted from her course, and as a result, in addition to the sixty-three men, women and children saved by the *New World*, another twenty or so travellers survived.

Chapter Seven

…a huge and crowded ship on fire at sea is the very embodiment of intense suffering and despair: with its blazing deck, densely thronged with men, women, and children, who know that whether they stand where they are, or leap into the yawning void beneath, death is their inevitable doom. Many in this case did 'anticipate their grave' by throwing themselves into the waves; others were crushed to death in the mass which eagerly struggled to elude the advancing element; others again clung to the masts, which broke beneath their unusual burden, and fell with them overboard; while the greater number, after enduring inconceivable suffering, were rescued by the vessels which at length arrived to their assistance. The Prince de Joinville it appears was in one of these, and exerted himself nobly in giving assistance to the perishing crew. He ought to be prouder in being thus privileged to save human beings from the jaws of death, than if he had accomplished his ancient boast of humbling the navy of 'perfidious Albion.'

(*Dumfries and Galloway Standard,* 30 August 1848)

Peril with pilots, near the coast of North Wales, afternoon, Thursday 24 August 1848

While other vessels sped to the rescue of those trapped on or near the *Ocean Monarch*, and survivors clutched unknown children to their chests and comforted complete strangers, another sixteen were struggling in supposed safety. The men and women who crowded into the ship's waist boat as it launched in the initial chaos, or jumped into the water and were then pulled in, had been deposited by First Mate Bragdon on board one of the pilot boats plying its trade in the area. It was the only reasonable option for them at the time, but they still didn't feel safe, and with good reason.

At first the party of passengers and crew were relieved to be out of the sinking waist boat and away from the shrieks and smoke of the *Ocean Monarch*. Among them was an Irishman who had pulled his sister from the water, reaching through the water until he caught a handful of her hair, yanking her above the surface as her body sank. Women rarely if ever cut their hair, and generally wore tight and restrictive clothes on their torso and many layers of thick petticoats on their lower half to give them the coveted silhouette of a hand bell. Usually the weight and the bulk of the skirts made it impossible to swim but some women's clothing had burned off, freeing their legs somewhat when – if – they reached the water around the ship. Other women wore very little in the first place, perhaps a cotton or linen shift, as they had retired to their berths with seasickness.

Occasionally the layers of skirts trapped sufficient pockets of air to enable women to stay afloat until they were rescued, as in the case of another Irish passenger from the *Ocean Monarch*. According to the *Belfast Commercial Chronicle* of 30 August 1848, a journalist

> *conversed with a young unmarried woman, from the county Leitrim who* [was] *almost dead when brought* [on board] *the Affonso, and certainly her account of her miraculous rescue is most surprising. She stated to us that long after the fire had broken out somebody on deck – she thinks a female – tumbled her overboard, probably thinking that death by drowning would be a far preferable death for her than death by burning; but more probable still, the action was prompted by those maddening, and almost inexplicable, feelings by which persons in sight of dreadful and impending ruin are agitated.*
>
> *The young woman, however, after plunging into the water, was borne upon the tops of the waves. She seems to have floated. Sometimes she was ascending, and at others descending. At length she caught hold of a hand. It was the hand of a dying woman. They seized each other with a sort of death grasp, and for some time it was a kind of struggle with them as to who should be the conqueror or last survivor of the two. The dying woman, however, who had been shattered about the head, from having been no doubt frequently driven against the hull of the burning vessel, breathed her last. Her head sank, but her body floated on the water. Our female informant held on by that dead body, and was absolutely saved*

> *by it. It bore her up for a considerable length of time, until at length she was taken on board the Affonso, where she was put into a warm bed, and had brandy and other restoratives administered to her.*

As well as the Irish siblings, Bragdon and his fellow rescuers had deposited another eight passengers and six crewmen on the pilot boat. They outnumbered the two pilots and their lad but were so weak and traumatised they were completely at their mercy. Usually, this would not have been an issue.

Edward Rogers was one of the seamen now on the *Pilot Queen of Chester*, which usually sailed around the Dee estuary. He was the one who actually cut the *Ocean Monarch*'s stern boat adrift, and as he later recalled in the *London Daily News* of 1 September 1848, they were then 'at the mercy of the wind and waves'. As he pointed out, forestalling any critics who might have suggested they should have returned to the *Ocean Monarch* to collect more people, they 'had only one oar, and could neither steer nor pull till the Chester pilot boat picked us up. ... After they picked us up they picked up the other boat in which the mate [Jotham Bragdon] and Mr Powell were.'

At this point they had been perhaps three or four miles to the windward of the wreck. Rogers thought 'they might have worked up. They gave the mate their oars, however, and would have had to go against both wind and tide.' The passengers in particular now wanted to return to land. They were tired, cold, soaked to the skin, traumatised and sick. The motion of the pilot boat on the waves was more pronounced than that of the much larger *Ocean Monarch*, and their seasickness was debilitating and deeply unpleasant.

Henry Powell was already an invalid before the awful circumstances of the wreck. He was a successful capitalist from London whose family had originally immigrated to the US in 1835 when Henry was 14. His father William had founded a lace factory in Belgium, and the Powell Valve and Brassworks Company in Cincinnati in 1846, and was known for making 'the first brass faucet west of the Allegh[e]ny Mountains'. Henry was one of three brothers and he had taken a second class cabin passage on the *Ocean Monarch* in an effort to rejoin his family in Cincinnati, Ohio. A man who was used to a certain degree of respect and privilege, what he was about to experience on board the *Pilot Queen* would anger him greatly.

As he told the *Carnarvon and Denbigh Herald and North and South Wales Independent* of 2 September 1848,

> *As soon as I got on board, I, with several other passengers, went below; we stripped off our wet clothes and tumbled into the berths for warmth, most of us being dreadfully seasick at the time. In about an hour after I heard a loud quarrel upon deck. I immediately dressed myself in a seaman's old torn jacket and trousers, wrapped a blanket round my chest, and proceeded above. It appeared that the men belonging to the pilot boat were determined to take us no farther, their excuse being that it was too dangerous to approach the coast.*

This simply was not true. As a coroner later stated in the *Southern Reporter and Cork Commercial Courier* of 5 September 1848, 'This I should remark, is a notorious falsehood, for the coast along the[r]e is quite accessible at all times.' But the reluctant passengers were in no position to make the pilots change their course. Several of the passengers who had managed to retain a coin or two on their person had begged the pilots to return them to land, offering to pay them a shilling each in an effort to make it worth their while since common decency clearly wasn't sufficient reason to do so. One respectable-looking young man, noted for his appearance of cleanliness by the others, even offered them a whole sovereign as recompense for his safe delivery to a nearby port or harbour, but heard nothing but excuses in return. Seaman Rogers, who remained on deck, grew increasingly concerned. According to the *London Daily News* of 1 September 1848, he later stated that the older of the pilots 'was tacking and trying to get to windward; he said he would put us ashore at Hilbre Island; but instead of doing so he kept veering and picking up things, among them a main gallant yard quite new'.

Hilbre Island is actually an archipelago of three small islands near the south-west tip of the Wirral, the peninsula jutting between Wales and Liverpool. At low tide they can be reached from the mainland on foot, and if the survivors had been set down there they would have been noticed and could easily have reached the Green Lodge Hotel at Hoylake, and the warmth and sustenance they so desperately needed. Instead the pilots continued to traverse the area in search of wreckage and luggage, something they could arguably have engaged in after depositing their unwilling passengers on land.

Pilots lived difficult lives but that was no excuse for this behaviour. As Henry Powell later stated in the *Carnarvon and Denbigh Herald and North and South Wales Independent* of 2 September 1848, 'The opinion of our party, however, was, that their object was to return to the neighbourhood of the burning ship, and pick up all the articles they could find. They had already secured several boxes [and] one trunk belonging to one of the cabin passengers'. Edward Rogers noted that pilot John Bennion, 41, pulled the trunk from the water when they were about five or six miles from the Welsh coast, and 'afterwards picked up two oars and a ladder. He kept tacking and would put us neither at one place nor another', (*London Daily News*, 1 September 1848).

This changed when an Irish fishing smack came in sight; Bithell and Bennion agreed to take them to it but insisted they were to keep the boat their visitors had arrived in. This led to the 'tremendous scuffle' that roused Henry Powell and most of the other passengers from the berths below. When Powell stepped on deck he was dismayed to find some of the wet clothes he had stripped off there earlier had now disappeared, and the shirt he did find was now missing its gold studs. There was a tangle of clothing, sails, rigging, ropes, and wood on deck along with the trunk Bennion had retrieved. Seaman Rogers and some of the others argued with the pilots about this mishandling of their fellow travellers' property and insisted on being put aboard the Irish vessel now approaching them and keeping the *Ocean Monarch*'s boat, too. The pilots had a little boat beside their vessel in addition to the one originally belonging to the *Ocean Monarch*, and while the rest of their passengers were distracted, one of them placed the trunk inside then slipped away, out of reach. This prompted one of the rescued sailors to exclaim, 'Damn it, what a shame to let that fellow take away that trunk', but there was nothing they could realistically have done to prevent it.

At this point the situation on deck appeared to many to be growing increasingly dangerous. Eventually the older pilot, Thomas Bithell, agreed to transport his unwilling passengers across to the fishing smack and the crowd of weak and traumatised survivors filed overboard into the *Ocean Monarch*'s boat. He demanded payment from each of them, a shilling apiece – fifteen shillings in total – but many wore only a shirt or their undergarments and didn't have any valuables on them. Everything they owned was back on the ship. Ship surgeon William Ellis, originally from Belfast, had lost all his instruments and books as well as his diploma from the Royal College of Surgeons. Others had lost family members and friends, their letters of introduction, money, goods, clothing, and personal mementoes. They were lucky not to have also lost their lives.

It was almost too much for Henry Powell. He was the last to leave the cabin apart from a naked young man who was too weak to dress himself and join the exodus above. In his frail state Powell couldn't bear to relinquish the pilots' blanket just yet, it's tatty material protecting him from the chill air. One of the pilots noticed it round the young man's shoulders and grabbed at it in a fury, exclaiming 'God damn ye, give that here!' Powell begged, 'No, don't take it from me!' and instead offered the man, who should have acted as his protector instead of tormentor, the silver lever watch he wore around his neck – the last of his possessions. It was worth a lot more than the five shillings the pilot demanded of him in exchange for allowing him the use of the blanket, and as Powell sarcastically noted, 'the articles we had left in their possession repaid them well for the mercy we received at their hands,' (*Carnarvon and Denbigh Herald and North and South Wales Independent*, 2 September 1848).

The fishing smack *Queen*, of Wicklow, received the unhappy party on board and immediately made them as comfortable as possible. As the passengers and seamen settled into their new quarters, they realised they had left one of their number behind in the cabin. Upon hearing of their ordeal, and the apparently wealthy young man currently lying in the *Pilot Queen*'s cabin, the fishermen commented that 'We might rely on't that if that young gentleman had money on him the 'Wallasey wrackers' would soon murder him for it.' According to a greatly disquieted Henry Powell, they 'concluded their remarks by observing, "That we had no idea of the black work going on in these quarters."' The two Irishmen treated the survivors with every kindness before landing them at Seacombe at around 7 pm. There they were handled in 'a very hospitable manner' by 'Messrs. Parry of the hotel', (*Carnarvon and Denbigh Herald and North and South Wales Independent*, 2 September 1848). An hour later they took the eight o'clock ferry across to Liverpool, the other passengers taking up a collection for the survivors amounting to £2. 4*s*. which was divided among them. Upon their arrival in the busy port of Liverpool, fifteen hours after their departure that morning, they reported their concerns regarding their fellow survivor to the police there. No one had heard a word about him, and he hadn't been landed by the *Pilot Queen* elsewhere.

Among the party of survivors were the *Ocean Monarch*'s surgeon, William Ellis of Belfast, and Second Mate William Perry Gibbs, as well as 20-year-old William Greenough who had shared a berth with the young man they had left behind. Different names were given to the police and the press in the confusion, including 'Coombes', but it was eventually established that the missing passenger was a handloom weaver from Huddersfield called John Sheard. This 24-year-old was now missing feared murdered. The wrecking of the *Ocean Monarch* was turning out to be a worse tragedy than anyone could ever have suspected.

*****

While ships collected survivors from the blazing wreck and the water around it, telegraphers passed messages along the coast warning of casualties and the loss of cargo. People clustered on the beach and promontories round Llandudno to watch the final throes of the rescue efforts, and another man and woman were missing feared dead, although they were actually safe, if not entirely well. Ships sent boats to port filled with survivors, or called back themselves, but one vessel had already delivered twenty-two others to the *Afonso* and the sea was running too high to safely allow them to turn back again. When the *Sea Queen* sailed past another two survivors bobbing on the waves, the decision was made to retrieve them from the water but then, instead of returning them to another vessel or a port in England or Wales, to carry them onwards to New York. A boat was sent down and a rope thrown to each, then the pair were pulled on board and transferred to the ship. No one in the United Kingdom or Ireland knew that Mary Ann Smyth and William Jackson were alive and on their way to America. They, along with nearly 200 of their fellow travellers, were feared dead.

William Jackson had been travelling with his young family from Sheffield for Boston. As the 31-year-old pawnbroker related in a letter home which was liberally quoted in the *Northampton Mercury* of 28 October 1848, he had been on deck near the captain when the steward ran up the stairs to raise the alarm.

> *You may guess what my feelings were at that moment. I ran down into my berth and fetched my family on deck. It burst out into a flame directly, and there appeared nothing but death, either by fire or water, staring us in the face. I took charge of Willy and Richard, and my wife took charge of Elizabeth. We determined to keep together, and did so for a considerable time; but there was so much confusion that we found it to be impossible to do so. We kept making our way over to the fore part of the ship out of the way of the fire; and as there were two other ships in sight, we entertained some hopes of being saved.*

Sadly this wasn't to be.

> *The heat became so intense that we were obliged to get over the bows of the ship, and hang by the ropes and chains; but I had not been there long before the ropes that sustained me and the two children gave way, and we were all going to the bottom together. My wife entreated me to try and save myself, if I could not save the children, so I was obliged to let go both of the dear lambs at one moment, in order to try and save myself, for the sake of those who were still left with a hope of being saved.*

And with that, Willy, 4, and his 19-month-old brother Richard, plunged out of their father's arms and into the roiling water below. As he later recalled,

> *I then got hold of another rope, and hung by it. I only saw my wife and Elizabeth once after this; they were then upon what is called the jibboom – a strong piece of wood that sticks out over the front of the ship. They appeared in a very safe position, and I felt almost certain they would be saved.*

There were so many people, lying three and four thick along the ropes and chains criss-crossing the front of the ship, clutching at each other's hair, limbs, and clothing, that Jackson soon lost sight of his wife and daughter. The noise was overwhelming, with the fire roaring and crackling all around, the waves surging below, wreckage knocking against the hull, and the screams and coughs of those still alive and afraid. At about 3.30 pm he was pulled to safety.

Portions of his letter home were reproduced in the *Sheffield Independent* of 21 October 1848, including his explanation of how he now came to be penniless having boarded the *Ocean Monarch* as a relatively prosperous man,

> *I had taken my money and wrapped it up, and put it into one of the boxes, thinking it would be safer there than in my pocket, as we had a nice room to ourselves, that we could lock up, and, my money being in gold, it seemed to drag my pocket so much.*

This may have saved his life, but it meant when he was taken on board the *Sea Queen* with just the clothing he had on his back he faced a long and treacherous voyage where he was entirely dependent upon the charity of others. Luckily the Nitherward family of Ireland took pity on him. Joseph and Mary, both 40, and their daughters Eliza, 12, and Ann, 10, were immigrating to America and allowed him the use of their berth and blankets. This generous and selfless family also shared their provisions with him and attempted to comfort him as he wept for his boys. Mary Ann Smyth appears to have been made similarly welcome.

As far as what remained of their families and friends were concerned, they were both missing presumed dead. All William could do was hope and pray his wife and little girl were among the living.

Chapter Eight

One of those startling calamities which, even in the midst of political convulsions, stand out as points upon which to fix the links of chronology, occurred on Thursday ... No language of ours can add to the melancholy interest with which these details will be perused. ... It is premature to criticise the conduct of those to whom blame has attached in connexion with the sad affair. It is more gratifying to be able to render undivided praise to the gallantry of the brave foreigners, the Marquis de Lisbon, the Prince de Joinville, the Duke d'Aumale, and Admiral Grenfell, and the not less gallant Briton – Mr Littledale – who so nobly and successfully exerted themselves in the preservation of life. The whole circumstance was one which displayed not merely the romance of real terror, but the romance of real generosity; and will as long be chronicled for the lesson it teaches, as for the interest it will sustain for coming generations.

(*Belfast News-Letter*, 29 August 1848)

Returning to the Liverpool area, from about 8 pm, Thursday 24 August 1848

One by one, the captains and crew agreed that nothing more could be done. Some of the rescuers were scorched and blistered, their flesh blackened from the fire as well as the times they had collided with people and objects. The berths on their vessels were full of the battered, burnt, and bruised survivors. Some were sobbing for lost loved ones, others were desperate to return to shore in case friends and family had been retrieved from the water near the wreck by another vessel. Cabin passenger Anna Roper was among them, hoping at least one of her children had survived the turmoil. She had already lost her youngest daughter to the waves but didn't know what had become of 3-year-old Lissy. While the rescue was in full force, seamen and other volunteers swapped on and off the little boats, and took breaks on other ships. Before they retrieved their boats from the water and heaved anchor, the captains had to make sure their crew and no other (apart from hands from the *Ocean Monarch*) were on their ships.

Many of the rescuers and survivors were cold and wet, in need of more food, drinks, and blankets than the galleys and cupboards could provide. Kindly crewmen stripped off their outer layers and shivered through their work in order to clothe the men, women, and children now in their care. As the Brazilian vice consul for Liverpool, J. R. Froes stated at the subsequent inquest, 'many of [the people on the *Afonso*], for the relief of others, divested themselves almost completely of clothing.' Provisions intended for a party, as on the *Afonso*, or a trans-Atlantic voyage, as on the *New World*, were doled out to all and sundry, more than many of the poorer passengers could have dreamed of in normal circumstances.

With the final delivery of survivors to the nearby steamer *Prince of Wales*, including Samuel Fielding and little girl Lissy from the burning bowsprit, Frederick Jerome and his fellow rescuers rowed to the *Afonso*. They were greeted with a heroes' welcome. On Jerome's arrival on deck he was greeted with hearty handshakes from the Prince de Joinville and his equally impressed brother, the Duke d'Aumale. They pressed gold coins upon him and the other rescuers and spoke loudly and highly of their brave deeds, the heroes rewarded with the charity of the elite.

As the *Carnarvon and Denbigh Herald and North and South Wales Independent* of 2 September 1848 reported in a somewhat obsequious manner, the Prince and the Duke,

> *behaved most gallantly, humanely, and charitably, using their best exertions to rescue the sufferers from impending death, and distributing all the money they had with them in their endeavours. The Princess was naturally dreadfully affected with the frightful appearance of all around. Too much praise cannot be given to Admiral Grenfell for his coolness and bravery. … All the survivors who were taken on board the Affonso speak in the warmest terms of praise of her noble commander, and of her most benevolent crew. Everything that the frigate had on board was liberally and bountifully supplied to them. Biscuit and bread, meat and vegetables, brandy and wine, all were handed about with*

> *unbounded profusion and we need scarcely say that these esculents and drinkables were most acceptable to the wretched sufferers, all of whom were drenched with wet, parched with thirst, and most of whom were literally in a state of nudity.*
>
> *And, talking of nudity, this most humane crew supplied to the best of their ability the wants of the survivors in this respect. To one they gave a coat, to another trousers, and to another a shirt, until, at length, in this way, every one brought on board the frigate had some essential requisite of clothing supplied. When the Affonso arrived in the Mersey she anchored in the Sloyne, and the distinguished company landed at the new stage, in one of the ferry steamers. The passengers who were saved were transferred to the President steamer, and landed at the Prince's Pierhead, doubtless with the view of being near to the Northern Hospital, whither those who were burned and otherwise injured were conveyed.*
>
> *On landing they presented a sad pitiable spectacle. Many of the men and women were almost in a state of nudity. Some of them had their hands bandaged, and some their arms, legs, and other parts of their bodies bound up, having been injured by their contact with spars in the water, by knocking against the boats, and in other ways. All the sufferers,* [many] *of whom were emigrants from the South of Ireland, have lost their luggage, clothes, and everything which they possessed. Many of them when landed were nearly naked, and had borrowed coats, jackets, and other articles of wearing apparel, in order to protect them from the effect of the cold. A number of policemen's top-coats and other articles of apparel were sent from the Dock Police-office, for the use of the unfortunate people, as they were landed at the pierhead from the different vessels which conveyed them into port.*

They were met there by the district superintendent and a group of policemen who sought to provide reassurance and establish order among the traumatised survivors thronging the docks. It took a while to find doctors to attend to the injured and unwell, there being none available at the Northern Hospital. The men raced through the busy streets radiating from the docks and obtained three from the Dispensary instead, then returned to the ship. As J. R. Froes stated later,

> *we got surgeons for the wounded and disabled, and saw that they were all well looked after. There were very few of those with us seriously injured. I think out of 156 we got off, not more than ten have been much wounded. It is very difficult to estimate the exact loss of life.*

What Mr Froes saw as 'much wounded' may have differed somewhat from the opinions of the survivors themselves, many of whom struggled to move without soreness and had bruising yet to bloom across their skin. One man had a compound fracture of the leg, his bones poking through the skin and putting him at great risk of suppuration, amputation, and deadly infection. Luckily his exposure to saltwater was in his favour.

Many had painful burns on their hands, heads, and feet. This was something, sadly, that the surgeons would have been very familiar with. According to *The Transactions of the Provincial Medical and Surgical Association, Volume 18*, 'In the large manufacturing towns children are frequently burnt to death during the absence of their parents at work,' and there were many thousands of burns serious enough to require medical attention in the United Kingdom every year. Treatments varied enormously but may have involved blood-letting, purgatives, and the application of creams, oils, liniments, treacle, gin, lavender water, flour, and cotton wool to the surface of the burn. This might be scraped off every so often and reapplied to the raw skin left underneath. Some physicians recommended wiping turpentine over the burned skin, which sometimes hurt so much that extra pain relief would be required and might have a worse effect on the patient overall. Poultices were also commonly applied, and according to *Transactions* these could include substances such as oatmeal or cow dung as a principal ingredient. Laudanum, ammonia, wine, and brandy would be taken 'internally' while physicians watched for the silent shivering that could indicate a poor outcome for their patient. Shock was a major killer but that, along with infection, was poorly understood.

As with the man with the broken leg, those with burns may not have realised that their immersion in salt water would help to save them from infection. At that time, cold water, whether with or without salt, was not considered helpful in the treatment of burns. Instead it was seen as a form of quackery.

Among the burns victims requiring treatment were the Booker family from Sheffield. Farmer James Booker of Bent's Green, Eccleshill, had been travelling with his son and daughter to America while their mother remained at home. They lost everything but their lives on the wreck. According to the *Leeds Intelligencer* of 9 September 1848, their escape 'was mainly the result of their own courageous exertions, and is an instance of the great importance and value of presence of mind, aided by firmness of purpose.'

Mary Booker, 24, managed to stay with her father and younger brother, 17-year-old Edwin. She,

> *had a rope tied round her waist by her brother while on board the burning vessel; she was then lowered into the sea, her father and brother holding by the rope; a boat being at hand, her brother sprang into it, her father in the meantime continuing to hold by the rope.*

James was 61, but years of work as a farmer and a grinder allowed him to take her weight alone. Mary was dangling at the end of the rope, at risk of drowning or being battered against the hull or pierced by wreckage. Luckily,

> *After much exertion on the part of her brother, she was got into the boat, apparently in a drowning state, and then taken on board the Affonso, which was at hand for the purpose of receiving as many as were brought to it. Her brother was then received on board the same vessel. Mr Booker, the father, let himself down from the Ocean Monarch by a burning cable, and as a matter of course his hands were severely scorched. He was taken into the Bangor packet, and from thence was transferred to the Affonso.*

When the small party of survivors landed from Seacombe after their unpleasant encounter with the Dee pilots, they eagerly sought out their fellow sufferers and news of the living and the lost. According to the *North Wales Chronicle and Advertiser for the Principality* of 29 August 1848,

> *When* [the crewmen among the party] *landed at the pierhead, some of their messmates, who had arrived in the yacht, greeted the new comers in the most tender terms, and the meeting of these hardy sons of Neptune,*

> *after their 'hair-breadth 'scape' is described as one of the most affecting. The men actually hugged each in a rough, but honest embrace, and tears were drawn from many of the spectators who witnessed the touching scene. The men inquired eagerly after others of their comrades, and tears, both of joy and sorrow, ran down their cheeks.*

Of the approximately 400 people who left Liverpool on the *Ocean Monarch* that morning, 209 arrived back at the docks the same evening. Another twenty were still on board the *Prince of Wales* as the steamer carried on with its journey to Bangor, and would be returned the following day. Mary Ann Smyth and William Jackson, currently on their way to New York, were counted among the roughly 170 men, women, and children still missing and feared dead. For a shipwreck so close to shore in the middle of a summer's day, near a busy port with plenty of other vessels in sight, the death toll was truly shocking.

The body of the little girl who died as she was handed up to the second mate on the *Prince of Wales* steamer was removed from the ship and carried to the agency house on George's pier at Menai Bridge for storage until an inquest could be arranged. On Anglesey, a kindly local druggist, Mr Thomas, worked with the ill and injured through the night, alleviating their suffering where he could, administering comfort and medicine to people who should have been asleep in their berths on their way to America.

As the somewhat melodramatic *Friends' Review, Vol. 1* said,

> *the Ocean Monarch, laden with men, and women, and little ones, set out from England's shores for the world's asylum of the west, and full of hope the proud ship flew over her ocean way: but the hills of Carnarvon were illumined that night by another light than that of moon or stars, and the wails* [of the people involved] *filled her night winds. One hundred and* [seventy] *victims perished in the waves, and the blackened hull of a mighty ship was their monument.*

But even this wouldn't remain visible for long.

While many of the survivors rested in borrowed beds at the workhouse or with friends and family nearby, and some groaned with pain and grief, what was left of the *Ocean Monarch* kept the sky aglow near Llandudno. As the clearly upset Reverend Remington recalled in *The Sailor's Magazine*, 1848, the direction of the wind meant the ship he was on had to repeatedly sail close to the site of the disaster. All around them were bits of wreckage knocking against the hull, bodies barely glimpsed below the surface of the water, cabbages and clothing. The *New World* was no longer racing the *Ocean Monarch*, but was full of people mourning its loss. The Reverend told the journalist,

> *The wind being ahead, we had to tack back and forth, so that we came quite near the burning wreck frequently during the afternoon and evening. At about 1 o'clock at night, we were receding farther and farther from this scene of horror. – I remained upon deck until after mid-night, expecting every moment the light to disappear. It grew more and more dim, both from our increasing distance, and its own diminution. Shortly after, it disappeared altogether.*

This sinking was witnessed by another vessel, which had remained nearby throughout the evening. According to the *Carnarvon and Denbigh Herald and North and South Wales Independent* of 2 September 1848,

> *The Ocean Monarch went down at her anchors, on Friday morning, at half-past one o'clock. The weather was fine, with a gentle breeze from the westward. The captain of the steam-tug Liver, who was about thirty yards from the wreck when it sank, says, that with the exception of the solid timbers about the stem, on which was the figure-head representing Neptune, with his trident, in almost perfect state, the fire had consumed the whole of the upper works to within a few inches of the water's edge. Indeed, so even had been the work of destruction round the sides of the vessel, that it appeared to have been wrought by carpenters. The sea first made its way into the after part of the ship and as she gradually settled herself into the bosom of the deep, large volumes of flames, with a hissing and crackling noise rushed into the air, till at length, being completely ingulfed* [*sic*], *she disappeared in about fourteen fathoms, causing a heavy swell for the moment. When the sea became settled nothing was to be seen of the wreck save a few pieces of burnt timber and some spars floating near the spot. Thus ended the sad but eventful career*

> *of this once noble vessel. Little more than twelve hours had elapsed since she was viewed with admiration by seamen as they passed her pursuing her course to the west in all her majesty and splendour, containing within her beautifully-formed hull* [about] *396 souls, who had then every reason to expect a favourable issue to their intended voyage.*

And with that last surge of the sea, this once magnificent ship sank with the remains of many of those hopeful travellers still trapped on board.

*****

Friday morning brought the first inquest for those involved with the wreck. This took place, according to the *North Wales Chronicle and Advertiser for the Principality* (29 August 1848), before William Jones, Esq., the coroner for Anglesey, and 'a respectable jury' at the agency house, George's pier, Menai Bridge. The subject of the inquest, specifically, was the little girl who died in her rescuer's arms, her salvation from the water coming mere minutes too late. Several of the sailors and would-be emigrants gave evidence, including James Batty, First Mate of the *Prince of Wales*, who pulled her from the water and was the last to see her open her eyes. As he recalled for the people assembled in the room, because of the smoke 'When we first saw the vessel [we] thought it a steamer coming down before the wind, but on finding it to be on fire we bore down upon her.' At that point, the *Ocean Monarch* had been about fifteen miles away. As far as the child whose body lay before them was concerned, they may as well have been on the moon.

The heroic fustian weaver from Glossop, Derbyshire, who refused to surrender little Lissy to the waves, was one of those examined. His hands were white with bandages, concealing severe burns and protecting them from dirt and the stares of those present. As the paper related to their readers,

> *One of the jurors put the question what inducement a man at his time of life could possibly have to undertake so long a voyage, to which he replied, 'I am a widower and have two daughters doing well in America. At their request, I was on my way to join them.' 'I suppose you will not make another attempt,' rejoined the juror. The old man shook his head doubtingly, adding, 'I am not quite certain of that neither.'*

Having ascertained from other witnesses and survivors that the captain and crew of the burning ship had been sober and sensible, and did their best to extinguish the fire, the coroner spoke with the jury. Their verdict regarding the death of the anonymous child was 'Accidentally Drowned'. They made a point of adding that in the opinion of the jury, 'the greatest credit was due to the commander, officers, and crew of the *Prince of Wales* for the prompt and efficient assistance rendered to the passengers on board the burning vessel'.

After reliving their ordeal before the jury, it was time for the survivors to return to Liverpool, and see if any of their family and friends had also made it to land alive. The *Prince of Wales* 'which had been detained better than an hour beyond her stated time for starting, got under weigh shortly after the inquisition had been brought to a close'. Many of the local people, who had so generously sought to support the survivors with donations of money, medicines, food, and clothing, waved them off.

As journalists recounted in the *North Wales Chronicle and Advertiser for the Principality* of 29 August 1848, reporters went on board the *Prince of Wales* to spend time with the victims of this terrible tragedy, which they could safely assume would continue to fill the papers for weeks to come. They related to their readers that

> *On the quarter deck, seated on a lady's knee, we saw an interesting blue eyed girl from three to four years old, saved from the wreck, who said her name was 'Lissy', and that she had a sister called 'Jane' (supposed to be the deceased* [child discussed at the inquest]*.) Three other children, Sophia and Sarah Ann Hill, sisters, and a third who said her name was 'Johanna', were among the saved also, and in the same part of the vessel.*

Sophia and Sarah Ann had lost all their hair as well as their mother, whom they had watched drown and drift away before they were rescued. Her auburn hair would have made her body stand out among the many others nearby.

With the first of several inquests pertaining to the tragedy now complete, this group of survivors now headed back to Liverpool. The forlorn travellers were treated to a sumptuous breakfast below decks on the steamer as it puffed along parallel to the Welsh coast. It would have been a struggle to eat and drink with bandaged hands, and throats sore from smoke, but they managed. Whether the survivors turned away from their view of the water as they approached the wreck and the detritus cluttering the surface above it is not recorded. Some may have looked out for luggage, belongings, and the remains of their beloved, but it would be entirely understandable if they looked inwards to their rescuers instead. Many certainly stayed below deck where it was relatively warm and cosy, thanks to the heat emanating from the boiler.

The journalists continued their virtual tour of the steamer for their readers, many of whom would have been frantically scouring the papers for reassuring details that their loved ones were still alive:

> *In the fore-cabin we conversed with other survivors of the ill-fated Ocean Monarch, whom we found in the act of partaking of a substantial breakfast. … Sixteen persons, adults and children, returned in the Prince of Wales to Liverpool, whose wants from the time of their being taken on board were liberally supplied by Capt. Dani. Many of them had burnt hands or other injuries, sustained in the fearful struggle for life.*

Meanwhile, back in Liverpool, those who could make it to the steamer's usual docking area did so. There they quizzed each other on who was seen where and when, hoping to hear details of those taken aboard the steamer as a breeze blew off the turgid brown waters of the Mersey and masts rocked like metronomes in the docks. As the *Carnarvon and Denbigh Herald and North and South Wales Independent* of 2 September 1848 later reported,

> *Many of those who have been bereaved by this melancholy disaster, those whose relations or friends were missing, clung to the hope that they were amongst those saved by the Prince of Wales steamer, which had proceeded on her voyage. The Prince of Wales, which had been anxiously expected about three in the afternoon, hove in sight shortly after five, and there was an eager and painful rush made by the crowd to learn what passengers she had saved. On the vessel's approach the gallant captain, who stood upon the paddle-box, was hailed with a round of hearty and spontaneous cheering, a gratifying and becoming*

> *tribute to the exertions of himself and crew. Great disappointment was felt, however, on its becoming known that the great majority of those whom the vessel had been the means of saving had been placed on board the Brazilian frigate, and were already here.*

A long and desperate night and day of hoping against hope for the arrival of certain faces at the dock had proved fruitless for many, including those on board the steamer. As the journalists continued,

> *The poor creatures were huddled together for warmth in the engine-room. They had themselves more inquiries to make about missing friends than ability to answer the many eager questions put. They spoke in high terms of the kindness with which they had been treated on board the Prince of Wales. One of the party had been picked up floating on a spar, nearly three miles from the scene of the disaster.*

Captain Dani and his wife brought with them Mr W. E. Timothy, the City of Dublin Company's agent, and a Mr Thomas Dew. They carried the very valuable contributions from people in Menai Bridge which totalled the 'handsome sum' of £56 18*s* 3*d*. This had been raised in a matter of hours by the kindly locals as well as visitors to the area such as 'A gentleman and lady staying at the George Hotel, Mr and Miss Ford, [the former contributing] £10, the latter £5. Every one was ready with his mite to mitigate the rigours of so disastrous a calamity.' Upon their arrival in Liverpool, this money was paid over to Mr Rushton, the Stipendiary Magistrate there, 'to be added to the fund now being collected in that town for the same object'.

In addition to this good news, there was one very special reunion made possible by the arrival of the *Prince of Wales* steamer. Lissy Roper, the pretty 3-year-old who had spent so many hours clinging to a stranger as the fire raged ever closer, was about to see her mother. The little girl's sister Jane had been the subject of that morning's inquest in Menai Bridge. Anna Roper, 28, of Bilston near Birmingham, was confined to the Northern Hospital and terribly worried about the fate of her young children. Mrs Dani, the captain's wife who had done her best to care for the girls on the steamer, took little Lissy in a cab to the ward. Lissy was exhausted, but the bounce of the cab through the streets and the noise of the horse's hooves would have helped her stay awake. According to the newspaper, 'The poor child had the horrors of the scene so strongly impressed on its mind, that during sleep it was evidently, in imagination, again amid the terrors from which it had been rescued, frequently starting, screaming, and muttering exclamations of alarm.' As the journalists told their readers, '[her] reception by the mother may be more easily imagined than described'. Sadly for the other girls, they 'were not fortunate enough to meet with their parents, who are it is feared, among the lost'.

It would have been wholly acceptable for Captain Dani to have been recompensed for the food, drink, blankets, and passage he lavished on the survivors in his care, but to his credit he refused to even consider accepting a farthing to cover his expenses. As the paper approvingly detailed in their article, 'Captain Dani generously refused to accept any remuneration out of the funds collected at the Bridge or elsewhere, towards the spirits, provisions, &c., which he so abundantly supplied the poor sufferers with, during the time they remained on board his vessel.'

He was not alone in his kindness. Aside from giving money to Frederick Jerome and rescuers from other vessels after their efforts to remove survivors from the wreck, the Prince de Joinville and his party had shared their food, drink and clothing with those brought aboard the *Afonso*. Upon leaving the warship for his quarters at Mr Birchenough's Railway Hotel on Lime Street, he also left 10*l*. for two seamen, Francisco da Silva and Joav Candido 'who exerted themselves courageously during the dreadful scene'. One of them was much scorched. Another participant in the rescue attempts, 40-year-old Chevalier Lisboa, 'Brazilian Minister to our court, forwarded 100*l*. for the crew of the frigate *Affonso*. This fact was communicated to them, when they one and all refused to receive the money, expressing a desire that it should be handed over for the benefit of the sufferers.' The Brazilian Consulate was besieged by people inquiring after friends and relatives and worked hard to allay fears or confirm bad news wherever possible.

Despite the general atmosphere of poverty and despair in many areas of the city, people still pulled together to contribute for the unfortunate survivors who had lost virtually everything they had in the wreck. The journalists explained it thus,

> *one feeling seems to pervade all classes in the town, one of deep commiseration for the sudden misfortune which has caused so much*

> *suffering, singled with a desire to alleviate as far as possible the afflictions of the survivors. All classes participate in the emotions of sympathy which the disaster has generated, and the suggestions and movements for providing the means of mitigating the distress, as far as human means can accomplish it, are numerous.*

For many of the people now living in the North West, there was a sense that it could very easily have been them or their families struggling along the seafront wearing everything they owned.

Luckily for many of the survivors, a 'benevolent gentleman, who does not like to have his good deeds observed, [and] will thank us but little for calling public attention to his conduct in relation to the recent dreadful occurrence' was on the Brazilian frigate at the time of the wreck.

> *Mr Lynn was on board the Affonso, superintending the arrangements for the entertainment of the distinguished party who were in her. He and his lady were indefatigable in their attention to the sufferers rescued from the unfortunate ship, administering to their wants in every way possible with an active philanthrophy* [sic] *which reflects upon them the highest honour, and which will gain them the love and esteem of all who hear of their exertions. Mr Lynn's general conduct did not end on landing the poor people safely on terra firma. He got* [some of] *them comfortably lodged at the police-station, Prince's Dock, and supplied them gratuitously, on Friday, with tea, coffee, soup, and meat, for which act he has the warmest thanks of every feeling mortal.*

Mr and Mrs Lynn weren't the only generous hoteliers to take more than a professional interest in the survivors now in their care. Cabin passenger Henry Powell, who was already an invalid when he took his berth in the *Ocean Monarch*, may not have survived his period of prolonged exposure to the cold and damp aboard the *Pilot Queen* without them. He later gave an 'Interesting And Important Statement' to the press,

> *I think I owe it as a debt of gratitude to express my sincerest thanks, in a public manner, for the kindness and attention which I have received at the hands of Mr Parry, of the hotel at Seacombe, from the time that*

> *I landed at seven o'clock on Thursday evening last up to the present moment. Being in a delicate state of health, I suffered much from the exposure to wet and cold for seven or eight hours; but, through the hospitality of this gentleman and his good lady, I am fast recovering from my indisposition. On my entering their house I was immediately provided with every comfort and the attendance of their medical adviser, with constant solicitude for my welfare on the part of my kind host and hostess. I wanted for nothing and felt as though I was more under the protection of parents than that of strangers. I can only thank them for all they have done.*

Powell also made a point of stimulating interest in the press regarding his mistreatment on the *Pilot Queen* and the likely fate of the man he last saw there, lying naked and alone below deck. As one journalist said when commenting on Powell's statement, it was 'very remarkable, considering the time that has elapsed since the accident, that he has not yet been heard of … very grave suspicions are beginning to be entertained'.

Chapter Nine

Although we gave last week as correct and full an account of the destruction of the Ocean Monarch, *as time and space would permit, our report, as might be expected, was obtained under circumstances that could no more exclude error than they could supply omissions. … The intense anxiety and curiosity such a catastrophe was sure to excite, must be pleaded in extenuation of the many garbled and false statements that have crept into contemporaneous prints: but it is matter of regret that any journalist should be so rash as to prefer accusatory and damnatory charges upon hear-say evidence, that has not had time to stand the test of scrutiny. Facts may be misstated by the most careful writer, when his sources of information are scant and partial … The most grievous charges have been made against Captain Murdoch: and his mate and crew have been spoken of as though their behaviour to the passengers was cruel in the extreme: but all the survivors and spectators of the horrid scene, all who stood in the best position for knowing the facts of the case, unite in awarding to the commander of the ill fated emigrant ship, that tribute of respect and regard which first rate seamanship, unbroken presence of mind, considerate kindness, unselfish gallantry, and truly British courage, imperiously demand.*

(*Carnarvon and Denbigh Herald and North and South Wales Independent*, 2 September 1848)

Recovering in the Liverpool area, late Friday 25 to Sunday 27 August 1848

Captain Murdock felt vile. He was physically, mentally, and emotionally exhausted by the disaster that happened under his command. He returned to William Lynn's renowned Waterloo Hotel on Ranelagh Street near the docks, a popular haunt of American sea captains which had many of their portraits hung on the walls. Lynn and his second wife, Mary Anne, had helped many survivors on the *Afonso*. He was famous for setting up both the Grand National and the Waterloo Cup, and his establishment appealed to mariners and well-heeled businessmen alike. As cabin passenger James K. Fellows recalled in his memoir, when he reached this beautiful red-brick hotel where he also took a room until an alternate passage could be arranged, he 'found the house surrounded by an excited crowd, mostly seamen, calling and yelling for the *brave* captain, who had abandoned his ship … Some called him a drunkard, others a coward, but no epithet was strong enough to bring him out'. Fellows wrote that,

> *thousands of seamen and others were gathered in and about the Waterloo Hotel – head-quarters for ship-masters – discussing the bravery of Captain Murdock. He did not make his appearance, although there in his room, where he remained several days as a safe retreat. Captain Murdock, as I remember him, was a fine-looking man, of good address, though I have not seen him since he was clinging to the spar.*

What Fellows and the crowd of men and women baying for his blood didn't realise was that the reason the captain of the unfortunate *Ocean Monarch* remained in his room was because he was sick. The 41-year-old was lucky to be alive, indeed his rescuers had believed he might not survive the journey back to Liverpool as he was near death when pulled from the water and was at first unable to move from the deck unaided. Despite some of the traumatised survivors wishing for pistols to use against him, and loudly making their feelings heard outside, the captain mustered his energy and put together a statement in which he expressed his regret for the loss of the people on board and clarified his reasons for remaining in his bedroom, 'I have been quite ill for the past twenty-four hours, and confined to my bed, but I am now much better.'

The *Reading Mercury* of 26 August 1848 quoted liberally from his account, revealing the torment of a haunted man, whose commands had gone unheard in the chaos of the wreck. It had been 'a scene of the utmost confusion, noise, and disorder. My orders could not be heard.' He explained the loss of so many of his passengers, saying,

> *The flames* [burst] *with immense fury from the stern and centre of the vessel. So great was the heat in these parts, that the passengers, male and female, men, women, and children crowded to the forepart of the vessel. In their maddened despair women jumped overboard with their offspring in their arms, and sunk to rise no more. Men followed their wives in frenzy and were lost. Groups of men, women, and children also precipitated themselves into the water, in the vain hope of self-preservation, but the waters closed over many of them for ever. I pointed out to them that there were several vessels around us, but howls of lamentation and cries for help were the only answers which I could obtain to my entreaties. … The shrieks of terror and alarm baffle description. Maddened by despair, and in the vain hope of being rescued they knew not how, numbers again jumped overboard.*

This was no cold, clinical report, but a passionate account of dire tragedy from a seasoned captain clearly disturbed by this great loss. It was the first of several communications from him printed in the press, and perhaps the most emotional. As another paper commented, 'There is a simple beauty in the Captain's statement, it is the moral beauty of plain unvarnished truth', (*Carnarvon and Denbigh Herald and North and South Wales Independent*, 2 September 1848).

Some of the newspapers had already included vicious attacks upon his character and his actions in their articles on the wreck. Grief-stricken survivors gave interviews loaded with vitriol, raging at the person they viewed as responsible for their loss. One passenger, printer Joshua Wilson of Manchester, was quoted in the *Manchester Times* of 26 August 1848 as saying,

> *The captain lent no assistance at all* [during the fire]*; but cursed and swore, and blamed the steerage passengers, saying that it was their fault. Some of the passengers then asked him what was to be done, to which he replied that he was not their captain then, as the vessel was on fire. … The captain then delivered himself of a few more oaths, and disappeared, where I know not; but I believe he threw himself overboard.*

Despite a desperate struggle to reach his loved ones as they floundered in the water, Wilson lost his wife and child. John Bell backed him up in his accusations, saying,

> *before the fire broke out, Mr Wilson's child was crying, and* [the captain] *stamped his foot and told the mother to throw it overboard. For the slightest thing, he struck and swore at the steerage passengers. The noise and confusion on board the burning ship were dreadful. … I lost my wife.*

Luckily for Captain Murdock, many of the men who sailed with him wrote their own letters and sent them to the press. Surgeon William Ellis joined with a fellow cabin passenger, Boston artist Nathaniel Southworth, in writing a rebuttal, which the paper introduced by saying,

> *Several reports, relative to the conduct of Captain Murdoch, prejudicial and untrue, having got abroad, we insert the following testimonials from the crew and passengers:- Having seen a statement* [attacking] *the character of Captain Murdoch, of the Ocean Monarch, we, whose names are undersigned, feel it our duty to contradict such statement, being fully convinced that while we were on board Captain M. acted with the greatest coolness and propriety; and we believe, had the passengers acted under his direction many would have been saved who have now perished. It is stated that Captain Murdoch said that he was no longer captain of the ship, and also that he cursed and swore at the passengers. This is entirely false. We heard him tell them to keep quiet, and they would be all saved, and encourage them every way in his power.*

(*Carnarvon and Denbigh Herald and North and South Wales Independent*, 2 September 1848).

Another cabin passenger, Thomas Henry, was also prompted to write a letter to the press to defend the captain and crew from allegations of misconduct and a lack of moral fibre, which was printed alongside Ellis and Southworth's similarly supportive address.

> *Captain Murdoch is very unjustly censured. The statement, by whomsoever given, is wilfully or maliciously false for I particularly noticed his conduct from the first alarm, and I was very near him, until I jumped overboard myself; and I could see neither cowardice nor unseamanlike conduct in his actions.*

The paper went on to include another document they had received, and also commented that,

> *The following declaration, in reference to Captain Murdoch, has been spontaneously made. The original document of it bears the signatures of the first and the second mates, the carpenter, the whole of the* [surviving] *crew, and of thirty passengers, and many more signatures could have been obtained, as the passengers were exceedingly anxious to refute the calumny which has been issued against the captain.*

It echoed the sentiments of the other letters included in the article, and went on to say,

> *we saw not even the sign of cowardice in him, and that he used his utmost exertions and every endeavour to save all the lives possible, and that he did not leave the ship until all means in his power of saving life were at an end, and that it also became necessary for all who could to save themselves on articles thrown over, in order to make room for others, as the crowd were so thick that many were being crowded overboard at that time.*

From the many accounts available from witnesses on different parts of the ship, it appears clear that Captain Murdock did what he could for all on board, whether rich or poor, and that what some passengers took great offence at, others understood to be the actions of a man used to having his orders obeyed, and for good reason. The captain was an icon of faith for passengers and crew alike, the person with knowledge and experience entrusted with hundreds of lives and tons of valuable cargo. He was expected to know what to do, and when and how to do it, to ensure the safe passage of those in his care. Whether they were a grizzled mariner with decades of experience or an up-and-coming young man, they held a position of absolute godlike authority on board their ship and with that role came the crippling weight of personal as well as corporate responsibility when anything went wrong and these enormous hopes and expectations were dashed. A lot of a captain's power on board their ship came from the absolute obedience shown them by their crew, but if his orders were ignored or, as in this case, went unheard, the situation would quickly deteriorate. Some survivors sought a name to blame, but others, perhaps less traumatised by the events on the *Ocean Monarch*, were more understanding.

One cabin passenger, the ailing but perceptive Henry Powell, explained in a lengthy statement of his experiences that day, that,

> [I] *believe him to be free from all blame. It has been said that he took no notice of the fire after he was informed of its existence. Apparently to some, perhaps, he did not, but his immediate impulse was to place the ship in such a position as to keep the fire abaft* [to the rear of the ship, with the wind blowing it away from the rest of the vessel] *as much as possible, and was paying more attention to this part of his business than to the fire itself, and whilst ordering the working of the ship, was also giving directions for the extinguishing of the flames. This, no one can doubt, was the only proper course for him to adopt. With regard to what has been said about his having used rough language to some of the passengers, I certainly did hear him insist upon some of those almost maddened with fright to keep quiet, in a rough seamanlike manner, as they very much interfered with the execution of his orders. There is every excuse for this on the part of the captain. I firmly believe that the consternation among the crew was caused more by the yells and shrieks of the steerage passengers than by the fire itself. You will, perhaps, be surprised, sir, that I am enabled to go so minutely into particulars, but I can conscientiously affirm that I never for one moment lost my presence of mind, and, therefore, was perhaps better able to take notice of all that transpired, whilst I was on board, than many of my fellow-travellers.*

The journalists sought to talk to the passengers and crew in person where possible. The tragedy of the *Ocean Monarch* had shocked the United Kingdom and Ireland, as well as readers abroad, and the newspapers were keen to include as many details as they could. The *United Service Gazette* of 26 August 1848 reported, on Friday:

> *We visited the places where the unfortunate survivors have taken up their temporary residence. Never did we witness such squalid masses of human beings. Most of them are women, some with burns on their necks and shoulders, produced by the blazing masts and spars, and others with black eyes, and contused wounds upon various parts of their persons, caused by frequent surges on the tops of the waves against broken spars and the hull of the burning wreck.*

Almost a dozen victims lay in the Northern Hospital, recovering from the trauma of the wreck, while Mary Ann Smyth and William Jackson sailed ever further from home, unbeknownst to anyone in Liverpool who still counted them among the lost. The lists of the missing were enormous, with huge varieties in spellings and ages between newspapers. Bodies continued to decompose, bloating with gas and rising to the surface of the sea once again. Some floated near fishing vessels and were hooked onto the boats, others washed ashore, and among these were – occasionally – people who could be identified, and mourned.

As the *Liverpool Mercury* of 29 August 1848 detailed for their readers, a number of bodies were brought to Hoylake, Birkenhead. The paper included a letter signed 'B. Sherwood' which said,

> *We have had brought in here, from the unfortunate ship the* Ocean Monarch, *13 bodies, picked up in the Welsh Deep by our fishing-boats, viz. there are two children from one to two years old; a man about 60; a lad, 13, lame in the left ankle; a girl about six or seven, had on a black velvet frock and trousers, the lower part tartan plaid; and eight grown women, say from 20 to 60 years; two of the eight last mentioned were named Julia Dunning and Mary Jones. I have placed the bodies at the Punchbowl, Shaw's old house, they have been washed, and I have laid sails to put them on, and covered them over with my old colours.*

It is unclear if Julia had been travelling with family or friends. Mary was emigrating from Irlam, near Manchester, with her husband, 48-year-old

The Cork Examiner.

1,137.)—PRICE—SIX-PENCE. **WEDNESDAY EVENING, AUGUST 16, 1848.** SUBSCRIPTIONS, {TO THE TOW[N] {TO THE COUN[TRY]

SALES.

PONEY PHAETON & LIGHT DRAG FOR SALE.

BOTH in excellent condition, and will be found worthy the attention of parties wanting such vehicles. Apply to JULIAN'S Coach Factory, 12, South Mall. August 16, 1848.

THE NEW CORN SCYTHE.

H. E. & G. SEYMOUR beg to call attention to the above, with which One Man, with ease, can cut down from 1½ to 2 Imperial Acres, per day, laying the Swath so that it can be gathered easily in even Sheaves.

CORK HARDWARE AND IRONMONGERY WAREHOUSE, 67, PATRICK-STREET.

July, 12th, 1848.

COFFEE AS IN FRANCE.

IT is a Fact beyond Dispute that, in order to obtain really Fine Coffee, there must be a combination of the various kinds; and to produce strength and flavour certain proportions should be mixed, according to their different properties; thus it is we have become celebrated for our DELICIOUS COFFEE at 1s. 8d., which is the astonishment and delight of all who have tasted it, being the produce of Four Countries, selected and mixed by rule peculiar to our Establishment, in proportions not known to any other house.

From experiments we have made on the various kinds of Coffee, we have arrived at the fact that no one kind possesses strength and flavour. If we select a very strong Coffee it is wanting in flavour; by the same rule we find the finest and most flavourous are generally want-

SHIPPING.

NOTICE TO PASSENGERS.

IT is arranged that a limited number of engaged BOSTON PASSENGERS, leaving Cork on SATURDAY Morning next, the 19th AUGUST, will be received on board the OCEAN MONARCH directly on their arrival.

LIKEWISE—A like number of NEW YORK ENGAGED PASSENGERS will be received on board the JAVA, sailing for NEW YORK on the 20th day of August.

D. KENNELLY & CO., CORK.

TO SUCCEED *the* OCEAN MONARCH.

THE HOPE, SOULE, Commander, in Truth 1300 Tons, Sailing from LIVERPOOL for BOSTON on the 28th of August. Passengers should be in Cork on SATURDAY Morning, and apply to Messrs. HARNDEN & Co., or, D. KENNELLY & CO., CORK.

Nota Bene.—In CORK, LIVERPOOL, or BOSTON, Passage by the BOSTON LINERS can only be obtained through this connection.

FOR BOSTON,

THE TRAIN LINE PACKET OF THE 20th.

THE largest Packet Ship out of Boston, and Boston Built, the "OCEAN MONARCH," MURDOCK, Commander; in truth 1800 Tons, sailing from LIVERPOOL for BOSTON, on the 20th of August.

THE MARKETS.

CORK CORN EXCHANGE—AUG. 16, 1848.

Barrels.	THIS DAY.	Currency.
— White Wheat	00s 9d to 29s 0d	00s 0d—20 Stone.
1 Red Wheat	29s 0d to 00s 0d	00s 0d—20 do.
— Ditto	00s 0d to 00s 0d	
— Barley	00s 0d to 00s 0d	00s 0d—16 do.
— Ditto	00s 0d to 00s 0d	
57 Bere	11s 4d to 11s 6d	00s 0d
40 Oats	12s 0d to 14s 0d	00s 0d—14 do.
77 Ditto..New	12s 0d to 13s 6d	
0 Pigs	00s 0d to 00s 0d	—00s 0d per cwt.

Seed Oats.. 00s 0d to 00s 0d.

Quantity Sold at the Highest Price.

0 Barrels White Wheat; 0 Red do.; 0 Barley; 45 Bere; 17 Oats; 0 Pigs.

Barrels.	YESTERDAY.	Currency.
9 White Wheat	29s 0d to 00s 0d	00s 0d—20 Stone.
7 Red Wheat	27s 6d to 00s 0d	00s 0d—20
— Ditto	00s 0d to 00s 0d	
— Barley	00s 0d to 00s 0d	00s 0d—16 do.
— Ditto	00s 0d to 00s 0d	
35 Bere	11s 4d to 11s 6d	00s 0d
34 Oats	12s 6d to 14s 0d	00s 0d—14 do.
30 Ditto..New	11s 8d to 13s 4d	
0 Pigs	00s 0d to 00s 0d	—00s 0d per cwt.

Seed Wheat..27s 3d to 00s 0d.

Quantity Sold at the Highest Price.

0 Barrels White Wheat; 00 Red, ditto; 0 Barley; 22 Bere; 10 Oats; 0 Pigs.

PRICES OF BUTTER SATURDAY

CASK		CURRENCY.	
First Quality	81s	First Quality	73s
Second Quality	77s	Second Quality	68s
Third Quality	76s	Third Quality	67s
Fourth Quality	73s	Fourth Quality	64s
Fifth Quality	69s	Fifth Quality	60s
Sixth Quality	59s	Sixth Quality	50s

Advert for the *Ocean Monarch*, the "largest Packet Ship out of Boston, and Boston Built", which was originally supposed to sail from Liverpool for Boston on 20 August. *Cork Examiner*, 16 August 1848. *(Newspaper image © The British Library Board. All rights reserved. With thanks to The British Newspaper Archive www.britishnewspaperarchive.co.uk)*

McKay's shipyard, East Boston, image taken by Southworth and Hawes c.1855, 8 years after the *Ocean Monarch* was built here. *(Museum of Fine Arts, Boston)*

View of Boston in 1848 from East Boston, artist Edwin Whitefield. *(Boston Pictorial Archive, Boston Public Library)*

View of Liverpool, from *Pictorial Liverpool* 4th edition, 1848. This port acted as a funnel for many would-be emigrants, including thousands of famine victims. *(Liverpool Record Office, Liverpool Libraries)*

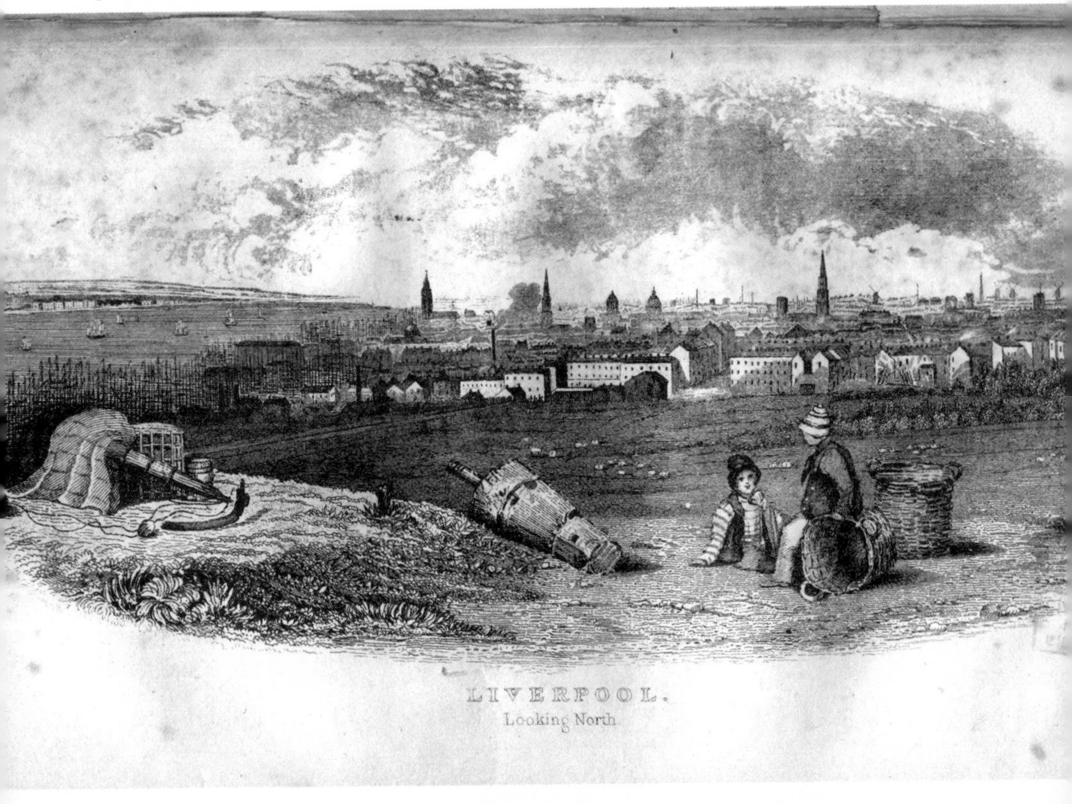

LIVERPOOL.

Looking North

'Sketch in a House at Fahley's Quay, Ennis - The Widow Connor and Her Dying Child' (a wood engraving from an English newspaper of 1850), shows the appalling hardship many people faced during the Irish Famine and explains, in part, why so many fled overseas. *(Alamy)*

Passenger Mary Ann Taylor, seated front row, surrounded by her family c.1889. Mary Ann lost her first two children and her teeth in the wreck. Despite misgivings, she left Leeds and after yet more trauma finally settled in Massachusetts, America. She was known for her kindness and went on to have many more children. *(John C. Schumacher-Hardy)*

Cabin passenger James K. Fellows, the generous jeweller who first realised the ship was alight. *(Lowell Historical Society)*

Burning of the Ocean Monarch of Boston **by Nathaniel Currier and James Merritt Ives. Michele and Donald D'Amour Museum of Fine Arts, Springfield, Massachusetts. Gift of Lenore B. and Sidney A. Alpert, supplemented with Museum Acquisition Funds.**
(Photography by David Stansbury)

An annotated engraving of the wreck and rescue, based on a sketch by the Prince de Joinville, from a pamphlet printed by William McCall, 1848. *(Liverpool Record Office, Liverpool Libraries)*

Frederick Henry Jerome, who made a habit of being a hero and braved the *Ocean Monarch* without a stitch of clothing to protect him from the blaze. *(Hazel Eckett)*

Royal rescuers: the artistic French hero Francois d'Orleans, Prince de Joinville, and his brother Prince Henri, Duc d'Aumale. *(Alamy)*

Liverpool Shipwreck & Humane Society medal awarded to rescuers, front and back.
(Courtesy of the Liverpool Shipwreck & Humane Society)

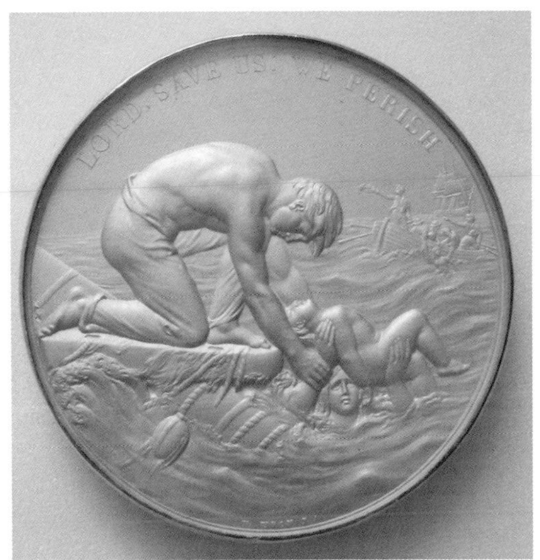

POLICE NOTICE.

OCEAN MONARCH.

TEN POUNDS REWARD.

MISSING,

From the Ocean Monarch, and supposed to be Drowned,

JAMES SMITH BACON,

HAD Booked as First-Cabin Passenger, in the name of JAMES ANDREWS;—Thirty-eight years of age, 5 feet 11 inches high, stout, fair complexion, light hair, rather large whiskers; marks on the back of the neck of having been recently cupped. Wore a Mourning Ring, with his own name in full engraved on it. Supposed to have been dressed in Black. Linen marked, I. S. B., or I. B. Supposed to have had a considerable sum of Money on his person.

The above Reward of Ten Pounds will be paid to any Person or Persons who shall give such information as will lead to the recovery of the said JAMES ANDREWS, DEAD or LIVING, on application to the Head Constable, Central Police Office, Liverpool; or to Mr. WILLIAM FONTAINE, East Street, Hoxton, London.

Central Police Office, Liverpool,
August 30th, 1848.

Police notice included in *North Wales Chronicle*, 5 September 1848, offering ten pounds for information leading to the recovery of James Smith Bacon alias James Andrews, "DEAD or LIVING". *Newspaper image © The British Library Board. All rights reserved. With thanks to The British Newspaper Archive (www.britishnewspaperarchive.co.uk)*

James Smith Bacon's grave in Abney Park Cemetery, London. He is buried with his mother and his 3-year-old son, George Albert, who died in 1845. It is unclear why he is listed as "Jessie" not "James".

The modern memorial in Abergele, Wales. James Smith Bacon was buried here for a few days before his body was claimed by relatives and re-interred in Abney Park Cemetery, London. *(George Frost)*

OCEAN MONARCH MEMORIAL
Here, 9 unnamed crew members/passengers
of the Ocean Monarch were buried
on the 13th and 15th of September 1848.
Their bodies were washed ashore on the beach
at Pensarn, following the sinking of the
American emigrant ship which caught fire and sank.
218 passengers were saved but 178 perished.

Erected 2016

COFEB YR OCEAN MONARCH
Yma, y claddwyd 9 aelod o'r criw/teithwyr di-enw
o'r Ocean Monarch ar y 13eg a'r 15fed o Fedi 1848.
Golchwyd eu cyrff i'r lan ym Mhensarn wedi'r gwch
Americannaidd ymfudol fynd ar dân a suddo.
Achubwyd 218 o'r teithwyr, ond collodd 178 eu bywydau

Codwyd y Gofeb 2016

John Henry Walter, son of the doomed Mary Ann, who treasured his mother's book and kept it as a "mascotte" when he immigrated to Australia. This image is from 1878, 30 years after his mother and sister died at sea. *(Mandy Gwan)*

The grave of 26-year-old Alice Wrigley in All Hallows, Bispham, England. Alice is one of the very few victims to have a named memorial, and she shares the graveyard with several anonymous passengers and crew from the wreck.
(Tamsin Johns-Chapman)

St Tudno's graveyard, Llandudno, where an unnamed victim is buried, looking towards the wrecksite.

Blue cups recovered from wreck. *(Chris Holden)*

Soup tureen and ladle recovered from wreck. *(Chris Holden)*

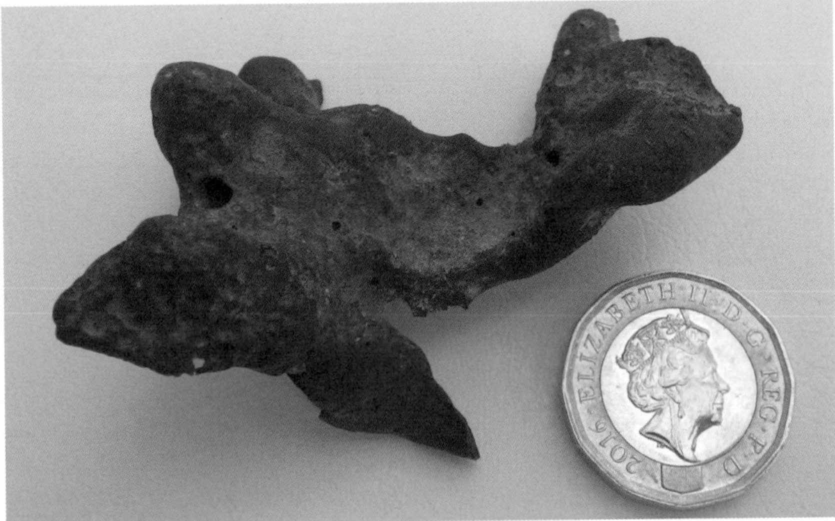

A scrap of melted metal from the wreck. *(Chris Holden)*

This cup and other items recovered from the wreck and pictured here were carried in the hold as cargo, and escaped the ravages of the fire. *(Chris Holden)*

Edward Jones, who was a farmer. He survived the wreck and was among the few who came to know where the remains of a loved one ended up.

More bodies were retrieved from the water soon after the disaster.

> *On Friday night a steamer brought up the bodies of five passengers which had been previously picked up by some boatmen outside. They were conveyed to the shed for the reception of the unclaimed dead, at the south end of the Prince's Dock. Two of the bodies are females, one of them aged, an old man, and two children. The younger female was given up to her friends. The bodies were much cut and bruised about the upper parts, and one of the children had apparently been much scorched on one side of its face. They appeared to have been steerage passengers.*

A physician from Manchester had discussed the appearance of drowning victims at a trial a few years earlier:

> *If the body of a person drowned had remained half an hour in the water, the skin would be cold and pallid. ... The countenances of persons drowned are generally placid and pale. It was not a general rule that the eyes remained open under such circumstances, but should not take the appearance of them into account whether they were half open or not. ... Mucus generally issues from the mouth of drowned persons. Much would depend upon the struggling of the patient in the water, if a drowning case, as to the rigidity of the muscles. The quicker a party were drowned, the greater would be the rigidity.*
>
> *(Liverpool Mercury, 3 April 1846).*

This failed to mention the action of hungry fish upon a body, which, along with burns, other injuries and general decomposition, would also hinder identification of the bodies which would soon litter the shores around this area of coast.

The five bodies held in the shed for 'the unclaimed dead' belonged to Mary Tobin, Geoffrey Lynch, Ellen Teirney, Elizabeth Atherton, and an unknown boy. Despite their battered appearance, visiting relatives and friends were able to determine their loved ones from hair colour and style, clothing, and what remained of their features. Mary's sister, Johanna, identified her sibling that Friday night as the young woman lying in the shed and according to the *Liverpool Mercury* of 29 August 1848, later told an inquest 'I saw my sister going down the side of the ship by means of a rope, and that was the last time I saw her alive.' She saw the rest of the bodies in the dead house on Saturday, when she removed her sister and had her buried.

Geoffrey Lynch, 58, was the 'old man'. His passage broker, Charles Hill, identified his remains on Saturday. Lynch had been one of the second cabin passengers, and died while attempting to save the lives of the women he had promised a friend he would protect from harm. His sacrifice was, unfortunately, somewhat in vain. David Murphy, of Killarney, Ireland, told the inquest he 'was intimately acquainted with' the deceased, who had been travelling to Boston with Murphy's mother and three sisters. Two of his sisters survived but his mother and other sibling died in the wreck. The 'aged' female was Ellen Teirney, of Omagh, in Northern Ireland. Her son James was a labourer living in Liverpool, and he described leaving his mother on the *Ocean Monarch* the Sunday before the ship departed, only to see her again laid out in the dead house. It is unclear who identified the little girl as Elizabeth Atherton, her family or friends may have been too upset to discuss her death with journalists or the jury at the inquest.

As the captain recovered in his hotel room, and others mourned their terrible losses, James K. Fellows was making plans. His name had been published by the papers along with many others, and this proved beneficial to the American jeweller, who was now even more keen to return home. He later wrote in his memoir,

> *I was surrounded by strange faces, with but a shilling in my pocket, but was soon called on by a friend, a member of the Middlesex Bar (Hon. Seth Ames, of Lowell, now on the Supreme Bench of the Commonwealth), who kindly offered me sympathy and aid. But as my letter of credit was not exhausted, I drew forty pounds for my passage and a trifle for clothing – for I was without hat or boots – and went on board the Hibernia, of the Cunard Line, the following Saturday, bound for Boston.*

The Cunard Line set the standard for safety, comfort, and cuisine. Although survivors were being offered replacement voyages by Harnden & Co., Fellows wasn't the only one to opt for a speedier – and possibly safer – exit from England. As he recalled,

> *There was one other of the rescued on board, a Boston artist, who had spent two years in collecting and copying in Italy, but he had lost all, and had taken second-cabin passage. On my making the fact known, however, he was ushered into the first cabin by the captain, without money or price.*

Luckily for Nathaniel Southworth, he could now relax with someone who understood exactly what he had been through as they crossed the Atlantic. The majority of the others who wished to carry on with their journeys, however, had no choice but to wait to take the replacement voyages, on the *Hope* on Monday or the *Sunbeam* on the following Sunday.

Many were too traumatised to try again, for a while at least. According to the *Roscommon Messenger* of 6 September 1848,

> *Great numbers of the saved, however, have been so terrified by what they have witnessed and suffered, that they on Friday* [the day after the disaster] *called at the office in Waterloo-road for the passage money they had paid, and it was promptly refunded to them; the passage-money amounted in the aggregate to £1,300.*

This was the equivalent of approximately £120,000 today, an enormous sum even when divided between almost 190 people. In addition to this, an Emigration Commissioner came to Liverpool with £200 for the survivors. It couldn't replace their loved ones, or the tools, books, and cargo necessary to provide them with a livelihood, but this money at least meant they could pay for provisions and comfortable lodgings, and letters home.

As dozens of bodies floated ever closer to the coast, and worried friends travelled to Liverpool in hopes of good news, the survivors were still struggling just to keep themselves covered and warm. Even though it was late August, Liverpool, like many other coastal cities, would have been chilly for the unclothed, and men and women alike may have felt uncomfortable without their heads covered with a hat or shawl no matter how hot it was. People who suffered such great misfortune through no fault of their own, in a well-publicised tragedy, would usually receive assistance from a combination of sources including private individuals, local and national charities, religious bodies, and the state. There would also often be some form of recompense from the maritime industry via the brokers, owners, etc. or at least a substitute passage on another ship. Whatever survivors received, it was unlikely to fully compensate them for their losses, even if the press did cannily publicise the generosity of the local 'great and good' in their response to the shipwreck victims' plight, making it more than worth their while to donate goods or money.

The *Liverpool Mercury* of 29 August 1848 reported that thankfully the shipping agent for the *Ocean Monarch* worked to aid the survivors in their comparative nakedness:

> *With the view of obtaining a complete muster of the survivors, so that their names, for the satisfaction of their relatives and friends, might be recorded, and that the plans of relief which public generosity is so freely contributing might be duly administered to them, the Messrs. Harnden called on Sunday a meeting of the whole of the passengers that could be found, at their offices, in Waterloo road. Nearly 150 drew up. Although private charity had in the meantime provided clothing for many, and had otherwise done much, a majority of the poor wretches were in the most wretched and destitute condition. One poor woman who was present had lost not less than five of her children; and it was pitiable to hear the recital of personal loss and peril which each poor sufferer had to tell. The poor creatures who assembled were taken under the charge of two of Messrs. Harnden's clerks to the Central Police-office, in High-street, where clothing of the most miscellaneous kind (contributions of which had been poured in with a liberal hand) were distributed to the sufferers by Mr Superintendent Clough.*

They added, 'as affording some hope to those who have missing relatives of friends' that the list of names now held by the shipping agent and shared in the press was not yet complete 'as several whose names are as yet unrecorded are confined by contusions and other injuries in lodging houses in various parts of the town'.

That same day, Captain Murdock was busy writing reports and a statement, gathering his thoughts, and penning a letter, reprinted in the *Carnarvon and Denbigh Herald and North and South Wales Independent* of 2 September 1848,

> *to render my thanks to Mr Thomas Littledale, the owner of the yacht Queen of the Ocean, and his friends … the master, and crew, for their indefatigable exertions in rescuing us from a watery grave, and also for their humane assistance rendered to us while on board the yacht. While thus expressing my thanks, I cannot refrain at the same time from also expressing my admiration of the skilful and seamanlike manner in which the Queen of the Ocean was handled.*

He also spent time defending his fellow sea captains. As the *Carnarvon and Denbigh Herald and North and South Wales Independent* of 2 September 1848, put it in their somewhat biting article on coverage of the wreck, 'Finding that calumny could not cling to [Captain Murdock], the next effort of foul tongues was directed against the commanders of the Orion and the Cambria steamers'. The men in charge of the opposition steamers were also under attack in public and in the press. If the much-maligned Murdock had chosen not to intervene, or had added to the scorn poured upon Captains Hunter and McKellar, he would no doubt have completely shifted the focus from himself as an object of contempt in some quarters. But he was an honourable fellow, and instead made a point of rectifying what he saw as a wrong.

His letter to the editor of the *Albion* was reprinted in many newspapers, including the *Carnarvon and Denbigh Herald and North and South Wales Independent* of 2 September 1848, and described as 'manly and satisfactory' and 'A letter which by all right minded men will be regarded as most emphatically and conclusively exculpatory'. It read,

> *SIR, – I have just read an article in the London 'Times,' and also some observations made in the House of Commons, by Mr Hume, tending to cast serious reflection on the conduct of the captains of the steamers Cambria and Orion, for not having rendered their assistance in rescuing the passengers of my ill-fated ship, and, as I believe these imputations were made under a misapprehension of the facts, I am most*

> *anxious to relieve them from any unfair share of blame. I know that both vessels had passed me several miles before the fire was observed by them, and, against wind and tide, it would have taken an hour and a half for them to reach me and being greatly crowded on their decks as I understand they were, by passengers, and seeing a large steamer and two other vessels close at hand, without knowing the emergency of the case from the number of emigrants on board, they might fairly suppose that I should have received ample assistance before they could have rendered any service to us. I do not, therefore, attach blame to them, and I should wish through the medium of your journal to express thus much to the public.*

The *Morning Post* of 28 August 1848 along with many other papers had carried the story,

> *Mr Hume said* [the *Ocean Monarch*] *was passed at the time* [of the fire] *by the Orion and Cambrian* [*sic*] *steamers, and they afforded her no assistance. It was painful to think that our own subjects should pass her by without affording any relief, and that we should be indebted to the heroic exertions of the Prince de Joinville and the Duc D'Aumale, who risked their lives to save our people. (Hear, hear.)*

Joseph Hume was a doctor from Angus, Scotland, and his comments in his role of radical MP had greatly embarrassed the captains of the steamers.

He and the other prominent critics, once provided with further information, retracted their condemnation of the commanders of the steamers. The *Carnarvon and Denbigh Herald and North and South Wales Independent* of 2 September 1848 included details of this along with a rebuke for their fellow newspapermen,

> *it is discreet and dignified on the part of Captain Hunter* [of the *Cambria*] *to pass over in silence those journalists who have been so prone to suggest evil; it may not be amiss in us, as a contemporary writer, to remind certain gentlemen that there is a wide difference between the involuntary mis-statement of a fact, and the voluntary utterance of a condemnatory inference or opinion. All public writers, be they ever*

> *so discreet or benevolent, are incident to the former error, because they are liable to be misled by incorrect information: but the latter mistake is the wilful offspring of indiscretion and malignity. Its rashness forms no excuse, for it is the morbid result of self-conceit and disregard to the reputation of those whom it attacks. If the writer of an article in the 'Times' of Saturday be capable of shame: there is plenty of room for the exercise of that feeling.*

It took some time for the syndicated versions of the retractions and letters of support to spread and some found it easier to believe the initial reports of skulduggery and cowardice than the more complicated accounts of difficult decisions made amid chaos, trauma, and tragedy. Despite Captain Murdock and other people's efforts, at the inquest the following day, as the *Liverpool Mercury* reported on 29 August 1848,

> *The coroner proceeded to say, he knew of no law that compelled a man to jeopardise his life in saving the lives of others. If he did all he could to preserve the ship, and afterwards found that his own life would be jeopardised, it was only a question of gallantry, how long further he should continue to use his exertions in saving life. He knew of no law either to compel one vessel to go to the rescue of another, but the man who would deliberately pass another vessel in danger, and not render assistance, particularly when such assistance could be rendered without risk or danger to himself – that man was the most despicable creature on the face of the earth, and if amenable to no human tribunal, he must be amenable to a higher – a heavenly tribunal, and was liable to the lash of public censure.*

Some of the passengers currently being sought by friends and family were also about to be blasted with public censure. But their seekers had to find them – or discover what happened to them – first. While the sods settled above Mary Tobin's hasty grave, Johanna mourned her sister and prepared for the inquest on Monday, and Lissy Roper grew used to her mother's appearance in hospital, jeweller James K. Fellows settled into his quarters on the *Hibernia* and hoped for a pleasant voyage. With all but a handful of the cabin passengers and crew alive despite the tragedy on the previous

Thursday, Fellows seems to have assumed that the cause of the fire would be determined easily enough in his absence. He was wrong.

Back on dry land, there was another mystery begging to be solved. Among the scores of people suspected to have died in the wreck, one man in particular stood out for all the wrong reasons. The naked passenger held aboard the Welsh pilot boat had disappeared, or perhaps, as many feared, been returned to the water in an effort to hide a crime, adding an extra element of horror to the tragedy of the *Ocean Monarch*. The press fanned the flames of discontent and urged someone, anyone, to come forward and show the public this poor man had not been murdered. If they didn't, the pilots could face the death penalty.

Chapter Ten

...there is one circumstance connected with the escape of our party that ought to be published as a lasting disgrace to the pilot boat [which] *took us on board but more for the purpose of robbing than from any motives of humanity, as was afterwards proved. ... When we left this pilot-boat, the Pilot Queen, of Chester, (her name cannot be made too public), one of the passengers was left below in one of the berths perfectly naked, too ill to dress himself in time to leave with us. He was a very respectable looking young man, and had money about him, as I myself heard him offer the men a sovereign to take him on shore. In the confusion, hurry, and quarrel he was left behind, nor has he since been heard of. When we named the circumstance to the men belonging to the fishing smack, their reply was, 'If they find out that he's got money about him, they'll murder him and throw him overboard. They'll never think to be found out' and concluded their remarks by observing, 'That we had no idea of the black work going on in these quarters.' These remarks I heard myself, nor can I divest my mind of the uneasiness I have since felt, with regard to the fate of this young man. I hope every inquiry will be made to trace him out. ... I shall feel a satisfaction in giving praise to those to whom praise is due, and exposing those who, supposing their conduct to have been such as there seems too much reason for believing it to have been, cannot be too severely punished.*

(*Carnarvon and Denbigh Herald and North and South Wales Independent*, 2 September 1848)

Searching for the missing, Liverpool, Monday 28 August – Friday 1 September 1848

As the public and the press came to terms with the tragedy, many questions arose. What happened and why? Could the fire have been prevented? Who was to blame? Who would help those affected by such a terrible event? Was this likely to happen again – was it safe to board emigrant ships or better to stay at home? And, crucially for those not present in Liverpool, who lived and who died?

There was still no sign of the passenger last seen naked below deck on the *Pilot Queen of Chester*. Rumours swirled of murder most foul, heroes turning to villainy for the sake of a few coins, and a body disposed of in the deep. The men accused of this heinous act, Thomas Bithell and John Bennion, carried on as normal in their homes near Flint on the North Wales coast. Thomas was the more senior of the pair of pilots at 54 years old. A father of six, his eldest son, also Thomas, had followed in his footsteps and was also employed as a pilot on the Dee. They came from a long line of fishermen, renowned for their skills and success at sea. His fellow pilot and suspected accomplice was a father of five. John Bennion was the son of a collier, and his wife, Mary, also worked as a pilot. A railway station had opened a few months prior at Flint, raising hopes of prosperity in the area and aiding people – like detective officers Tuck and Bates – who wished to visit the area in a hurry.

Three full days had passed since the wrecking of the *Ocean Monarch* and subsequent rescues, and despite numerous enquiries among the people living along the coast nearby, no one claimed to have seen or heard from the missing survivor. Henry Powell, the prosperous albeit sickly cabin passenger still smarting from his rude treatment at the hands of the Dee pilots, grew ever more certain of his fellow survivor's dire fate and subsequent burial at sea. He, along with other respectable gentlemen including the ship's surgeon, William Ellis, continued to ask questions via the press, and expressed their grave concerns to the police and Mr Cook, the superintendent of the pilot service in Liverpool. Having made it clear to journalists and readers that the men currently under suspicion of murder worked on the Dee and were nothing to do with the generally well-respected Liverpool pilots, Cook along with the police instigated a formal investigation into their actions. The police also offered a reward of £10 for any information received regarding the young man currently missing and feared dead.

The search for the missing passenger was hampered from the outset by confusion over his identity. William Greenough, who also escaped the *Pilot Queen*, was sure the naked and near-unconscious young man left shivering below deck was his berth mate from the *Ocean Monarch*, 20-year-old John

Coombes. They may only have known each other for a couple of days, and Greenough would probably have been traumatised by his narrow escape from the ship, but his identification was almost all the investigators and press had to go on. It was ascertained that Coombes was from Liverpool, where his father ran a shoe shop, and therefore it was expected that he would have made himself known to friends and family locally if he had indeed survived the wreck. No one raised suspicions regarding his behaviour prior to leaving home, unlike others on board who may have taken advantage of an assumption of death in order to start a new life. These included joiner and builder John Atkinson from North-street, Leeds, who was alleged to have defaulted his creditors, or the wife and daughter of Mr Murphy from Killarney, Ireland, who had stolen money from the bank where he worked then sent for his family to join him in America.

Others who left the *Pilot Queen* in favour of the Irish fishing smack gave an entirely different name to concerned authorities, but even this was spelled a myriad of ways in the press. Information regarding the whereabouts of John Sherne, Shurr, Surr, or Sheard was also being sought, again to no avail. But the pilots lived in Wales and this was also where they worked from, so any official investigation which crossed the jealously preserved boundaries of jurisdictions had the potential for considerable political upset and outrage. Something clearly had to be done, but the matters of how and whom by were less certain.

While some searched for Shurr and Coombes, others in London were anxious to hear news of their own loved ones, although in this case they knew that if any name was given it was likely to be false. Emmeline Bacon and her brothers-in-law were fairly sure her errant husband had fled England on the *Ocean Monarch* along with the workhouse schoolmistress and her daughter, but they had no idea if the fugitives were among the survivors clustered in the lodging houses of Liverpool awaiting a replacement voyage or if they had perished in the blaze. That Monday Emmeline's brothers-in-law decided, through discussion with the workhouse Board of Guardians, that the only way to discover the fate of James Smith Bacon was to travel to the North West themselves.

As urgent inquiries continued to be made regarding the lost and the living, the body of the toddler who died in the arms of Mate Batty was being buried in Llandysillo churchyard near Anglesey. This little girl, most likely Jane

Roper whose mother was currently restricted to the Northern Hospital in Liverpool and comforted by the presence of blue-eyed Lissy, was the first to receive an anonymous burial after the disaster, but was certainly not the last.

In Hoylake, on the coast of the Wirral near Liverpool, the second of several inquests on victims of the *Ocean Monarch* was about to begin. Inquests were held as soon as possible after the discovery of a body thought to have died in sudden or suspicious circumstances, in the nearest suitable location or occasionally in the open air. Pubs and inns were popular venues for these public affairs as their parlours were often the only places with enough room for everyone involved, and sometimes had cellars or cold stores where the body could be stored until the inquest was held. Some inquests were more perfunctory than others, depending on the circumstances, the person holding the inquest, and the state of the body. The comparative chill of a cellar would slow the process of decomposition but, especially in summer, speed was definitely of the essence. Inquests were open to the public and presided over by the local coroner, who was often a lawyer by training and would choose a dozen able men to act as jurors. Unlike at a trial, these men could ask questions of witnesses as they pursued a suitable verdict and, in cases like this, attempted to identify the remains lying before them.

One of the bodies had already been buried, that of Mary Tobin, but plenty still remained including a baby in 'long clothes', according to one visitor. Green Lodge Hotel was the ideal setting for such a grim enterprise, situated on Stanley Road near the sea, with a broad drive of pale stones and a sweep of lawn curving in front of its clean façade. Run by John Ball, guests staying at the hotel were offered the privilege of rabbit shooting on the warrens nearby. This elegant building had originally been constructed as a shooting box by the Lord of the Manor. Initially a low building with a thatched roof, it now stretched over three storeys and had outbuildings and stables nearby, allowing ease of access to the local gentry attending that day.

The place was packed full of survivors thanks to a sympathetic publican. According to the *Bolton Chronicle* of 2 September 1848, 'a great number of the passengers by the Ocean Monarch went to Holylake [*sic*], Mr Gouch, of Woodside Hotel, having in the kindest manner conveyed them there and back free of cost.'

The jury consisted of Thomas Phillips, who acted as foreman, and fourteen men, well respected within their community: Walter Gilfillan,

William Borris, John Kellitt, Thomas Foulkes, James Bleasdale, Thomas Austin, Richard Rowlinson, Robert Norris, Thomas Ellison, John Charters, John Johnson, James Edmondson, and Robert Mercer. They sat before Coroner Philip Finch Curry and listened as the details of the wreck and the discovery of the bodies they had examined were laid out before them. They were encouraged to ask questions of the witnesses and clarify any vague statements made before them, especially regarding a person's character, motivations, or any actions which may have caused death or injury, and lost or saved lives. After a day of gathering evidence and hearing the awful accounts of what happened on the wreck, the inquest was adjourned, allowing the County Coroner and jurors to mull over what they had heard and agree their verdict.

Coroner Curry, 42, was not himself a doctor but his father had been a surgeon in the Royal Navy and Philip had received some medical training himself in addition to training as an attorney. One of triplets born to a successful family on the Isle of Man, he suffered with epilepsy, although this was something he attempted to conceal, and despite occasional ill health had served as coroner for the Borough since 1836. A deeply religious man, he was sometimes criticised for using inquests as an opportunity to sermonise to those present. Nevertheless, he was very experienced and well respected within the community, and the friends and relatives of the people discussed that day could be assured of his commitment to reaching a true and fair verdict.

The bodies were fast decomposing and as soon as the coroner and jury had examined them to their satisfaction they were taken to be buried in the pleasant surrounds of Holy Trinity Church in Hoylake. During the viewing of the corpses, one had been identified as Mary Jones, 48, from Manchester. Her farmer husband, Edward, had survived the shipwreck that killed his wife. Margaret Shereane, 52, was buried nearby. She and her husband had been travelling from Glossop, Derbyshire, where he worked as a shopkeeper. Another ten bodies were buried in two plots beside them, unidentified and unclaimed. They may have been on board alone, or fellow travellers who might have identified them perhaps died in the wreck too. A local woman later wrote, 'The fearful injuries from burning which many had received prevented the last offices being paid to the corpses before interment, and they were deposited in whatever clothing was upon them', (*Twixt Mersey and Dee*, 1897). Details and personal artefacts such as jewellery, money, and keys would have been retained in case of enquiry later. News travelled slowly and if the people laid to rest in the grounds of the beautiful church had come from Ireland, Scotland, or a rural area of England then it could take weeks for those who knew them to discover the details, and several days more to travel to West Kirby. For the sake of hygiene and decency the bodies had to be interred as soon as possible.

Across the water from the hotel, pilots Bithell and Bennion continued with their lives on land, blissfully ignorant of the plans being formulated against them in Liverpool and unaware that their activities would be rudely interrupted the following day. The trunk they had hauled on board the *Pilot Queen* was huge and heavy, and they were keen to find out what was within. That morning Bennion went to Messrs. Mathers' leadworks at Bagillt, a little west of Flint, and found a clerk to ask about it. According to the *Liverpool Mercury* of 12 September 1848, this clerk, Joseph Hughes, later deposed,

> *Bennion came to me, near the office, and said, 'We have picked up a box, and we have got it on board; I should be very glad to get some one to see it opened.' I said the best way would be to get a respectable man to see it opened, Mr Buckley or Mr Henry. Mr Buckley, when apprised of it, said 'he would be very glad to see it opened'.*

Bennion was delighted, and soon returned. As Hughes recalled, 'The box was brought to the works in a cart, and opened in my presence. It was full of clothes, very wet and offensive.'

Although the box had held together throughout its few hours in the sea, water had managed to seep in and the contents were now a stinking mess. The respectable witness to this discovery, prosperous local farmer John Francis Buckley, corroborated the clerk's statement, saying:

> *About noon Bennion came to our private office, and we had the box opened by our carpenter. The box was not full. I recommended the linen to be washed, and the articles of clothing to be put out to dry. Bennion remarked that he would like them put in the trunk, so that he might take them with him to Liverpool on Wednesday. I promised to see them made up, and an inventory taken. I advised him to take them to his wife, to see them washed, &c., which he did.*

The carpenter, Charles Jones, backed him up, saying,

> [I] *was called to open the trunk produced. There was only one nail to fasten the lock; it was very fast in, and did not appear as if it had been previously forced open.* [I] *would have used such a nail to fasten such a lock. It was hard work to take the nail out; it was clenched.*

With the trunk open and, it appeared, approval granted for him to act on his desire to empty the contents, John Bennion returned home with his booty. Soon the clothing was washed and hanging to dry, and the trunk itself left open to air the sour stink out. What he intended to do with the contents in Liverpool – if he did indeed intend to take them there – is unclear. Along with his fellow pilot Thomas Bithell, John Bennion would reach Liverpool sooner than he thought, but not in the circumstances he hoped.

Tuesday brought three unwelcome visitors to Flint, policemen Bates, Tuck, and Inch. They had been despatched from Liverpool in search of Bithell, Bennion, and the truth about their reluctant passenger who had now been missing for five long days.

The policemen went in search of the pilots and found Thomas Bithell in the hilly market town of Holywell nearby. When Bates asked him about the previous Thursday and told him to list what he picked up the pilot was initially somewhat coy and evasive, only admitting to retrieving some spars and rigging, nothing else. Bates smelled a rat. Luckily for the policemen, the boy who had been on board the *Pilot Queen* that day, John Foulkes, was nearby. The 13-year-old may not have realised it, but his answers differed significantly from the pilot's. He told Bates the trunk was at Bithell's house. Officer Tuck, who had been in the army before joining the police force, challenged Bithell with this new information, and the pilot assured him it was standard salvage work. When the policemen remained unconvinced, he even asked them to turn a blind eye to the trunk. His wheedling attempts at persuasion failed to win them over, and the questions continued.

According to the *Liverpool Mail* of 2 September 1848, the pilot had 'expressed a wish that a correct inventory of the articles saved would be taken, and that they would give him (the prisoner) as much as possible. "If," said he, "there is anything else, say nothing about it; the trunk has nothing to do with the insurance."' They returned to his house and found the trunk lying there, emptied of its contents apart from a few papers, and a jacket and trousers hanging drying along with a few other items of clothing which had just been washed.

They apprehended John Bennion on board a vessel lying on the Dee. His reaction was telling. Upon being told what the police wanted him for, he responded that he ought to have salvage rights for what they had taken from the sea that day – and also claimed to have only pulled spars and rigging from the water. He insisted this counted as lawful salvage and told them he expected a good deal for his retrieval of these items. Bennion initially denied taking the trunk, then asked what Bithell had said. As the *Liverpool Mail* of 2 September 1848 reported, the pilot 'hinted that there was something wrong: it was Bethell [*sic*] who picked up the trunk, and had brought trouble upon them'.

Alcohol may have changed his mind about discretion being the better part of valour, and was apparently supplied by the police questioning him in an effort to loosen his tongue. Either way, they discovered that the valuable silver watch held by the pilots in exchange for the tatty blanket used by Henry Powell had been taken to a watchmaker-cum-pawnbroker in Holywell and pledged by Bennion's wife, Mary. Eventually, the pilots agreed they had taken the trunk but it had been the day after the wreck and rescue, and would be a separate matter to salvage, which they were obliged to report. The pilots were arrested for theft and dragged from their wives and children. There was still no sign of the missing passenger.

*****

As Mary Bennion and Elizabeth Bithell comforted their children on the banks of the Dee, across the estuary, on the Wirral, another child was receiving attention of a very different nature. One of the bodies at the inquest had been identified by family members from Sheffield and was being buried in a graveyard sheltered by sand dunes and the church of Holy Trinity, Hoylake. Elizabeth Jackson, age 5, had last been seen by her father as her mother held her tight against the jib-boom at the front of the ship. He hoped and prayed she and his wife were safe as he sailed towards New York, but unfortunately this was in vain. She was already dead. Elizabeth suffered terrible injuries to the back of her head, the skull bashed in with great force, and would, with luck, have been unconscious at the time of her death.

People wanted answers. How did this happen, who was to blame, who would pay to cover the losses involved, and how would they stop a similar tragedy from happening again? As *The Welshman* later reported, Mr Hume asked about this very matter in the House of Commons on Monday 28 August, only to receive an answer that proved wholly dissatisfactory to many of their readers.

> *Mr Labouchere, in reply to a question from Mr Hume relative to the loss of the Ocean Monarch, said that the Board of Trade had only power to inquire into the cases of British steamers. The Ocean Monarch was a sailing vessel and a foreigner, and the Board of Trade had, therefore, no power to interfere.*
>
> *(1 September 1848).*

Because the *Ocean Monarch* was American built and owned, returning to a home port in the US and captained by the American Captain Murdock, the only questions that could be answered were those posed at the inquests now taking place along the English and Welsh coast on bodies recovered from the water and the shore. Unfortunately, there would be no shortage of corpses, some more upsetting than others.

The jury at Hoylake had returned a verdict of 'accidentally drowned through the burning of the *Ocean Monarch*' regarding the bodies received there, and also expressed their approval of the efforts made by the captain and crew as they attempted to rescue their passengers. Meanwhile, another inquest was under way in Liverpool on the bodies of Mary Tobin, Geoffrey Lynch, Ellen Teirney, 15-month-old Elizabeth Atherton, and the unidentified boy who had been lying in the dead house for the past few days. Among the allegations made were accusations of negligence and inhumanity.

Having established some of the basic facts of the fire and the subsequent shipwreck the day before, along with the identification of the bodies inspected by those present, the focus of the inquest was now turning towards the cause of the fire and what could have been done to prevent such an appalling loss of life. Captain Murdock and his officers were soon cleared of accusations of cowardice and abandonment, but the captains of the steamers which continued their journeys past the blazing emigrant ship faced a gruelling inquisition.

It seemed obvious to many that if these ships had adjusted course and come closer to the *Ocean Monarch* then many more lives would have been saved, but, as the captain's statements and other accounts revealed, this was a gross oversimplification of the truth. Admiral Grenfell, whose efforts in the metal paddle-box of the *Afonso* saved so many people, attended with Captain Evans and other people of influence in the city. The room was packed with survivors, journalists, and the family and friends of those involved, as well as people curious about the tragedy or keen to witness the steamer captains' anticipated rollicking. The court was so crowded that many huddled round the door outside, too. One by one, sailors from the various vessels involved that day came forward to swear an oath of honesty then speak to the throng.

A fireman from the *Afonso*, George Lee, who ordinarily helped to keep the fires blazing and under control on the steam frigate, said,

> *a quarter of an hour before I heard the alarm of fire I saw the two Bangor steamers running in; they were on our larboard bow, about a mile and a half off in shore; they could only have been about five miles and a half or six miles from the burning ship; when I first got on deck after hearing the alarm of fire, I saw these two steamers both pursuing their inward course; they were then on our larboard quarter, and the distance between them and the burning ship would be increased to nine miles;* [I] *never saw the steamers alter their course, or make any attempt to render assistance to the burning ship.*

According to the *Freeman's Journal* of 31 August 1848, he then continued,

> *there was nothing either in the state of the tide or the state of the weather to prevent these steam-boats rendering assistance … If there had been other boats there before we got to the vessel more lives might have been saved. … The Bangor boats* [the steamers] *could have been at the burning ship at least an hour before the Affonso.*

This was a point that many critics of the steamer captains kept coming back to: if the *Cambria* and *Orion* had only diverted their course towards the *Ocean Monarch*, more lives would have been saved.

George Aitken, a passenger on board the *Cambria*, took the stand and was examined by Mr Wright. Aitken had been standing on the stage between the paddle-boxes with Captain Hunter and a Mr Melling, about fifteen minutes after passing the *Ocean Monarch*. He saw smoke coming from the vessel, and heard the captain ask Mr Melling for his glass, and exclaim, 'There is a ship on fire, what shall we do?' According to the *Morning Chronicle* of 4 September 1848, Aitken told the court,

> *At this time* [we] *were about eight or nine miles distant from the ship. The steamer was a-head of the* Cambria, *on the larboard bow. … There was a good deal of anxiety manifested on board by the passengers; the captain went aft, and made a signal to the* Affonso *that there was a ship on fire. Just at this period a heavy shower of rain came on, and when it had cleared away they found that they had headed the* Orion, *and were then nearly abreast of the* Prince of Wales. *A number of passengers were standing on the bridge with Captain Hunter, and the general impression was that there was not much danger to the people on the burning ship, as there was so much assistance going towards her.*

In answer to a question from Captain Evans, this witness said they were not aware at the time that the vessel on fire was an emigrant ship.

Captain John Hunter of the *Cambria* was next to be examined by Captain Evans, and his answers largely agreed with Aitken's statement. He had been working that route for six years and in that time '[he] had been instrumental in saving lives in four instances, and the persons so saved amounted to upwards of one hundred. … Had [he] known the ship on fire was an emigrant vessel, [he] would have thrown [his] cargo overboard and gone to her assistance.' His attention had been drawn to the *Ocean Monarch* when a passenger told him there was a ship firing a gun at the Great Ormes Head, prompting him to look that way through his glass. Captain Hunter stated he had then ordered the signal-box up, and hoisted the number requesting that the ships he could see, the *Prince of Wales* and the *Afonso*, give assistance to the westward vessel. He also denied that the *Cambria* and the *Orion* had been racing each other.

As would be expected of any complex situation, the accounts given did not agree on every detail but there were enough similarities to provide a fairly comprehensive overview of the events that day. There were some minor disagreements throughout the inquest regarding who saw which vessels in which area and when, as well as whether the right flags were hoisted – and sighted – when they should have been, but overall it seemed clear that the captains of steamers crowded with livestock and passengers made understandable choices and were not grossly at fault.

However, one of the owners of the *Cambria*, Mr Price, declared that the inquest was seeking to incriminate the captain of his steamer and managed to repeatedly antagonise the coroner and others present, leading Mr Wright to declare that Price's repeated allegations against them amounted to a charge of perjury against several of the witnesses. This did not work in the ship owner's favour.

After a very long Friday covering over twelve hours of interrogation and statements, the *Morning Chronicle* of 4 September 1848 reported on the conclusion of the inquest, and the heroic one-armed Admiral Grenfell's closing statement. He,

> *rose and thanked the jury for the kindness and attention they had displayed throughout the inquiry. He had thought it his duty to attend at the inquest, having been an eye-witness of the melancholy catastrophe, and having seen a multitude of helpless creatures lose their lives, not from the want of boats, but from the want of a few sailors to assist them from their perilous situation. Previous to hearing the evidence, he had formed an opinion prejudicial to Captain Murdoch and the crew, but, after the investigation, the unfavourable impressions he had formed were utterly removed, and he now recalled anything and everything he might have said hurtful to the feelings of Captain Murdoch.*

At this, Coroner Curry proceeded to charge the jury, guiding them in their duties.

> *After some complimentary observations to Admiral Grenfell and Captain Evans for the assistance they afforded in the inquiry, the coroner said he would apply the evidence to several persons upon whom responsibility was imposed; first, the captain, and then the first and second mates of the ship, and then to the moral responsibility attaching to those who fell short of their duty in not rendering that assistance*

> *within their power – he alluded to the Cambria and Orion. Until the conclusion of the case that day, it had been his intention to have directed their notice to the evidence relative to this, without offering any opinion upon it; but when he found that an opportunity had been afforded to the owners of these vessels to have produced any evidence they had liked – when Mr Wright would have rendered them any assistance he could have done – when, instead of this, they were met by upbraidings, it was with a very bad grace that Mr Price (one of the owners of the Cambria) came there and used the expressions he had done – that there had been an attempt to criminate Captain Hunter.*

Clearly angered by these suspicions of a stitch-up, Coroner Curry carried on,

> *if Mr Wright had wished to have criminated Captain Hunter, he might very easily have carried this out. Captain Hunter had said he was not aware that the ship on fire was an emigrant ship. Why, if she was not an emigrant vessel, it was not difficult to have discovered that she must have been a troop ship, or some vessel having an extraordinary number of passengers on board. Captain Hunter never so much as stopped his engines, or made towards her, but seeing other vessels go in the direction, pursued his course; but at the very time the discussion spoken of, as occurring between Captain Hunter and those on board, the Cambria was drawing close upon the Orion, the opposition boat.*

This was a very telling detail. The coroner, choosing his words very carefully, pointed out to those present that he,

> *did not say this was a fact, but he would say, that until it was explained away, there had been an attempt by the Cambria to get to Liverpool before the Orion. With reference to the Orion, the chief mate was present, and in answer to whether he had any questions to ask, he said he had nothing to say.*

This could be interpreted as an attitude of 'least said, soonest mended'. Whether the competition that seems to have developed between the steamers actually affected the decisions made by those captains or not, this and Mr Price's obnoxious tirade did not do anything to endear them to the people in court or reading about the inquest in the newspapers.

The coroner then identified another target for public vitriol which may have diverted some of the negative attention from the steamer captains. He 'in the severest terms, denounced the conduct of the crew of the Pilot Queen', currently locked up nearby. Coroner Curry ended his address with fulsome praise for the heroes who saved so many lives that day,

> *nothing could be more gratifying than the account given by an officer of such standing in the navy as Admiral Grenfell. He (the coroner) felt assured that to such men as Capt. Murdoch and Mr Bragdon, their reputations were dearer to them than their lives, and it would not have escaped the observation of the jury, when Capt. Evans got up to second, as it were, the tribute that he (the coroner) was about to pay Capt. Murdoch, that his heart was full – in fact his eyes showed them how sensitive he was when he said that had he a ship, Capt. Murdoch should have the command.*

Having praised the beleaguered captain of the *Ocean Monarch*, the coroner then

> *complimented Mr Littledale, the chief mate of the Prince of Wales, the captain of the Affonso, and others, and instructed the jury that their verdict must be one of accidental death, and they might accompany this with any remarks relative to the different individuals who had taken any part during the melancholy occurrence in rendering assistance, or who by their apathy had failed to render the assistance within their power.*

The jury retired to discuss the evidence heard and the coroner's guidance, then returned after an absence of only fifteen minutes, a little after 9 pm. They found that Mary Tobin and the other bodies previously on view in the dead house,

> *came to their deaths from being accidentally drowned, consequent on the Ocean Monarch taking fire. And at the same time the jury would show*

> *their marked approbation of the conduct of the captain, and particularly of that of the first mate, of the Ocean Monarch, during that most trying scene; as also the noble and praiseworthy efforts of the distinguished individuals who signalised themselves at that awful catastrophe, as well as the officers and men under their command. Further, they wished to express their disapprobation of the conduct of the masters of the two steamers, Orion and Cambria, who might, they were led to believe, have rendered most efficient service to the ill-fated people on board.*

As at Hoylake two days earlier, Captain Murdock was officially cleared of blame at the conclusion of the inquest in Liverpool. Accidents were unfortunately a part of life, something to be avoided if possible but generally not dwelled on as most people were not in a position that allowed them to demand safer conditions or more care to be taken. Injuries and fatalities were common and, depending on a person's age, location, and occupation, more or less to be expected. Some survivors would always view Murdock as somehow responsible for the deaths of their loved ones, or the terror they themselves experienced during the wreck, but overall his name was now clear and he was free to get on with his life. Criticism of the captains of the *Orion* and *Cambria* would, however, continue to linger – and the Dee pilots were accused of far worse.

Chapter Eleven

One of the most scandalous, and if true, certainly the most barbarous act which has for a long time occurred on the Cheshire coast, took place during the period when the unfortunate ship, Ocean Monarch, was being consumed by fire. The facss [sic] are briefly these; – A number of the passengers and crew were picked up from one of the ship's boats by the Pilot Queen, of Chester; subsequently a trunk, containing clothing, was also picked up – the trunk was pillaged, and to screen themselves from the consequences of this act (wretched, who otherwise might have rendered 'good service' at the wreck) resolved to get rid of the passengers whom they put on board. They put them on board a fishing smack, and one man was obliged to give his watch in exchange for an old blanket, and some of the others compelled to pay 1s. 'a head' as salvage for their bodies! But the worst feature yet remains to be told: A young man (possessed of a considerable quantity of money) was left behind, being too sick to be then removed. He, poor fellow, has never been heard of since.

(*Limerick Reporter*, 5 September 1848)

Trial and investigation, North Wales and North West England, late August to early September 1848

As burnt bodies and wreckage continued to wash up with the tides along the coast, and survivors suffered in hospitals nearby, two Welshmen were hauled from the dank and uncomfortable Bridewell between Exchange Street West and Rumford Street to face a hostile reception in a Liverpool court. As one paper, the *Carnarvon and Denbigh Herald and North and South Independent* (17 November 1849) later put it, they had been 'incarcerated in a loathsome dungeon … swarming with vermin, in the Liverpool police gaol', a stark and unpleasant contrast to their homes overlooking the River Dee.

Thomas Bithell and John Bennion were charged with robbery at the Police Court in a room packed with unsympathetic onlookers, including Mayor Horsfall and Alderman Turner. The crime they were accused of repulsed the Victorian public and the room was filled with journalists and local people keen to hear the duo's testimonies and those of their victims, and, most importantly, find out what exactly happened to the missing man. This unfortunate traveller, whose identity remained undetermined, was thought to be somewhere offshore. Rumours in the press led many to believe he had been disposed of by the pilots after they removed the substantial amount of money still on his person after he escaped from the burning emigrant ship.

First the court, led by stipendiary magistrate Edward Rushton, investigated the alleged robbery. Rushton, 52, was the son of a well known anti-slavery campaigner, and known to be able and humane. An educated man, he had been a printer and stationer and also trained as a lawyer before being called to the bar in 1831. Rushton was a leading member of the reform party in Liverpool and ardent social reformer, who advocated for prison reform and the compassionate treatment of juvenile offenders. Luckily for the defendants whose cases were heard in his court, he was also against the death penalty.

As the pilots and their families would know, murder carried a capital sentence. If Bithell and Bennion could not prove to the court's satisfaction that the young man last seen naked on their boat had been alive when he left them, they faced being hanged in public. Robbery was also classed as a felony carrying a sentence of between ten and fifteen years' transportation overseas – often a death sentence in itself. Either way, the pilots were in terrible trouble, especially since the magistrate overseeing their case was very keen to protect emigrants, who were regarded as some of the most vulnerable people around. The Welshmen were represented by William Davenport, 56, an attorney-at-law more used to cases involving property and bankruptcy, which is perhaps why he did not challenge the legality of their arrest in Wales.

The survivors they picked up the previous Thursday were sworn in and the court fell silent as the men gave evidence. As the *Morning Advertiser* of 2 September 1848 reported, cabin passenger Henry Powell was among them,

> *but he was so weak from the effects of his sufferings as to be almost inaudible. The purport of his statement was that, in the confusion on*

> *board the Ocean Monarch, he jumped into the water and gained a boat. The boat drifted away, and, ultimately, he was taken on board the pilot Queen, of Chester. It appeared to him that this vessel might have been of service in rendering assistance to the people on board the wreck, but the crew directed their attention to picking up the floating rigging. He and others stripped off their wet clothes and got into the berths. Subsequently* [the reluctant passengers] *ordered the men to put them aboard an Irish vessel, but previous to this witness saw a man glide into a boat into which a trunk belonging to the Ocean Monarch had been placed.*

Powell also detailed the exchange of his valuable silver watch, which he had been in the habit of wearing round his neck, for the worn old blanket he had wished to borrow from the pilots in order to protect his near-naked body from the cold. This was not a crime, but the lack of humanity displayed by the pilots in such dire circumstances did not reflect well upon their characters.

Over the course of Tuesday, Wednesday, and Thursday, while Coroner Curry was hearing evidence at the inquest nearby, other survivors were being interviewed in the police court, including crewman Adam Jones. The trunk at the heart of the case, which the Liverpool police officers had removed from Bithell's house, along with what they could find of its contents, was produced. It was stamped 'Richard Young, Portsmouth, Virginia', which Jones had assumed was the maker's mark when he purchased it in Boston. Jones examined the trunk and, according to the *London Daily News* of 1 September 1848, 'found missing two pairs of trousers, a shirt, two black silk handkerchiefs, and a spotted coloured handkerchief; some pictures, and things of that kind... [He testified that it] was locked at the time he heaved it overboard.' The *Liverpool Mercury* of 2 September 1848 included further testimony from Adam Jones, where he said the trunk also included a pair of patent leather boots and a white shirt belonging to his messmate, William Walker. This crewman also appeared, and confirmed that he had given Jones a shirt to store in the trunk now on display in the courtroom, and saw him place it inside the night before the wreck.

Crucially, when the pilots had returned a report of items salvaged from the wreck to the principal officer of the Coast Service in order to fulfil their legal obligations and formally be eligible for reward for this service, there was no mention of the trunk on the list. They had also told the police it was something they retrieved the day after the wreck when many witnesses, including the lad in their employ, had seen otherwise.

John Foulkes, 13, testified that he helped Bennion haul the trunk aboard the pilot boat on the day of the wreck, and afterwards assisted him to take it to his house at Dee Bank, Flint. Interestingly, under cross examination he revealed that he helped get the trunk out of the hold when the magistrate's clerk of Holywell came to see it, suggesting that there was some kind of official knowledge – and implicit approval – regarding the pilots' retention of the box. The lad's evidence wasn't all to the detriment of the pilots who had, till then, employed him on their vessel. As Foulkes recalled, he and Bithell put the young man currently considered missing into a small boat and took him to the *Taliesin* steamer, which was on its way from Rhyl to Liverpool. Foulkes saw him safely on board, and told the court that at this point the shipwreck survivor had on a jacket, and gave 10*s* to Bithell.

Henry Powell, who had instigated the investigation into the pilots' conduct in the first place, told the court that although there had been a young man on board the *Taliesin* who was originally on the *Ocean Monarch*, this was not the person he left on the pilot boat. Until the man in question was found, whether alive or dead, this would remain in contention.

Another of the passengers who spent time on the pilot boat claimed to have known the missing man. William Greenough, 20, had shared a berth with his fellow survivor. He named him as Joseph Surr and despite inquiring after him since, could not find him. Greenough agreed with other evidence heard, his erstwhile bunkmate had indeed carried a large sum of money on him when last seen.

Police officers Bates and Tuck testified regarding their visit to Wales to apprehend the defendants, summarising their conversations with the pilots and initial denials of having anything to do with the trunk or its contents. Other witnesses gave evidence that backed up information already given regarding the pilots taking the trunk from the water, removing its contents, and last seeing the young man below decks on the *Pilot Queen*.

Judge Rushton remarked that the prisoners, as 'pilots on the River Dee, – men whom the unfortunate sufferers by the burning ship ought to depend upon for succour [*sic*] above all others, – had turned robbers … [and] that the young man who was said to be missing must be accounted for as soon as possible', (*Leeds Intelligencer*, 2 September 1848). He was furious that anyone, let alone people in their trusted position as pilots, would take such advantage of the vulnerable survivors of a shipwreck. Their actions were completely contrary to the notions of chivalry and selflessness held so dear at the time.

At this Greenough stepped forward and claimed, according to the *London Daily News* of 1 September 1848, 'there was a young man, Henry Fisher, in court, who could prove that a relative of his was taken on board the pilot-boat; every inquiry had been made, however, concerning him, but nothing could be learned.' How this relative could prove this was not specified in the reports, but the judge seemed satisfied of his truthfulness. 'Here a young man, residing at no. 11, Paisley-street, stepped forward,' according to the *Morning Advertiser* of 2 September 1848, 'and stated to the magistrate that he was acquainted with Joseph Searle (the young man who is the subject of the inquiry [with yet another variant of his name]), and that no tidings had as yet been heard of him, though great pains had been taken to discover what had become of him. He confirmed the surmises relative to his having a large sum of money on his person.'

Every night, the pilots were remanded into the custody of the Liverpool police, and slept in cells stinking of sweat and urine, miles away from the warmth of their wives. They were facing a possible death sentence or transportation and it was obvious that the press and the public were baying for blood. Their position as pilots meant that, as with many other maritime occupations, there were certain standards of behaviour expected, especially when lives were in peril. It was also obvious that the judge held no sympathies for their plight. As the *Limerick Reporter* of 5 September 1848 told their readers,

> *Mr Rushton, after commenting in the most severe terms on the conduct of the pilots, and assuring them that this man must be produced alive, or they should suffer the consequences, remanded the case in order that inquiry might be made on board the* [*Taliesin* steamer] *and on the Welsh coast for this man whom they said they put on board.*

It was a glimmer of hope for Bithell and Bennion, but the investigation was completely out of their hands. Luckily for them, the newspaper reports on their conduct were passed far and wide throughout the UK and Ireland, and this included the Yorkshire town of Huddersfield.

On Saturday morning, the defendants were again brought to the stuffy courtroom, a horrible contrast to their usual life outdoors. There had been rumours throughout the previous evening that the missing man was alive and well, and the *Liverpool Mail* of 2 September 1848 reported that the Head Constable of Liverpool,

> *Mr Dowling said, he had reasons for believing that the passenger, who was supposed to have been drowned by the prisoners, was in some way accounted for, inasmuch as a person answering his description had been landed, and possibly there might be reasons for his non-appearance. There was, however, further evidence with regard to the robbery.*

With so many possible names and spellings suggested, the judge wisely insisted upon seeing the man in court for himself before closing that particular inquiry. As for the additional evidence regarding the trunk, someone named only as 'an intelligent seaman belonging to the crew of the Ocean Monarch', probably Second Mate Gibbs, had added accounts of violence to the evidence already heard.

According to his testimony, 'He told [the pilots] they would, of course, have salvage for the portions of the wreck which they might save, and they would also be rewarded for saving the lives of the seamen and passengers. Notwithstanding this they forcibly took the trunk from the Ocean Monarch's boat.' To do this to people already suffering from the effects of the fire and their time in the water was despicable.

When the court reconvened, there was a pleasant surprise in store. John Sheard, 24, last seen lying seasick and naked in a berth on the *Pilot Queen* was now fit enough to give evidence to his being alive and well. He testified in front of the surely greatly relieved pilots that they treated him with 'great kindness' and he offered them half a sovereign upon his departure from their company for the *Taliesin* steamer as a mark of his gratitude for their assistance. John, like his father, was a handloom weaver. He had rushed home to Huddersfield upon landing, not thinking for a moment that his disappearance from the port area would cause such worry in the area or have such enormous repercussions for the pilots. When he became aware of his 'murder' at their hands he immediately returned to Liverpool, arriving on Friday night and showing up at the commencement of that day's proceedings.

As the *Liverpool Mail* reported on 2 September 1848, the judge then said that since

> *the missing passenger were clearly accounted for, he had some doubts as to whether he had further jurisdiction in the matter. No doubt, the trunk which had been alluded to had been picked up on the high seas by the prisoners, and then the question would arise as to the county nearest to which the felony had been committed.*

Although the pilots were now completely cleared of all suspicion of murder, they still faced further questioning on the accusations of robbery, a serious allegation in and of itself. This seemed an open and shut case, for, as the paper continued, 'It was clearly proved that the trunk had been emptied of its contents when found by the police-officers.'

The men may not have committed murder but the testimonies Judge Rushton had heard so far had greatly displeased him. According to the paper, he,

> *said that this was one of the most inhuman cases that had come within his knowledge. There could be no doubt that a felony had been committed; and he hoped that Mr Dowling would prosecute the other inquiry. In the meantime he would remand the prisoners till the following day, and remit the prisoners in the custody of the two Liverpool officers for examination before the magistrates at Flint.*

First, however, the judge instructed that the silver watch pawned in Holywell be returned to Henry Powell – and that the tatty old blanket be restored to the pilots. He admitted that this might not be within his remit as judge, but he did it anyway.

*****

A passing captain on his way from Waterford to Liverpool watched part of the *Ocean Monarch* bob on the water, still tethered to the spot by the ship's cables and anchors, right in the way of vessels en route to and from Liverpool.

Warning buoys marked the spot, and larger pieces of wreckage which posed a risk to ships in the area were retrieved where possible. As the *North Wales Chronicle and Advertiser for the Principality* reported on 5 September 1848,

> *The blackened masts and some of the spars of the Ocean Monarch ship, with portions of the rigging attached, were towed into the river … by one of the steam tugs, which found them floating near the spot where the remains of the vessel went down. They were floated into the Prince's Basin, where they remain.*

Pieces of wood from the *Ocean Monarch* were bought for use in the manufacture of macabre mementoes which would then be sold to benefit the victims of the disaster, or for personal gain.

Divers were directed to salvage what they could from the wreck, an always risky and often grim task, especially when it was likely there would still be corpses trapped below deck. Some cargo was recovered but the fire and/or water had ruined much of it. Bodies continued to float up from the depths as decomposition bloated their bellies and rendered the remains buoyant. Some were hauled on board fishing smacks along with their catch, an unwelcome surprise amid the fish in their nets. Others drifted on shore or bobbed against boats until they could be pulled into the vessel and passed to the authorities in port. Friends and relatives unable to make the sometimes lengthy and expensive journey to the coast to look at bodies before they were decently disposed of, would scour newspapers for details of height, hair, and clothing. This included the abandoned workhouse mistress, Emmeline Bacon, her employers and family.

No one had heard from James Smith Bacon or his partner in flight, Mary Ann Walter, since before the wreck. Nobody had seen the girl. Following several frantic days in London, Bacon's brothers-in-law decided to act upon the assumption that he had either survived the wreck and gone into hiding, or, more probably, died and been recovered from the water. Minutes of a meeting held by the Guardian Board of St Luke's Workhouse state: 'various circumstances had occurred leading to an idea that the Master and Schoolmistress had both perished'. Emmeline's brothers needed to confirm, if at all possible, whether Emmeline was a widow, and if her errant husband's will could now be processed.

These well-to-do gentlemen, one a surgeon, one the owner of a tallow factory, boarded a fast train to Liverpool in Euston Square, London, at 10 am on the Tuesday following the wreck. While Henry Powell gave evidence against the Welsh pilots in the Police Court, fellow Londoners James Baker and William Fontaine discussed their plans and concerns with another passenger on the train, Sir John Jervis. As luck would have it, the Attorney General was travelling in their carriage and amenable to their plight. As they later recounted in a statement for the Board of Guardians, 'upon our communicating to him the painful mission in which we were engaged, he kindly offered us every assistance in his power to aid us in our search; when we arrived at the Adelaide Hotel, Liverpool, he wrote us a letter of introduction to Mr Rushton, the Police Magistrate of the Borough'.

Such powerful connections would prove very useful to these outraged relations, especially since Rushton was so well acquainted with the case. The letter they passed to him worked wonders. As Bacon's brothers-in-law explained to the Board of Guardians,

> *we had an interview with that Gentleman at his private residence in the country the same afternoon; Mr Rushton immediately expressed his willingness to cooperate with us, gave us a letter to Mr Dowling, the Head Constable of Liverpool, who gave instructions to the Police Force that they should accompany us, if required, and hold themselves in readiness for our service. We lost no time in obtaining an interview with Captain Murdoch, Mr Ellis, Surgeon, and several other Persons who were on board the Ocean Monarch at the time the ship was on fire.*

They also spoke with Bacon's fellow cabin passengers including Whiston Bristow and Henry Powell, and the agents for the ship. 'From All parties we received the greatest courtesy, accompanied with cheerful promises of assistance.' Now they were in the North West, and had a better idea of who to speak with and where, Bacon's relations embarked on their manhunt with determination and enthusiasm.

> *From the time we left Euston Square on Tuesday, the 29th ultimo, up to and including Saturday the 2nd instant, we were journeying from morning till night in search of Mr James Smith Bacon, and although*

it would be impossible to recollect every minute circumstance which occurred during our travels or the names of all the places we visited along the coasts of England and Wales; we, however, made notes at the time of every fact and circumstance which in our opinion helped us to complete the chain of evidence, which we were enabled to collect, as it were, link by link.

Having questioned survivors from the wreck and ascertained that Bacon, Walter, and the little girl had definitely been travelling on the *Ocean Monarch* at the time of the tragedy, the investigators moved on to the next part of their plan.

As soon as we had obtained sufficient information to justify us in adopting decisive measures, we caused several hundred large Posting Bills to be printed under the sanction of the Police Authorities of Liverpool, and forwarded by them to all the necessary Police Stations. We also proceeded by water, by rail, or by carriage conveyance, to the following (among other) places [including] *Hoylake, Birkenhead, Seacomb*[e], *Chester, Queen's Ferry, Flint, Holywell, Mostyn, Prestatyn, Ryhl* [*sic*], *Abergely Bay* [*sic*], *Conway, Aber, Bangor, and the Straits near Menai Bridge, and employed men to post Bills offering a reward of £10 to any person who would recover Mr Bacon either living or dead.*

These posters, like the adverts placed in local papers, said:

Copy. Police Notice. No. 443
Ocean Monarch
£10 Reward
Missing from the 'Ocean Monarch' and supposed to be drowned,
James Smith Bacon.
Had booked as First Cabin Passenger in the name of James Andrews;
Thirty eight years of age, 5 feet 11 inches high, stout, fair complexion, Light hair, rather large whiskers; marks on the back of the neck having been recently cupped. Wore a mourning ring, with his own name in full engraved upon it. Supposed to have been dressed in Black Linen marked I.S.B. or I.B. Supposed to have had a considerable sum of money on his person.

The above reward of £10 will be paid to any person or persons who shall give such information as will lead to the recovery of said James Andrews, dead or living, on application to the Head Constable, Central Police Office, High Street, Liverpool; or to Mr William Fontaine, East Street, Hoxton, London.
Central Police Office, Liverpool, August 30, 1848.

They soon heard from staff at the St George's Inn & Eagle Hotel on Fenwick Street, Liverpool, where Bacon had stayed in the days prior to his departure on the ill-fated emigrant ship, and took a number of statements which they returned to the Board of Guardians. According to the minutes of a meeting held at the workhouse on 6 September 1848, the gentlemen who took such an interest in safeguarding the welfare of the people in their care then directed their attention to Bacon's presumed widow, Emmeline. She was widowed, embarrassed, and now the sole provider for their five living children. The Board were not unsympathetic to her plight, but their plan of action was still relatively merciless beneath its veneer of civility.

Resolved – that this Board entertain, both individually and collectively, a strong desire to assist Mrs Bacon, but that they do not see any means by which they can do so. They feel that this Workhouse has been built for a Master, having a Wife who should perform the duty of Matron, and they also feel that the wellbeing of the establishment requires the appointment of a married man as Master, so that, as hitherto, the Matron should be the Wife of the Master. The Board, therefore, in the first place, beg to condole with Mrs Bacon, on her late loss; to express their desire that she will continue to aid as Matron (as the same salary as heretofore), the Preservation of Order and Propriety in the Workhouse, until the Board can elect a new Master and Matron, and instal [sic] *them into their office, and that the Overseers of the Poor be requested to arrange with the Vestry Clerk for the conduct of the House until the election can take place.*

As soon as they found a family to replace hers, she was out, but until then, she had to carry on as normal with her work.

The surviving members of the Bacon family were not the only ones to suffer as a result of Bacon's relationship with Mary Walter and her daughter.

John Walter, not yet 13, lost his mother and sister in the wreck while his father was in jail for sex offences. The book his mother gave him before she left to visit his supposedly ailing grandmother – who, thankfully, was now with him as he mourned – became one of his most treasured possessions. As he later wrote in a note which accompanied it, 'The shock [of the loss] was so great to my father that he took brain fever and was long time sick in fact was never the same man after.' He may have been unaware of his father's crime, or decided not to commit it to paper. As John recalled, 'The home was broke up and I had to go to work.' The elopement of his mother with what some papers including the *Preston Chronicle* of 30 September 1848 described as 'The Lothario of St. Luke's' had led to hellish repercussions for their loved ones, something they surely could not have anticipated when planning their flight.

The efforts of Bacon's brothers-in-law soon paid off. Among the many, many bodies washed ashore along the Welsh coast were seven corpses picked up around Abergele on Sunday 10 September. The *Albion* of 18 September 1848 contained detailed descriptions, including this one:

> *A man about six feet, about forty years of age, stout, light hair, teeth in the upper jaw irregular, and the two middle ones rather large. Had on a very good black dress coat, double-breasted black vest, black buckskin trousers, a dark plaid scarf, and white cotton stockings. His shirt was marked with the letters J. S. B. No.6, and on his feet were a pair of bluchers. Upon the body of this man were found the following articles:- A silver hunting watch, with a gold chain, two gold seals, and a gold watch key; also, a common linen purse, containing four sovereigns, four penny pieces, a penknife, a small silver vinaigrette, and a bunch of keys, (eight in number), a pocket book, and amongst other documents, a 'warrant, dated October 12th, 1847, under the hand and seal of Thomas James Arnold, Esq., one of the Metropolitan magistrates, for the apprehension of Edward Glass, charged on the oath of Thomas Bennett, constable of the parish of St. Luke, with having deserted his wife, Betsy, whereby he had committed an act of vagrancy.' Also, a printed ticket, of which this is a true copy:- 'Communist Covenant. We hereby covenant and declare that co-operation and association should succeed competition and private property, and believing that Communion of Goods was an element of*

> *the Original Model Christian Church at Jerusalem, we hereby call for its restoration as a religious duty. No. 63, 1848. John Parry, member, Gosdwyn Barny* [probably 'John Goodwyn Barmby'], *founder.*

The remains of Bacon and the other bodies retrieved at Abergele that day were examined, and their property removed and retained in case relatives claimed it later. They were buried there on Wednesday 13 September. Among those bodies lay the mother of the two little girls from Rochdale, now living with their grandparents there. Depending on their literacy and the availability of this report in their locality, they may never have discovered where their mother, last seen drowned near the *Ocean Monarch*, was buried. It appears from the description detailed in the newspaper that she lost some of her hair during the wreck, though not as much as her daughters.

> *A female, about thirty, with light auburn hair, about five feet two inches, hair lost, teeth of upper jaw lost. Had on a black merino dress, two gray flannel petticoats, two flannel jackets, black woollen stockings, and drab-coloured cloth boots. Found upon her three letters, two of which were addressed to 'Jonathan Lord, North Andover, State of Massachusetts, North America,' and the other to 'Mr Samuel Kershaw, Captain Horley's Mill, North Andover, Massachusetts;' also, a piece of leather, bearing the following address:- 'Mrs Rebecca Hill, passenger to Mr George Hill, with Andrew Hart, Middlesex Factory, Massachusetts, America;' also, a wedding ring and a contract paper for the Ocean Monarch, upon which appeared the name Rebecca Hill, 36, Sophia Hill, 8 ½, Sarah Anne Hill, 9 ½; likewise a clasper blue and red bead purse containing 10s. in silver, and a leather purse containing 3s. in silver &c.,.*

Unlike Rebecca Hill, Bacon's remains were soon claimed by his relatives. As *Bell's Life In London And Sporting Chronicle* reported on 24 September 1848, 'Some papers found in his pocket were sent to town, and his friends, recognising the clothes found upon him, procured his disinterment, and the body was brought by rail to London to the house of a relative until the hour for conveying it to its final resting-place.' Their request for his body to be laid out in his own home according to the usual mourning customs had been denied, as according to the minutes of a meeting at the workhouse on 15 September 1848, 'it appears exceedingly undesirable under all the circumstances of the case that such a course should be adopted and the Board therefore feels itself compelled to intimate to the friends of Mr Bacon its objection to such a course.' Apparently his brothers-in-law, Fontaine and Baker, accepted this, meaning his almost month-old corpse was instead displayed in a sympathetic family member's residence before his well-attended funeral on 19 September in Abney Park Cemetery, Clapton.

At this meeting, the clerk of the workhouse also read out a letter from a Mr Richard Ward which contained the following waspish postscript: 'PS – I hope for the future strict morality will be observed in the Workhouse – not only by the Poor but by all those whose duty it is to set good example. If this Postscript requires my explanation, I will give it if required.' It does not appear this was the case.

As families throughout the UK and Ireland settled into their new version of normality, draping themselves and their homes in black, or girded their loins and prepared to venture out to sea again, the newspapers continued to include details of bodies recovered from as far afield as the Isle of Man, Morecambe, and Beaumaris on the Welsh island of Anglesey. Those claimed and buried included Elizabeth Steele; John Atkinson of Bradford; Daniel Pollard of Huddersfield; Joseph Bladon of Birmingham; Emma Bell, James Healy, and James Ronayne of Manchester; Joseph Shaw of Glossop; William Pawson and his sister, Jane Roberts, of Leeds – who, like Bacon, was reinterred once her family knew where she was – and 30-year-old Esther Jackson of Sheffield. William Jackson, who last saw his wife clutching their daughter at the front of the ship, had survived his secret voyage to New York thanks to the generosity of the Nitherward family and the cherished hope that at least his wife and daughter had survived the wreck.

When he reached America and heard the news he was, understandably, completely devastated. As the *Northampton Mercury* of 28 October 1848 reported, he wrote home to Sheffield after a very rough passage of thirty-five days improved only by the charity and support of the captain and his fellow passengers.

> *For three days after I got on the Sea Queen I could not hold up my head; and but for the kindness of* [the Nitherwards] *I certainly must have*

> *died. …* [My wife and Elizabeth] *appeared in a very safe position, and I felt almost certain they would be saved; but I found by the New York papers, to my very great grief, that my hope was groundless.*

He wasn't the only one to have lost everything he held dear that day. One woman lost all five of her children, others lost their extended family and friends. After experiencing that kind of loss, it was difficult to know what to do or where to go.

Chapter Twelve

When we were on the Atlantic, and many miles from land, the galley of our own vessel took fire, and it was with great difficulty that the flames were extinguished. I know you can readily picture the scene. Cries, lamentations, and prayers were offered up, whilst some made ready to lower the various spars and loose timber on deck. But what could these have done? At the best, they could have saved only about 50 lives out of 675 – the number we landed safely at New York. However, with the able management of the seamen, the fire, which certainly occasioned more alarm than it need have done, was extinguished. None but those who have crossed the Atlantic, can sympathise with poor emigrants, who have great trials indeed to undergo, and deserve comfort and happiness after running such risk.

(Passenger account from the *New World*, *Bolton Chronicle*, 28 October 1848)

Onwards or home, United Kingdom and America, September 1848 onwards

While more than eighty of the bravest or most desperate survivors sailed across the Atlantic on the *Sunbeam*, on a far less eventful voyage than the one they had briefly experienced on the *Ocean Monarch*, the American jeweller James K. Fellows travelled to America with miniaturist Nathaniel Southworth. As Fellows wrote in his memoir years later, he got there on the *Hibernia* steamer two weeks after the disaster,

After a pleasant voyage, we landed at East Boston in due time, and having no baggage, I was the first to cross the ferry and inform Mr Train of the loss of his ship. Ocean cable despatches were unknown at that time. I was soon on board the train that took me to my friends, thankful

> *that my life had been spared; but I was minus my bag of valuables, my baggage, and a variety of curiosities and 'traps' which I had collected during my four months' travel. … Mr Train seemed very anxious to know of the management of Captain Murdock, and remarked that no ship was better provided with appliances for saving life.*

At the inquests and inquiries which continued in England and Wales as ever more bodies were retrieved from the sea, it was established that steerage smokers were not to blame for the fire, though many newspapers continued to portray their supposed carelessness and disobedience as the cause of the tragedy. Some passengers blamed the cook, their claims highlighting that he was black and lower class, and also accused him of gross acts of violence towards some of the women on deck as he attempted to escape the burning ship – accounts which appear baseless when compared with the many other witness statements of his exit and subsequent death. A few journalists opined that crewmen drawing off spirits in the spirit room of the ship while illuminating their work with naked flames sparked the tragedy, but, as with the wooden ventilators initially cited as the source of the fire, Captain Murdock denied having such a place on board. There was a store room below the cabin which housed kegs of wine and brandy along with food items, but no separate spirit room where vapours could dangerously build up as these commentators described.

James K. Fellows was an apparently astute and observant passenger who had breakfasted with the captain and his fellow cabin passengers just a few hours before the ship burst into flame. After listening to other survivors and thinking back on the awful events that day, he recounted in his memoir what appears to have been the most likely sequence of events.

> [The fire] *was caused by the boys while getting liquors from the store-room, as ordered by the captain. They slightly melted a lighted candle at the bottom and stuck it on a box of porter, leaving it burning, and closing the trap-door as they came away.*

Unfortunately, he left Liverpool before giving evidence or leaving a statement with any of the officials investigating the tragedy, and as a result, as the *Northern Whig* explained on 2 September 1848,

> *THE precise cause of the catastrophe, the news of which has already shocked so many thousand hearts, is not ascertained. Fire was the undoubted agent, but how it originated is unknown: in which part of the vessel it first appeared, – even that is a matter on which those saved from the wreck cannot altogether agree. Most probably it was caused by the carelessness of a single individual. If he have escaped, what must be his reflections! if engulfed in the sea, what a penalty he has paid! and what a warning does this event hold out against the indulgence of that heedlessness of consequences in seemingly little things which is the very habit of many people!*

*****

Well over a hundred of the missing passengers were buried in England and Wales. The majority remained anonymous and unclaimed. As the *Glasgow Herald* of 15 September 1848 explained to their readers, 'Bodies are daily washed ashore upon the banks of the Mersey. The coroner held inquests on two to-day, so revealed again to light.' Many other bodies would no doubt have been retrieved from the water in this busy area, especially as there were now pleasure trips run out to the wreck site with refreshments included for grieving visitors and the morbidly curious, but as the newspaper continued,

> *owing to a recent regulation of the town council, no witness before the coroner is to receive more than one shilling per day for his loss of time. This operates harshly in the case of labouring men, who are generally concerned in such cases, and renders this class extremely loath to come before the coroner. It is said a boatman passed three bodies floating on the water one day last week, but, owing to the knowledge of the loss he should sustain were he to bring them ashore, declined to touch them.*

Seasoned sailors would have had a certain degree of experience in dealing with the dead, hauling in decomposing bodies along with herring in their nets, or collecting drowned shipmates after accidents at sea. It was unpleasant but probably not as upsetting as it might be for someone less used to the appearance of a corpse after it had spent a while in the water, who might be walking along the shore and wondering what the crows were feasting on or why there was such an abominable stink, only to find a body on the beach. If the local council had not placed such a restriction on the financial compensation of witnesses, people like Jonathon Nicholson would perhaps have been spared the nightmarish sight of a coffin birth.

On Thursday 7 September, a fortnight after the *Ocean Monarch* caught fire, Nicholson had been staying at the Clifton Arms in Lytham, a little south of the popular resort of Blackpool. Owing to the recent addition of a railway line, the town was booming, and its long stretch of sand allowed visitors to indulge in scenic walks along the beach. This was something he may have come to regret. As his letter, included in the *Bolton Chronicle* of 9 September 1848, explained:

> *At six o'clock this (Friday) morning I went on the shore at Blackpool, the tide being at its height at half-past seven, during which time I saw three bodies worked up, all women: one with a silk dress on; the second with a plaid mourning dress on, a wedding ring, and hoop, I should say rather an expensive one; the third was dressed like an Irish reaper girl, with a straw hat and waistcoat, and in this instance the woman seems to have been delivered of a child, either at the time or after the accident took place. For an hour the body might be seen floating, and a bird picking on the top of it, only moving from it when it saw a breaker a-head, and it continued to do so until within a few yards of the beach. The baby seemed to be quite perfect.*
>
> *One* [body] *seems to be coming up now as the coach is starting for Lytham (half-past nine). A lady who was with me at the time the woman with the wedding ring and hoop on was taken up says, that from the description given, she will prove to be the woman whose children were saved, and saw their mother drowned and floating amongst the wreck. Being at Lytham now, I hear that there has been two taken up, a man and a woman. The man is now lying in an out-house belonging to the Clifton Arms, and is very much disfigured. More are expected up by the next tide.*

The saved children this onlooker referred to were probably Daniel Leary, 11, and his 7-year-old sister Catherine, who had been travelling from Tralee in Ireland when their mother died. They were naked when their rescuers took them on board the *Afonso* and lost every single thing they had in the wreck, except their lives. More details of the recovered corpses were included in the press including the *Glasgow Herald* of 15 September 1848, ostensibly to allow their audience the chance to identify the missing travellers, but also to satisfy their more prurient readers,

> *a number of other bodies were seen floating in with the tide, and the inhabitants generally assembled to secure them and convey them ashore for interment. From the confusion naturally attendant upon such an event, and the discoloration and disfigurement of the several bodies, it is difficult to give a definite description of each. The following particulars, however, collected on the spot, may be relied upon, and will, we hope, be the means of leading to the identification of some of the bodies, and of enabling surviving relatives and friends to pay their last mournful tribute of duty to the deceased. The bodies washed up at Blackpool, including the one on Wednesday evening, were seven in number, viz., four females, and three males. …*
>
> *Second Female. – This deceased is of slender make, having on her head a Dunstable bonnet, and a dress of blue hail showered print, blue cotton skirt or top petticoat, and a red flannel under-petticoat, and a red and white woollen plaid shawl. Under her dress she had on a man's waistcoat made of worsted cloth, with a small red flower on a light ground, and small metal buttons. On the wedding finger was a gold ring, marked in the inside with the initials 'G. W.' Round her neck was a double link of coral neck beads with a gold clasp, and her arms appeared much scorched. This female had been thrown into premature confinement, and was partly delivered of a child. She appears to be about 34* [some papers say 43, either way it would have been difficult to determine age after so long in the water] *years of age.*

No accounts survive including any mention of a woman seen to be in labour during the hours between the fire breaking out and the final travellers being rescued from the wreck. The bodies of several pregnant women were recovered from the water in the weeks after the tragedy, none of which were officially identified. This young woman stands out as unusual, however, because of the circumstances of her baby's 'birth'.

Technically known as 'postmortem fetal extrusion', or, more commonly, a coffin birth, this rarely witnessed phenomenon occurs after the death of the mother. Bodies begin the process of decomposition immediately after death, and the action of bacteria within the corpse can soon lead to a build-up of intra-abdominal gasses. As the flesh loosens and the pressure on the womb increases, the dead foetus is then partially or wholly expelled from the maternal body. In some cases, the whole uterus is ejected, turning inside out as it prolapses and emptying the contents into the area around it. This can only happen if the pressure outside of the body is less than that building up inside, e.g. if in the open air, a coffin, or the sea. In burials without a box, where the corpse has soil or rocks placed directly on top of it, the foetal remains can only be retained within the abdomen.

On Saturday 9 September mother and child were buried with several other women and a man recovered from the sands at the same time in the graveyard of Bispham All Hallows, a beautiful old church constructed of red sandstone and oak which had received the remains of many shipwreck victims over the years. Only one of the bodies from the *Ocean Monarch* was identified. Her gravestone reads,

> *Beneath this stone a sister lies:*
> *The Briny Waves have closed her eyes*
> *Unthinking at the morning light*
> *To sleep in Death's cold Arms at Night.*
> *The Strong must yield to Death's strong grasp*
> *But Jesus died, and rose and reigns …*
> *He'll raise Her sleeping Dust to life*
> *And bind The Tyrant Death in chains.*
> *In Memory Alice*
> *Wife of James Winsley. Aged 26 years*
> *Late of Bury*
> *Who perished at sea in the endeavour to escape*
> *from the Wreck of the* SHIP OCEAN MONARCH
> *when on Fire*
> *26* [*sic*] *August 1848*

Alice, originally from Scotland, had been travelling from the village of Gigg, near Bury, to America when she died. There is no mention of a child so it appears she was not the mother whose corpse was eaten by birds as she washed onto the beach.

That same Saturday saw another eleven bodies buried in the graveyards of Southport Christ Church, Warton St Oswald, Lytham St Anne's, and West Kirby. Twenty sets of remains were interred with little ceremony. It had been an exceptionally wet season but at least the soil was workable and it wasn't close enough to winter to bring frost and frozen ground for the workmen digging the (sometimes mass) graves.

Not all of the bodies recovered over the months following the fire were inspected closely enough to reveal detail that might allow loved ones to identify the rotting remains. According to one local newspaper, over twenty bodies were cast up on the beaches around Blackpool, Lytham, and Norbreck, along with charred timbers from the wreck. Although many were searched for information, revealing that one young man was likely named 'John Curly' and had a brother and sister in Massachusetts, as *Bell's New Weekly Messenger* told their readers on 24 September 1848,

> *Mr Palmer, who was officiating for Mr Gardner, the coroner for this district, refused to hold an inquest on* [some of] *the bodies, on the ground that it had been dispensed with at Blackpool, Lytham, and other places, and therefore ordered them to be buried. We hardly think this proceeding in accordance with the dictates of humanity, even if strict justice did not call for an investigation in such cases. The description of the bodies, and other particulars elicited at the inquiry, might attract the attention of the friends of the deceased, to whom, doubtless, it would be a source of melancholy satisfaction to know the last resting-place of their hapless relatives.*

Often the shifting tides brought other, less upsetting, relics from the wreck to the shores of England and Wales, and also returned Neptune to dry land. As the *Halifax Guardian* of 13 September 1848 reported,

> *By a strange mutation of events a portion of the figurehead, we believe, of this ill-fated emigrant ship, has found its way to Halifax. It was washed up … at South-shore, Blackpool, and was taken possession of by a lady from this town, who for some time had been watching it as it*

> *rolled among the surge.* [It] *proved to be a fine colossal head of Neptune (the monarch of the sea), surmounted by a gilt crown. The crown is partially destroyed, but the face and flowing beard are quite perfect, and the paint is hardly scratched; the head appears to have been severed from the rest of the body by a very violent blow, and which has much splintered the neck.*

As the newspaper explained for readers curious about how this head came to wash up so far from the wrecksite,

> *although Blackpool is a considerable distance from where the awful conflagration took place, yet as the force of the current is in that direction, it frequently occurs that portions of vessels wrecked off the Welsh coast are brought up by the tide on the sea coast near Fleetwood and Blackpool … a charred piece of the bowsprit of the ill fated ship was also washed up at Nut End (a small ferry opposite Fleetwood).*

They were lucky to have been able to identify the chunk of bowsprit as such. Having recounted their satisfaction in finding charred pieces of timber and tree nails at the high water mark on the eastern shore of Morecambe Bay, journalists at the *Lancaster Gazette* sniffily remarked on 2 September 1848 that,

> *At Hest Bank a rather considerable portion was cast up … We were unfortunately unable to have a look at this sad relic before it was broken up for the convenience of carriage, when it would have been easy to tell to what part of the vessel it belonged, but from what we can make of the fragments, it appears to us that they are part of the larboard side of the ship just above the counter. There is a long strip of external planking, with a portion of a timber attached, and this latter is very much burnt, the surface being charred to a considerable depth, and in some parts the original form is utterly destroyed, so as to present the appearance of a shapeless mess. This shows how furiously the fire raged in the interior of the vessel, and amongst her lower timbers. Amid this piece of wreck was found a small quantity of molten lead, curiously fused up with charcoal and other matters.*

Portions of the wreck were hauled up from beaches and sold off, the wood used to craft knick-knacks such as 'a most beautiful little stand with a spiral pillar and claw feet [in a cabinet maker's shop in Southport]. The wood is American white oak beautifully grained. A suitable inscription is engraved in boxwood and inlaid at the top', (*Southport Visitor*, 22 May 1851), as well as commemorative seals for watches, and even model ships for school fetes in Middleton.

Being able to buy mementoes of the wreck, such as postcards depicting the ship ablaze or wee boats made of wood recovered from the *Ocean Monarch* itself, allowed some people to experience a vicarious connection to the disaster while also giving money to benefit those directly affected by it. Activities such as dealing with bodies, fundraising for the less fortunate survivors and their families, and rewarding heroes also helped the public to feel less powerless against the might of the elements and the often callous government.

The mementoes presented to heroes involved with saving travellers from the wreck itself were items made of something other than wood from the ship. Surgeon William Ellis, who lost his certificate, books, and the tools of his trade was presented with a new set of instruments at a special dinner held in his honour. He married Mary Corrigan in St Peter's Church, Liverpool, around the same time, then disappears from the records. Thomas Littledale, owner of the yacht *Queen of the Ocean* which had raced to the aid of those on board and saved many lives, received a case of razors engraved with the inscription, 'In memory of the *Ocean Monarch*' and his name, from a cutlery manufacturer in Sheffield, and his friend John Aspinall Tobin, Esq., and the sailor Frederick Jerome received similarly personalised cases of their own beautifully carved razors.

It had been a truly multi-national rescue attempt, reflecting the great mix of cultures and countries represented in the Liverpool area and other ports of the time. *The Albion*, 4 September 1848, in an otherwise argumentative article rightly stated that,

> *it matters not a straw to what country the parties who were engaged in these acts* [of heroism] *belonged, for there were Brazilians, Englishmen, Frenchmen, Americans, Scotchmen, Welshmen, and perchance Irishmen, actively, courageously, and conspicuously engaged in doing all they could to rescue their fellow-beings from the dreadful fate which threatened them.*

If someone was being saved, whose hand was pulling them into a boat away from danger was irrelevant.

Many medals were awarded to the men involved in the rescue, some of whom were badly injured in their efforts to save lives. As *The Principality* stated on 8 September 1848,

> *Such deeds are far more worthy of honours than the victories of the most celebrated generals, who have by fire and sword succeeded in vanquishing the army of a neighbouring State. The Royal Humane Society have awarded* [Fred Jerome] *a splendid gold medal, and the Queen has directed that £50 be paid him out of the bounty fund. The Queen and Prince Albert have given a joint subscription of £100 for the relief of the sufferers. The Humane Society have also awarded gold medals to Thomas Littledale, Esq., owner of the yacht Queen of the Ocean; Admiral Grenfell, who was on board the Affonso; Captain Lisboa, commander of the Affonso; and, to Captain Dani, of the Prince of Wales steamer, whose gallant conduct was mentioned last week. Several other medals of the second and third class, have been awarded to the officers and seamen of the Affonso; to J. Bragdon, mate of the Ocean Monarch; and to many others, who, on account of the services rendered by them, were successful in rendering assistance to the unfortunate sufferers.*

Not everyone agreed that Jerome, who clambered naked onto the burning ship to rescue the men, women, and children still clinging to the burning bowsprit, deserved reward or recognition in addition to the handful of gold bestowed upon him by the Prince de Joinville as he ventured on board the *Afonso* with the survivors. Some felt he had been unfairly singled out among many similarly deserving heroes to the detriment of his fellow rescuers. Others reckoned he would neither appreciate nor appropriately utilise the honours coming to him, their remarks containing more than a whiff of jealousy and/or snobbery.

As the *Northern Whig* of 2 September 1848 opined for its readership,

> *...the heart swells with admiration as it contemplates human nature in the full activity of helpfulness. There is the sailor FREDERICK*

JEROME – long be his name remembered! – who plunged into the sea with a rope round his body, made for that part of the ship where trembling wretches who had not dared to cast themselves on spars, anticipated swift destruction, and with the calmness of a true hero slung down in succession [many] *of his fellow-creatures, nor ceased until the last of them was safe on board another vessel … BUT there were others busied to the extent of their power in saving human lives.*

The distinguished party on board the Brazilian steamer Affonso, and its gallant crew, well deserve the tribute of British gratitude. Those must have been scenes of deep interest when two sons of a royal house, a Brazilian naval officer of rank, and a British admiral leaped into the boats to superintend and personally help in rescuing their scorched and drowning fellow creatures, and when the hapless children picked up from the wreck were solicitously tended and cared for by delicate female descendants of royalty.

Assuredly no acknowledgments of British hospitality in affording refuge to the family of LOUIS PHILIPPE could be more graceful than was given in these acts of spontaneous benevolence on the part of his children. Into what different revelations with England has the gallant but fiery PRINCE DE JOINVILLE been brought from those which he contemplated when visions of deadly hostilities between France and this country floated before his eyes! We would engage that the pleasure he feels on reviewing the events of Thursday week transcends immeasurably that which he would have derived from the most complete naval victory over the people whom a distempered fancy had at one time represented as irreconcileably [*sic*] *hostile to his own countrymen.*

The exiled prince and his family were now afforded a new respect and affection by many, and for good reason. Regarding sailor Frederick Jerome, the *Anti-Slavery Bugle* of 6 October 1848 took a more practical tone when it told its readers,

The praise of the brave young sailor, Jerome, who saved the lives of [many] *persons from the burning wreck of the 'Ocean Monarch,' is now in the mouths of all men. …* [New York] *city government, not*

> *to be outdone in generosity* [by the people of England], *and in its appreciation of a noble deed by the people of England, who have loaded Jerome with gifts, have presented him with the freedom of the city in a box of gold. The freedom of a good sloop or schooner of his own, or half a dozen acres of land … would be gladly exchanged for the box – which is not half so good as a tin one to hold his tobacco, and we are puzzled to know to what other use he can put it – and for the freedom of the city which now means absolutely nothing, that we have ever heard of. However, the purpose was a good one, and the city fathers, and all others who have praised the intrepid sailor, honor themselves no less than him in recognizing and reverencing his heroic self-devotion.*

A letter included in the *Liverpool Journal* of 16 September 1848, signed 'A LANDSMAN', captured the concerns of some in its audience regarding what they felt was a flagrant misuse of the word 'hero',

> *Sorry would I be to detract from the merit which has been bestowed upon several noble names rendered familiar with the deplorable catastrophe; still I do think noble deed sought to be accounted first: the bestowing of a shirt upon the shirtless or clothing upon the naked, may be all very well in their way, but these were common acts, prompted by the common sympathy of our nature, and heartless indeed would he or she have been, who would not have extended them under the circumstances; and surely they ought not to be accounted before the noble daring of him who 'paused not at peril, but, humanely brave,' risked his own life in saving the lives of others.*
>
> *Punch has, with a telling sarcasm … castigated the public for the admiration evinced towards the great names, to the almost exclusion of the really meritorious, by bitterly rating the committee of the Underwriter's Rooms, for having granted the freedom of their establishment to the distinguished personages and overlooked the 'common sailor.' Now this, when properly viewed, is 'not so bad as it looks'. Such a compliment to a man in Jerome's station of life would have been useless and worse than meaningless; as swell for any utility to him, might they have created upon him the King of the Cannibal Islands, or have conferred upon him the order of the garter.*

Instead, in this time of abject poverty and need, the optimistic 'Landsman' suggested a subscription scheme whereby the sum of not more than one penny each was collected far and wide, as,

> *By this means a compliment would be conferred, which would convince the brave seaman that his exertions are rewarded by the genuine and general outpourings of a sympathising people; an amount would thus be accumulated which would enable him to buffet the rough surges of the sea of life, to steer his bark clear of the rocks and shoals of adversity, and when rendered unfit for further sea service, he may be laid snugly up in port, in a haven where the squalls of want shall never blow.*

Luckily for the recipients of financial rewards, this advice was roundly ignored. Plenty of people ranging from the greatly impoverished to the monarchy gave money for the benefit of the survivors and many thousands of pounds were raised in this fashion, saving some survivors from the workhouse or worse. Fundraising attempts included the raffle of a beautiful sketch in crayons of the wreck donated by the Prince de Joinville, who described his skilled representation of the rescue attempts he had been involved with as 'a mere trifle'. Regiments of soldiers and groups of singers and actors put on performances with all monies received being donated to the subscription fund or given directly to the sufferers residing in that area. Goods were donated by merchants and the well-to-do for charitable auctions, and fancy dinners laid on to celebrate their conspicuous benevolence which was lavishly praised in local papers by fawning journalists.

This money was not always distributed fairly, however, and in the case of the Neesom family, resulted in a court case. Mrs Blamire had been given the sum of £80 from the subscription fund to distribute to her three relatives. Instead of dividing this up as the treasurer had intended, she kept the majority of the money for herself and attempted to leave the area. As the *Manchester Courier and Lancashire General Advertiser* of 27 January 1849 reported, she 'had not only been guilty of gross breach of trust, but had endeavoured to make away with her property' and as a result he would 'make an order for her immediate execution against her goods, as well as commit her to prison for 40 days'. A grim humiliation for this greedy survivor, and something two men in Wales also involved in the wreck of the *Ocean Monarch* could no doubt relate to.

The much-derided pilots Bithell and Bennion had suffered the humiliating and uncomfortable experience of being taken back to Wales in handcuffs. Upon reaching the market town of Holywell they were bailed home to their families. These were well known and easily recognisable local men who came from large families thoroughly established in the area, and so they were not considered a flight risk. It seemed likely from the reports in the media that the pilots would be found guilty of the felonious act of robbery under legislation from 1837, 'An Act to amend the Laws relating to Robbery and Stealing from the Person'. Section VIII, 'Punishment for wrecking', specifically referred to the theft of 'Goods, Merchandizes, or Articles of any Kind belonging to [a wrecked] Ship or Vessel', the punishment being transportation 'beyond the Seas' for ten to fifteen years, or imprisonment for any term less than three years. Prison was not considered a punishment in itself, but a form of containment and accommodation for the guilty while they performed hard labour or awaited transportation or execution. Punishment or not, prison was a grim and claustrophobic affair, especially for men used to working in the open air with nothing but sky above them and a view stretching across many miles of sea from the mainland to the Isle of Man.

But, as the *London Daily News* summarised in a tone of indignation on 16 October 1849,

> *The case, however, on going before a jury, was stopped, and a verdict of acquittal taken. As to the charge of murder and stealing the watch, they* [had] *both ended in smoke, for the watch was proved to be a gift, and the supposed murdered man was found to be alive a few days after the arrest. It further appeared that* [Officers Bates and Tuck] *had concealed the circumstances of their being police-officers from the plaintiff. They were thought to be Custom-house officers, and the plaintiff complained of their kidnapping pilots from their homes in Wales, and taking them to Liverpool, without the previous sanction of a warrant from a magistrate.* [Apparently] *they were acting under the orders of Mr Whitty, the superintendent of the Liverpool Police.*

The aggrieved and embarrassed pilots, represented by either a more able, or less easily cowed, solicitor than at their original court appearances in

Liverpool, brought a counter-claim against the police officers who had hauled them from their homes in handcuffs. Bates and Tuck had neither jurisdiction nor a magistrate's warrant so when they detained the pilots and removed them to Liverpool for an unpleasant week in the Bridewell, technically they had done so as private citizens and were therefore guilty of false imprisonment. Their roles now reversed, the home crowd in Holywell loudly revelled in the decision to award the maximum damages the law allowed to Bithell and Bennion, 20*l*. It seems clear from the many accounts of both cases and the witness testimonies given that there was fault on both sides and private resentments and power plays afoot between the Welsh and English judges and gentlemen involved.

The pilots were free to carry on with their lives on the Welsh coast once more. As for the policemen involved with their case, Joseph Bates continued in his work of detection and policing, despite his very public chastening in court. The *Glasgow Herald* of 23 April 1855 announced,

> *An office of a very useful character has been opened* [called] *'Private Enquiry and Absconding Debtors Office.' Mr Bates is an exceedingly active man, of good business habits, and while he would scorn to act as a mere 'spy,' he will be found to render valuable assistance to parties who may become the dupe of swindlers, and other base and dishonest characters.*

He and his wife Margaret raised two sons in the Liverpool area, and he seems to have died (or possibly emigrated) sometime after 1861.

His fellow police officer, Samuel Tuck, led a less successful and straightforward life. He and his wife Eleanor had four children, at least two of whom survived infancy. He continued to work for the police in Liverpool but in 1852 was accused of stealing a shirt and went to trial, though he was eventually acquitted. He died age 59 in 1862 and is buried in Walton Park, Lancashire.

Their onetime quarry, John Bennion, appears to have become a publican, running the Royal Oak in Bagillt a few years after his ordeal in Liverpool. He and his wife Mary, who also gave her occupation as 'pilot' in the census of 1851, had a sixth child and continued to live in the Holywell area until his death aged about 67 in 1874. Thomas Bithell, his fellow sailor on the *Pilot*

Queen of Chester, also worked as a fisherman at times, and lived for another few years at least.

The pilots were used to a hard life at sea, working with sailors who were similarly tough and physically fit rather than in need of the care and attention required by the survivors they took on board their vessel on that fateful day. This had not been their finest moment as pilots or as men but they did not, as some of their reluctant passengers feared, drown anyone, and it appears that even their theft of personal items recovered from the water was largely approved of by local gentlemen whose judgment they and their peers would perhaps have considered representative of the legal system as a whole. That Bithell and Bennion were wrong in this matter and unkind to the survivors temporarily in their care was no doubt unpleasant and unhelpful for those involved, but it was not a crime.

Epilogue

The experience of such seasons as the last falls slightly upon the Legislature. They do not overlook the sufferings. They cannot plead ignorance of the deaths and sickness on emigrant vessels. They do not affect to doubt the intensity of the evil. They even vote a grant to the colonies for their extraordinary charges in curing the sick. Thus they afford the most appalling evidence that life is very cheap with them, and money greatly respected. Nothing will be done to prevent another moving village of emigrants being wrapped in fire on the waters. Nothing will be proposed to hinder another evening gale from laying a range of sea-coast in mourning again. On all these subjects the Legislature will be silent, unless the people rise, and say that life is preferable to money; and, reading right the lessons taught by the blazing ship, off Formby Light-house, and the reproaches seen in the pallid cheeks of the corpses strewn on the Eastern coast, or the warnings given by the broken boats, wrecked on the granite rocks, say that life is dearer than gold – that life must be saved if money should be lost – and that first, where mankind and their existence is staked, security must be sought; and next, but only next, economy.

(*Northern Whig*, 2 September 1848)

Afterwards

Newspapers including the *Northern Whig* of 2 September 1848 acknowledged the clarity of hindsight, saying,

It is, no doubt, very easy, after the full effects of any accident are seen, to point out the probable means by which it might have been prevented ... most people are aware, that, in emigrant ships, there is a great number of divisions run up with thin dry laths, and it is astonishing, that a greater number of accidents by fire do not occur.

They made a suggestion, which would not be acted upon, that 'It would be easy to obviate this danger; but the remedy would increase the cost of construction. The internal divisions of emigrant vessels might either be completed of iron, or covered with zinc, or a less expensive metal.'

Their coverage of the *Ocean Monarch* tragedy encouraged a practical review of the current arrangements for ships carrying this vulnerable human cargo,

> *the authorities should see that emigrant vessels should be so fitted up, not as at present, after the cheapest fashion, almost wholly irrespective of the safety of passengers; but at that cost, be it what it may, which would best protect the lives of poor thousands from being eaten to death by fire, often, indeed, created by their own carelessness, super added to the culpable structure of such vessels, in which the danger is only seen when it has attained such rapid growth that little chance of escape for life is left – property need not be dreamt of; – while the horrors of this dreadful situation are too often aggravated by the cowardice or stupidity of those in charge of the ships.*

Despite calls in public and in the press for increased safety measures at sea, little if anything actually changed as a result of the *Ocean Monarch* disaster. Suggestions put forward included lifeboats clad in metal, and more lifeboats to be provided – perhaps even enough for all travelling on the ship to safely remove themselves elsewhere should there be a fire, collision, or sinking. Other ideas included the installation of dedicated smoking lounges on the top deck for all those wishing to indulge in the luxury of a pipe, and the careful monitoring of all below deck in case anyone sneakily smoked and risked a repeat of the disaster, even though it is clear the fire on the *Ocean Monarch* was not sparked by someone smoking where they shouldn't. Many adverts used the accounts of the disaster to promote their fire extinguishing equipment and life preservers, correctly suggesting that a lot of those who died in the water that day would still be alive if they had been able to stay afloat until other vessels came close enough to pull them to a place of safety.

The *Newcastle Courant* of 8 September 1848 included a piece pulled from the *Manchester Guardian* intended to draw people's attention to the plight of all on board these ships, who were essentially unprotected from any fires which spread beyond their cooking areas or lights below deck,

> *PROMPT EXTINCTION OF FIRES ON SHIPBOARD. – The melancholy fate of the Ocean Monarch ought to awaken the attention of all parties concerned to the excessive risk of accidental fire which is incurred from the usually crowded state of passenger ships, and the careless manner in which loose straw and articles of light clothing are permitted to be about amongst thin deal partitions, exposed to all the casualties incidental to the assemblage of the thoughtless multitude who throng the berths. Few of these vessels are furnished with any apparatus for the extinction of fires, beyond a limited number of buckets and the ordinary number of pumps, which are totally inadequate for the purpose; yet, with an unlimited supply of water, it would not be difficult to arrange a pair of force pumps, or to carry two small fire engines, by which a continuous stream could be forced by jets through any crevice that might present itself near the source of the flames; whilst, by means of a hose pipe, the men working the engines could be kept out of the smoke and heat. Such pumps or engines could readily be made available as supplementary pumps in the event of springing a leak, and the expence* [sic] *would be a mere trifle in the cost of the ship.*

Still, little changed for those travelling across bodies of water in search of a better, longer, or at least *different* life. The elements of fire and water are no less lethal now than they were 170 years ago. Disasters such as that of the *Ocean Monarch* eventually forced people who put profits above practicality (and lives) to change their priorities, and bring in measures regarded by many then and now as simple common sense – a total misnomer as it's clearly not that common. A lot of people, though sadly not all, are now able to take adequate lifeboat and flotation vest provision for everyone on board for granted. Fire retardant materials, plentiful fire extinguishers, and effective alarm systems tend to be standard for vessels in many countries. Progress has been made but anyone who goes out on or below the water is still taking their life in their hands.

Heroes like Captain Lisboa of the *Afonso* worked to make life at sea as safe as possible. He went on to save two men whose boat was destroyed during a severe gale near Rio de Janeiro the following year despite this being likely to kill him, and was duly – and rightly – lauded in the press.

As the *London Evening Standard* stated on 26 August 1848,

> *It is impossible to exaggerate the horrors of that frightful calamity which occurred on the coast of Carnarvonshire* [*sic*] *on Thursday – the destruction of the emigrant ship Ocean Monarch at mid-day within a near sight of land … In reading the accounts of the deplorable event, the mind has not even that imperfect and perverse relief afforded by the discovery of some one who is to blame. The terrible misfortune was not one against which any vigilance could guard, and which no amount of skill or energy on the part of the unhappy crew and passengers could mitigate.*

As with any situation involving more than one person, there were many perspectives – often conflicting – on the events surrounding the shipwreck. Trauma and fear affect memory, and the chaos on board the ship led to confusion at the time and then in the retelling. Sometimes comparing accounts of the same event led to clarity, when, for example, someone's rescue or exit from an area of the ship meant they failed to see the return of the first mate, and therefore classed him as a coward. A few people seemed to exaggerate or fixate on certain aspects of the wreck, or lash out in their grief to blame people like the captain and mates who were meant to protect them from harm and deliver them safely across the sea.

Among them were three young friends from Nottingham. John Wesley Freckleton was a tailor who had been reduced to living in the workhouse in Radford, Nottinghamshire, several years earlier with his parents and siblings, before he sought to emigrate in 1848. His terror during the shipwreck may have coloured his perceptions somewhat, and this deeply religious Baptist wrote home to his mother and sisters the following day,

> *Thank God we are all safe. After having braved death in two of its most horrid forms we have, by the mercy of Him who rules the winds and the waves, been spared. All is gone but life and the little money I had left in my pocket – clothes, books, and all but life. I know you will receive me again though ruined in circumstances I have still a home with you, and I cannot go out again at present, if I ever do. I have nothing but the very worst clothes I took with me. … God assisted me. … I cannot, it is impossible, to give you any description of the awful scene. My heart now wrings at the thought of it: men, women, and children, struggling*

> *and sinking and dying in the waves. It is awful! awful! Never will the remembrance of the awful scene leave me. It is only by a miracle that my life and the lives of my companions have been saved. … if spared, I shall see you soon, and be able to give you more particulars. I do not repent going; I firmly believe it was for the best, it has proved otherwise, I submit. Remember me to my friends; my love to you all.*

Freckleton travelled across the Atlantic to Boston on the *Grenada* the following summer age 23, newly married to Mary Ann Hollis. They settled in the Kings area of Brooklyn and had five children. He switched to trading in dry goods and manufacturing, and died at home in 125 Butler Street, Brooklyn, in late 1890 aged 65. He is buried in Green-Wood Cemetery, NY.

His friends Elisha Bannister and James Walker, who clarified or rebutted some of the more outrageous statements made by John Freckleton, chose to remain in England. Elisha appears to have had three wives and at least eighteen children, and James seems to have lived to the age of 73 before dying in the spring of 1899 in Eastwood, Nottinghamshire.

The American jeweller James K. Fellows, who first drew attention to the fire as he relaxed after a hearty breakfast of celebration below decks on the *Ocean Monarch*, blamed the captain and many of his crew for the loss of his luggage, the ship, and so many lives. He expressed his views on this repeatedly, and it may have been Fellows who discussed the supposed cause of the shipwreck with 25-year-old Henry Oscar Houghton, who went on to become one of the founders of Houghton Mifflin publishing house. Houghton had an incredible memory and was temporarily working as an editor at the *Boston Evening Traveller*. According to J. C. Derby's *Fifty Years Among Authors, Books and Publishers* (Winter and Hatch, Connecticut, 1884), Houghton was on his way home to dinner when,

> *he fell in with one of the passengers of the ill-fated ship … who told him some of the particulars of the disaster, and how cowardly the captain had acted. The latter was an old man, a broken-down merchant, who had been put in charge of the ship for the sake of giving him a place.*

Captain Murdock, 41, was neither broken down nor old, and was given his position due to his experience and prowess, not out of sympathy for a non-existent plight. The anonymous informant also told the young editor of the actions of 'the colored stewardess'. Incensed by the details he heard from this survivor, and the 'pathetic story' of the shipwreck, 'the young editor returned to the office and wrote a long account, in which the captain was severely reprimanded and the stewardess highly praised'. Houghton attributed this story to a clergyman, and it caused a sensation. Fellows was not alone in his outrage at the events surrounding the shipwreck, but may, like Admiral Grenfell, have changed his mind had he remained in Liverpool to hear the evidence given at the inquests. He travelled to Europe several times, even after his awful experience on the *Ocean Monarch*, making his last trip overseas age 78, and also enjoyed an active home life with his wife, children, and grandchildren.

Fellows lived a long and useful life, devoting much of his wealth and resources to the benefit of others. A prominent businessman, he is still celebrated in his adopted hometown of Lowell, Massachusetts, for his donation of a site for the Lowell General Hospital, having purchased it for $30,000 in 1891 for the purpose. In his letter to the trustees detailing this generous gesture, Fellows stipulated his desire 'that you or your successors shall constantly keep at least one woman on the staff of attending physicians', and ended his letter by saying, 'That this hospital may be speedily found in operation and prove an enduring blessing for the relief of human suffering is my most earnest desire.'

A decent and temperate man, he had started to learn typesetting and the trade of printing as a lad but found it too arduous and instead became a watchmaker and jeweller and thus built his fortune. A local history publication from 1907, three years after his death of heart disease and 'old age' at 94, describes him as 'a man of the strict old-fashioned type of integrity, simple in his tastes, quiet in manner, abstemious in habits, and unimpeachable in rectitude of conduct. He will long be remembered as an upright citizen and a public benefactor.' His house still stands on Andover Street in Lowell, Massachusetts.

His fellow passenger on the *Hibernia*, Nathaniel Southworth, who Fellows helped to obtain more comfortable quarters, did not fare so well, though he appears to have been equally well loved and for good reason. Upon arriving in New York, he bumped into an old friend who, according to the *Vermont Phoenix* of 22 September 1848,

> *took out his pocket-book and spontaneously pressed upon him a sum of money for his relief. The next day came news of the great fire in Brooklyn; and on glancing at the newspapers, Mr Southworth learnt that his open-handed friend had been burnt out, losing all he was worth. Hurrying to his hotel, he had the satisfaction of restoring the donation, with an usury of grateful acknowledgments and sympathies, which happened to be all that he had it in his power to add.*

Southworth carried on with his work, producing intricately detailed miniature portraits and cementing his reputation as a gifted artist, but repeatedly pushed himself too hard. Ten years after the disaster which claimed so much of his work, this talented artist was suffering terribly with consumption. He moved in with his mother in Hingham but after she died he went to Paris for work and the sake of his health. This proved a fatal error. His habit of overworking combined with the unfavourable weather and his pulmonary tuberculosis, and instead of his health improving as he had hoped, he soon realised he was dying. Southworth took the next steamer to Boston in hopes of reaching his home and the familiar faces of his friends in Hingham but he died in the carriage just before reaching the house in 1858, age 52. An article about him in *The Crayon*, 1 June 1858, describes him as 'a good artist, pleasing in deportment and retiring in his manner; he possessed the warmest friendship of those who knew him well.' One of his intimate friends, G. S. Hilliard, said of him,

> *He was a man not widely known, but his ability as an artist, and his purity of life and amiable qualities as a man, entitle him to some tribute to his memory. … All through life he was remarkable for skill and neatness in handicraft work, but his spirit was that of the artist and not of the mechanic.*

His work is exhibited in Boston to this day.

Captain James Murdock, despite being cleared of all blame in the official inquiries and inquests which followed the sinking of the *Ocean Monarch*, immediately retired from the sea. He had been one of Enoch Train's 'crack' captains, an otherwise highly successful graduate of Partridge's Military Academy at Norwich, Vermont, studying alongside Gideon Welles, who became Lincoln's Secretary of the Navy during the American Civil War. Murdock had spent many years as a captain in the East India trade, and was used to hard work and difficult decisions, but his time in the water had nearly killed him. His health was ruined by the smoke and prolonged immersion and he suffered greatly with rheumatism for the rest of his life, dying in Massachusetts Hospital of heart disease and exhaustion age 76 in 1883. Like Southworth, he did not marry and left no known children.

Frederick Jerome, the naked sailor who saved so many from the burning bowsprit, continued to live an adventurous life of daring exploits and danger. He was granted the freedom of the city of Liverpool, awarded a gold medal from the Boston Humane Society in addition to the medal he received in England, and given money from many quarters as well as presents including a silver tankard from London. He liked to wear his medals, and spent time in the Wild West, searching for a fortune in the Californian Gold Rush, and fighting (and sometimes killing) members of the tribes already living there, and was an honorary member of the Pioneer Society of California. Owners of a vessel going to the Gold Rush advertised his presence on board in order to entice passengers to pay for passage on this ship. He may have chosen to receive money instead of medals but, as with so many stories about his colourful life, there is conflicting information available.

A few years later he appears to have married Elizabeth Horn at St Paul's Church, Portsea, Hampshire, England. Jerome went on to work in the US Marshals' Service and the Custom House Service, successfully oversaw the landing of building supplies for the Cape Medecino Lighthouse, and became First Officer on a northern ship during the American Civil War. This was burned, and he and his crew were taken prisoner by the Confederate privateer *Florida*. He plotted his escape only to be betrayed by a fellow prisoner to the guards, leading to him being placed in double irons and lashed to a gun. He was then transferred to another ship which was paid to take him to Peking. This could easily have been the end of him but when he landed he was noticed by a Japanese captain he had previously helped, who put him onto a ship back to Liverpool with food, money, and clothes.

In later life Fred Jerome saved yet more people from several other shipwrecks, and eventually retired with his second wife, Bridget, a music hall star from Halifax, Nova Scotia. The *Hampshire Telegraph and Sussex Chronicle* of 8 June 1899 described him as, 'a muscularly-built old sea-dog [who] wears a black suit of clothes and a light soft hat. He speaks with the approved slur of the Yankee [and] has a hearty and jolly laugh as he recounts the more humorous episodes of his career.' They travelled to his hometown of Portsmouth, England, towards the end of his life then returned to San Francisco where he died in 1900 at the age of 75. Although often awarded considerable sums of money for his endeavours, it seems this was not his primary interest. He appears to have simply had a taste for the adrenalin rush of adventure.

His fellow hero, Thomas Littledale, became the Mayor of Liverpool like his father before him – the youngest in over a century – and Chairman of the Dock Board. He was known to be an exceptionally nice man with a strong sense of civic duty, who made a positive impact on the area and those within it. The *Liverpool Mercury* of 1857 described him as, 'tall in person, most gentlemanly in his manners, generous and kind hearted; indeed, his good tempered face is an index of his mind … His general appearance and manner give the notion that he is a man of great modesty. … There are few members of the Council more generally popular…' He and his wife Julia went on to have six children, including the big game hunter and celebrated traveller Clement St George, who was presented with a 2ft-long silver cradle by local businessman when he was born, and named after the magnificent St George's Hall in the heart of Liverpool. Thomas Littledale died in London in 1861 at the age of 42 when his youngest child was just 4-years-old. He had travelled to London to seek medical advice, only to die of a heart ailment within the doctor's office. His funeral, meant to be a strictly private affair, was well attended by many non-family members despite terrible weather, who watched as he was interred in the recently built family vault at St John's Church, near Highfield House, Old Swan, West Derby. A keen sailor, without his swift and selfless assistance at the wreck, many more would have died, including Captain Murdock.

Francois Ferdinand Philippe Louis Marie D'Orleans, the Prince de Joinville, who had been exiled from France with his family a few months before he saved so many lives on the *Ocean Monarch*, continued to travel and went on to write about events he witnessed during the Virginia Campaign of the American Civil War. The Prince was recognised for his bravery and intellect, and it is clear from the picture he donated to raise money for the survivors of the tragedy that he was a man of many talents. He was eventually able to return home to France in 1873.

Captain Joaquim Marques Lisboa of the *Afonso* was presented with an engraved chronometer by the British government in recognition for his efforts during the rescue. The *Afonso* was involved in a battle in Pernambuco, Brazil, the following spring. About a hundred of the crew helped to repel the insurgents' attack, and approximately half of these crewmen were reported killed amid great slaughter.

Another hero, Whiston Henry Bristow, went on to marry Mary, a native of Vermont, in 1852 in Jefferson, Indiana. They had two sons and a daughter. Bristow's cousin also survived a shipwreck and went on to become the first prime minister of Cape Colony in South Africa, and was known as the 'Lion of Beaufort'. Whiston Bristow is buried in South Park Cemetery, Greensburg, Indiana, with his daughter Rose.

Whiston, who saved so many lives by braving the smoke below deck and moving the magazine of gunpowder, made a point of telling reporters about the anonymous stewardess who died in her efforts to prevent the *Ocean Monarch* from blowing up. It was a joint effort but generally only Bristow received recognition for their bravery. Her name is still unknown. Some newspapers, such as the *Hampshire Advertiser* of 9 September 1848, didn't even have the good grace to allow her selfless act of heroism to be acknowledged without tempering their praise with a dig at stewardesses in general, saying,

> *Few functionaries seem less removed from commonplace, less free from the baser and more sordid motives, than that class of female waiters in ships, who are styled 'stewardesses;' yet the frightful calamity which befell the Ocean Monarch suddenly displays one of that class courting death by an act of devotion on a par with the most heroic that have been recorded.*

As a woman of colour who worked on an emigrant ship, this heroine – as far as the press and much of society at the time was concerned – was not deemed worthy of interest, or even identification. She may have been married to one of the stewards, who also perished that day, and sadly remains unnamed despite making the ultimate sacrifice for her fellow travellers.

John Baptist Orange, who signed a letter with Whiston Bristow testifying to the good conduct of the captain and crew, became a successful horticulturist in Albion, Illinois and developed cream-coloured blackberries. The aptly named Orange opened his own nursery in Edwards County in 1857 and delighted in the growing conditions there. His strains of fruit plants are still available for sale today. He may have married twice and had five children, before dying of typhoid pneumonia in 1880 at the age of 58.

Many of the women on board that day vanish from the records immediately after the wreck, perhaps because of marriage or subsequent success in emigration, including 39-year-old Mary Cashman who lost all five of her children in the wreck and was last noticed bewailing their fate in an office in Liverpool. Another example is 28-year-old Johanna Ronayne from Manchester who lost her parents and three siblings on the wreck. Some women, however, told their stories to family members who thankfully recorded this oral history, such as Mary Ann Taylor, who was travelling to meet her husband in Oxford, Massachusetts with her very young children Sarah Ann and George; their bodies were lost to the sea when an Irishman untied their little corpses from her waist enabling her to be pulled free of the water. Mary lost her teeth, her children, and – understandably – her nerve in the wreck.

When her husband eventually learned of the tragedy he sent more money for her passage to join him but she refused to go to sea again. He made the voyage back to England the following year and persuaded her to accompany him on board a ship across the Atlantic. This ship also caught fire but the blaze was extinguished and they eventually made it to Massachusetts where her husband worked as an overseer of the weaving department in a large mill. The Taylors lived in Andover, Lawrence, Ware, Plymouth, and Dennyville, and had nine more children (seven of whom survived Mary Ann) and celebrated their Golden Wedding anniversary two years before she died. Mary Ann was known to be a very industrious woman, and was celebrated for her skill in healing the sick with herbs and simple remedies. She died in the home of her son at the age of 70 in 1894 after an illness spanning two years, and is buried in West Rutland Cemetery, Rutland, Massachusetts.

Sophia and Sarah Ann Hill, daughters of woollen weavers from Rochdale in the north of England, did not take the substitute passage offered and instead of travelling to be with their father in Andover, Massachusetts, they returned to Rochdale to live with their maternal grandparents. At a time when women and girls did not usually cut their hair, they would have stood out while the hair grew back on their scorched scalps. Both girls became weavers themselves, and Sophia married James Simpson in the summer of 1875. Sarah died a spinster in 1910 at the age of 70, Sophia died age 88 in 1926. Their early lives were hard and it is unclear what happened to the money due to them, or to their father. English newspaper reports from 1854 indicate he remarried and killed himself while awaiting trial for murdering their half sibling – apparently he tried to stab his new wife during a heated argument but, as she was holding their child at the time, missed and killed the child instead – however records in Massachusetts suggest he was actually found dead eight years later age 48.

Lissy Roper and her mother, Anna, disappear from the records after they left the Northern Hospital in Liverpool, but Lissy's rescuer, Samuel Fielding, appears to have made it to his daughters in America. There is a grave in Texas Cemetery, Clinton, Illinois for a Samuel Fielding of Hurst, near Glossop in England, who died age 79 in 1857 and is buried with his daughter Mary and her husband John Alsop. Samuel Fielding, an old fustian weaver who chose to put up with the terrible pain of being burned over a period of many hours in order to safeguard a 3-year-old stranger, was a quiet hero who, along with dozens of others who acted utterly selflessly that day, deserves to be remembered.

Another child seems to have survived, according to one uncorroborated account in the *Bolton Chronicle* of 28 October 1848. An unnamed journeyman printer on the *New World* wrote,

> [Our voyage] *was a remarkably good one – 30 days; only three deaths, very little sickness, and, on the whole, very favourable weather. You will be well aware that we saw the Ocean Monarch on fire. Never was a more awful sight witnessed. Fancy the state of our minds at that time. Most gladly would we have sacrificed all to have bid adieu to the New World at that time. We were not more than a mile from the burning wreck, and could see the poor passengers falling from the bowsprit and masts like apples from a tree. … In my opinion, there were men in our ship that deserved as much credit as* [Jerome] *does; I mean the third mate and another officer; they floated in the water for upwards of an hour, and saved many lives, including that of a very pretty child, about three years old, who was seen floating a long way from the wreck. They brought it to us, and have determined to keep it. I used to nurse it often.*

This may have been a reference to Mary Anna Coxe, who was rescued with her aunt and taken aboard the *New World* and onwards to New York, but the account implies the child was alone. Whoever this child was, and wherever they ended up, remains a mystery – one which even the child may have remained unaware of throughout their life.

Less of a mystery was the fate of the Scottish newlyweds, Alexander and Jane Dow, who made it to Alexander's family in Ryegate, Vermont, in early October, having spent time recovering from the trauma of their ordeal with friends in nearby Manchester. During the wreck, Alexander had attempted to keep a petrified Jane calm, but she panicked and leapt overboard, closely followed by her new husband. They managed to remain near the ship, clutching at ropes and wreckage and staying afloat together until they were pulled into one of the rescue boats, despite the waves repeatedly washing them off. Perhaps because they were situated closer to the top deck than many of the steerage passengers, all but a few of the cabin passengers survived compared to approximately fifty per cent of the others.

Cabin passenger James Smith Bacon perished while urging others to save his 'wife' Mary Ann Walter and her 9-year-old daughter, also Mary. His body was recovered and recognised but the whereabouts of the two Marys' remains is still a mystery. Bacon's wife, Emmeline, was soon evicted from her home in the workhouse to make room for the new master and mistress. She and her five children somehow managed, with the help of their family, to cope with their new situation. Her two eldest sons, James and John, moved to the Kings and Queens districts of New York and she joined them there some time after 1870. Emmeline 'Emily' Bacon, abandoned by her husband and embarrassed in the press, died in New York in early 1911 at around 97 years old. She is buried in Green-Wood Cemetery, Brooklyn, NY.

John Thomas Walter, the sex offender whose conviction and imprisonment in the summer of 1848 seems to have triggered the trio's flight, appears to have been altered by his experience in prison, very public humiliation in the press, and the death of his wife and daughter. His son John was forced to leave school and work, and became a master mariner abroad, immigrating to Australia in 1863 on the *Spitfire* and marrying twice having been widowed while still relatively young. He took his mother's book, which she gave him before leaving for Liverpool, wherever he went as 'a mascotte' and kept a cutting about the wreck tucked inside, along with a note for his own family explaining that his mother and sister had been lost on the wreck while travelling for their health. John junior settled in the Sydney area and died in Balmain, New South Wales, age 86 in 1922. Meanwhile, his father was half a world away. John Thomas Walter remarried almost exactly a year after his trial in London, and had another son, Thomas Henry four years later, who became an organ blower. Despite his criminal record, Walter seems to have continued to find work as a schoolmaster in London, and later became a caretaker and deacon of a local church, dying in Paddington age 82 in 1893.

Joseph Ratcliffe, the Chartist caught hiding by police below deck before the *Ocean Monarch* departed for Boston, was sentenced to be hanged by the neck despite the jury recommending leniency and the judge admitting in court that he was perfectly satisfied it wasn't Joseph who actually murdered Constable Bright. This death sentence was eventually commuted to transportation, and Ratcliffe and other Chartists were sent to Australia as punishment instead.

Henry Powell, who stood up for what he believed to be right and ensured there was a full investigation into the conduct of the pilots on the day of the disaster, even when he was so weak as to be almost inaudible in court, managed to return to America. His house still stands on Auburn Avenue, Mt Auburn, in Cincinnati, Ohio. He married another Londoner, Susan Berrall, in Marylebone in 1852, and had a daughter and three sons. Powell became a well-known capitalist who grew very rich while at the forefront of the brass-working business. He suffered greatly with chronic dyspepsia and this prompted his retirement from business before his death a few years later. According to the *Cincinnati Enquirer* of 10 July 1888,

> *He had been also twice operated upon for gravel* [kidney or gall stones], *both operations causing him the greatest misery. The last operation was performed several years ago, but ever since he had a great dread of a return of the gravel. During the past few months this feeling had grown with him, and about the last thing he said to his brother, Mr William E. Powell, when taking his departure from this city, was that he feared a return of the gravel. 'If it does ever return,' he said 'I know that I can not survive the attack – I know I can not,' and he shook his head sadly.*

While travelling with his daughter, Mary, to Europe, he appears to have suffered a turn for the worse. They ate dinner together and spent some time promenading on the deck, then when she had retired to her room for bed he left her a letter and jumped overboard to his death. Powell seems to have waited until the steamer was passing the spot where he escaped the *Ocean Monarch* forty years prior. As the newspaper continued, 'To this thrilling experience he has often referred, and it is thought that in his ill health and with the recollections of that event, a determination to end his life took possession of him and drove him to the desperate deed.' He was 67.

First Mate Jotham Bragdon, who pulled Powell from the water and into the *Ocean Monarch*'s leaky boat, returned a hero to his wife Julia and baby son, Irving, in Sullivan, Hancock, Maine. They went on to have two daughters, Ervilla and Margaret, and he became a captain in his own right. He was a good man who, according to records, died of "apoplexy" in 1879 at the age of 65. His remains are buried in the Coutant Vault in Saint Paul's Cemetery, Mount Vernon, New York, along with Ervilla. Some of the papers at the time of the shipwreck, including the *Illustrated London News* of 23 September 1848, printed a letter they introduced somewhat patronisingly as being from 'honest but unliterary Jotham Bragdon, 'late chief mate of the *Ocean Monarch*'' where he articulated feelings no doubt shared by many of his fellow survivors.

> *Being about to leave Liverpool, I take this opportunity to express my deep sense of gratitude to the inhabitants of Liverpool and its vicinity, also to the captains and officers of several ships in port, for their unbounded kindness to me since my escape from the ill-fated ship Ocean Monarch. While on board of the steam-frigate Affonso I received every attention; and, on my arrival on shore, the hand of friendship was offered by all; not the hand alone, but my friends contributed to my every want, which enables me to leave Liverpool in far more comfortable circumstances than I had hoped; a kindness I can never forget, and for which I shall feel under the greatest of obligations as long as my life is spared.*

Bragdon went on to describe his pleasure at receiving a medal from the Liverpool Shipwreck and Humane Society for his part in the rescue, ending with an effusive prayer for their bright future, and his statement of what was clearly a belief he lived by: 'what is really our duty [is] to save life and relieve suffering whenever it is in our power.'

Personal note

As someone at the *Cambridge Chronicle and Journal* wrote so perceptively on 9 September 1848,

> *The accounts of the loss of the 'Ocean Monarch' emigrant ship were exceedingly frightful; but we have no doubt that there are a thousand personal details connected with that deplorable event which would go to the heart of a reader far more surely and quickly than the most highly-coloured general description.*

With the passage of so many decades, a lot of those personal details and stories have been lost, but thanks to the work of sites like the British Newspaper Archive, enough remain to build a picture of the travellers on board that day.

Some information got to my heart more than I thought it would after so many years reading and writing about shipwrecks, making me tear up as I typed, but that's as it should be – it may seem pathetically maudlin but I think someone *should* weep for the lost, especially those whose whole families were wiped out in the tragedy, and the victims who remain anonymous even now. When I read of the boy, aged about 7, who was washed up wearing trousers with patched knees, I thought of my own son whose clothes sometimes wear through from playing outside, and wondered if this long dead child's mother grumbled while mending his clothes or ruffled his hair and resigned herself to it with a smile. They may have been handed down from an older sibling or cousin, or received from a charity, it's impossible to know. A girl of about the same age was also brought up by the tide. She still had on her new ankle-strap shoes and light blue socks, and I bet she was proud as punch to have them on for her big adventure overseas. Neither child was claimed, along with many others whose remains were interred in mass graves or rubbed to rough sand on the sea floor.

Agents in Liverpool gave 'the following interesting particulars' about the wreck in 1848:

> *The wreck lies in about nine fathoms at low water, on a hard, sandy bottom, and keeping tolerably free from sanding. The vessel appears to have gone down stern first, and it is supposed that the iron, hardware, &c., which weighed about 700 tons, slid aft, and carried away her stern at an angle of about 20 degrees. Two thirds of the ship is a mere shell, with large breaches in the sides, burnt through. These facts are evident from the divers having walked upon the keelson two-thirds the ship's length, beginning aft and proceeding to the bow. They say that at the after part and over the sides of the ship, the cargo lies in one mass. … Should the vessel be relieved of her weight at her stern, by the divers, or otherwise by her own working in rough weather, she may float and be run on shore.*

This never happened, and there is little to see there now. Divers still visit the wreck, where lobsters and conger eels hide from human visitors and fish flourish. Some of the contents were salvaged at the time of the disaster and again in 1987 when there were thoughts of raising it – and some kind of scandal regarding funding this endeavour. The wreck lies in about 13 metres of water, and some of the cargo – perhaps including parts of Thoreau's lost rocking horse, or Fellows's jewellery – remains trapped within what's left of the hull, secured by concretion. The *Ocean Monarch*, once counted among the three largest ships at sea, has been reduced to a length of 30 metres and a width of 10 metres. If diving there, you may see lumps of metal melted by the fire that killed so many, and plenty of broken plates. A trip to the top of the Great Orme, with its spectacular views across the wreck site in Liverpool Bay and on towards England and the Isle of Man, also reveals a graveyard. In it lie witnesses to the tragedy, who remained haunted by what they saw and heard that day, along with the body of a woman washed ashore from the wreck almost two months later. As *The Principality* told its readers on 20 October 1848, 'The poor remains were so decomposed and mutilated as to render it impossible even to guess at the age.'

Almost 50 years after the wreck, one of the mass graves for the victims appears to have been accidentally disturbed. Several artefacts were uncovered in Hoylake, as reported by local Hilda Gamlin in *'Twixt Mersey and Dee'* (1897), such as 'a splendid coil of black hair' and 'also coins of the realm and keys upon a ring that had evidently been in the pocket of one of the sufferers on the unfortunate vessel.'

Of the more than one hundred bodies which made it to shore for burial, only thirty were officially identified, and, from trawling through details recorded about otherwise anonymous victims as well as the various names lists and information in the newspapers at the time, I have tentatively identified a further six. As with all my shipwreck books, if anyone has any further information or questions regarding the wrecks or the people involved with these tragedies then I would encourage you to either email me at gillhoffs@hotmail.co.uk, contact me via @GillHoffs on twitter, or write to me through my publisher.

Despite my best attempts, plenty of questions remain unanswered, which is to be expected after 170 years. I would love to know the identity of the stewardesses who perished as they endeavoured to save the travellers in their care, who the little child was that made such a favourable impression on the passengers of the *New World*, and whether Mary Ann Walter's son understood what happened to his mother and sister – and what his father had done – and forgave them. The note he wrote inside his 'mascotte' when he passed that treasured book to his own son has a very loving tone towards his mother, and whether he deliberately revised their family history to protect her honour or his own, or genuinely remained unaware of the elopement, it appears John Walter held fond memories of his late mother.

The Bacon/Walter trio were probably the only first class passengers to die, and at least five of the people in second class also perished, meaning eight of the thirty-two travellers in this section were lost – a quarter, or possibly more, as five of them were unnamed and their fate is unspecified. Two of the crew of forty-two died along with the cooks, stewards and stewardesses whose names largely remain unknown, and of approximately 322 people travelling in steerage, only about 150 – less than half – survived. I had hoped to be able to narrow down the cause of the fire to a specific act or location on board but as I initially suspected, after so much time this has proved impossible. It is absolutely clear, however, that the steerage passengers were in no way to blame.

From discussions with a retired engineer who specialised in offshore fires and maritime incidents and kindly reviewed the circumstances of this event, it seems the *Ocean Monarch* along with most (if not all) wooden emigrant ships of the time was a disaster waiting to happen. It seems amazing that anyone reached their destinations at all. This ship was constructed from wood, full of flammable materials, and difficult to escape in a hurry, or even at all once at sea. All it took to start a tragedy was a candle left burning unnoticed, whether in the lazarette or, as seems most likely, the store full of booze. If this had been spotted earlier, if the ship had been close enough to shore to be run aground, if more people had – and used – personal buoyancy aids like cork vests, if a large ship had been able to approach more quickly and offer help, if the captain could be heard above the noise and his orders obeyed, if, if, if … the casualty rate would have been much, much lower. However, the most important component of their voyage, luck, was sadly lacking that day.

Strange as it may seem, there was another fire a few months later as a direct result of the *Ocean Monarch* tragedy, this time in inner city Glasgow. Many creative competitions and productions raised money for the travellers, some more successfully than others. These included poems of variable quality (which haven't aged particularly well), plays, and viewings of sketches. A dramatisation of the disaster was due to be performed at the newly built Adelphi Theatre, but during a rehearsal one lunchtime, while the actor playing Captain Murdock was directing his passengers not to smoke, he supposedly 'observed a sudden glare of light in the northwest corner of the upper gallery', according to the *Morning Post* of 18 November 1848, but before he could so much as shout out, the place had burst into flames. Soon the whole building was on fire along with some wooden sheds nearby, and panes of glass were shattering over 150yds away due to the heat. An unfortunate horse passing by had the hair burnt off its back, but no lives were lost so in comparison to the event the play was based on, there was a happy ending.

I really wish the people and livestock on board the actual *Ocean Monarch* that wet August day had been granted the same.

Gill Hoffs, 9 November 2017
Warrington

Acknowledgments

The lost story of the *Ocean Monarch* would still be swirling in my head rather than committed to the pages of this book if it weren't for the support and assistance of family, friends, and complete strangers. Any and all mistakes are my own, and no doubt due to a chronic shortage of chocolate, sleep, and cups of tea. Special thanks must go to Maureen Thomas, who generously shared her years of research with me upon hearing of my nascent book, and Colin Morgan, retired engineer and shipwreck book consultant extraordinaire. Additional thanks go to Angus and Mike for bearing with me while I covered various surfaces with notes, maps, pens, and the dust of a good few sandalwood incense sticks; the Ottersons, for fixing my wonky laptop before I threw it through the window and general internet support, biscuits, fried pizza and kindness; and the MacLeans, for cheerleading (minus pompoms and short skirts) and continual goodwill even when I subjected Gloria to a phone call about human gravy and ignored Archie while I typed on the sofa and munched his crisps.

Thank you to – in no particular order – the following lovely entities: Nutella, CocoPops, and Malteaser reindeer (these are literally Writer Fuel); Jennie Goloboy of Red Sofa Literary Agency for her support as an agent and a history fan; Jen Boyle for teaching me so much about writing history books; Katie Eaton and Heather Williams of Pen and Sword; Karyn Burnham; Suzie Grogan, Emma Briant and Nemma Wollenfang for author support; Emma Jobling for pepping me up from time to time; Darren White for feedback and always surprising me with the images he finds online (no, not THAT kind); Jenny Garside of Wyte Phantom, an incredible person all round; Coraline, Friendlycat, Echo, and the late great Tam-Cat; Craig Sherwood of Warrington Museum and Art Gallery, for his kind support and discussion of body preservation and inquests; Carly A. Silver, for her help with knitted underwear and naked sailors on twitter; Peter and Pat Day; Dr Mike Roberts; Chris Holden, of Calgo Publications; Deanna Groom; John

Lawson-Reay, vice-chairman of Llandudno and Colwyn Bay History Society; Jannis Nixon, parish administrator of Bispham All Hallows Parish Church; Peter Higginbotham of workhouses.org.uk; Steve Benson of Lancashire Family History and Heraldry Society; Revd James McGowan and Annette Thackray, very helpful people on the Isle of Man; @BlackPlumes1850; @Undine; Sarah Hoile; Marius Hollenga; Claire Wood; Chris Woodyard aka 'Mrs Daffodil'; Carol Evans; Mandy Gwan, a gracious and very helpful descendant; Jeff Sengstack; Kameron 'Kami' DeWulf; Theresa Ganly; Shirley Cox, without whose help I would not have met Maureen Thomas; John C. Schumacher-Hardy; Carole Thornton, for her generous and prompt assistance when I sought to learn more about the role of stewardess; Ellie Downer, of the *Barre Gazette*; Peter Newton; Jane Lanterman Shaw Elder, who made 'contributions in loving memory of my father, Robert Southworth Lanterman 1924–2010, the family genealogy enthusiast'; Helena Coney, for her generous assistance and sharing of research; Janine Whitcomb, Special Collections Archive Manager, UMC Center for Lowell History, who was wonderfully helpful with information on James K. Fellows; Debbie S. Hamm, Abraham Lincoln Presidential Library, who shared with me Fellows' book; Nick McParlin for medical advice and enthusiasm; Angela Buckley for discussions of Chartists and capital punishment; does anyone read the acknowledgments section unprompted? I doubt it. Send me an email with the word 'strawberry' and prove me wrong, I'll reply with a joke if you do; Geoff Topliss; Penny Rudkin, of Southampton Local Studies and Maritime Library; Josette Reeves and Katy of the University of Liverpool; James Gareth Davies of MOROL; Jeremy Scott; Claire King; Michael J. Malone; Mignon Ariel King; Nate Evuarherhe Jr., librarian in the V&A Museum, London; Katie Hughes, for map-spotting in Wales and enthusiastic support; Gail E. Wiese, of Norwich University Archives and Special Collections; Joanmarie Myers; Corrina Readioff; the ever-helpful, ever-kindly Dr Cathryn Pearce; Elaine Holman (Wilson) Benjamin; Jourdan and Alan Fraser Houston, who kindly shared their excellent 'Ships Afire at Sea' article; Jerry Alsup; Helena Smart and Roger Hull of Liverpool Record Office; Dave Bridson of the Liverpool History Society facebook group; Tutti Jackson, of the Ohio History Connection; Mark Parsons; Mark Britton, of the London History Forum facebook group; Ian Flood, for his enthusiasm and wreck information; Dr Jonathan A. Green, Senior Lecturer in Marine

Biology, University of Liverpool, for not minding when a stranger asked him about bird crap; T.M. Upchurch for letting me discuss grisly details and cowpat poultices with her late at night; Shane Simmons for letting me pour my heart out over much deliciousness; Keirstan Pawson, Violet Fenn, Sarah Collie, and Joanna Delooze for being supportive sweethearts; Pat Watt, Diane Watt, Heike Bauer, Lynne McKerr, and Ivan Walton for cheering me on; Tamsin Johns-Chapman, for food, fun, and frolics; John Clarke for pies and praise (very much appreciated); and Roland Moore for another beautiful hand-carved jigsaw – thank you for my cat, and your supportive and entertaining emails.

I have a horrible feeling I've neglected to mention someone here who deserves hugs and plaudits (or at least their name in print). Let me know if it's you and I'll send you a Twix.

If anyone reading this section is wondering if they should contact an author (not necessarily me) I really, really recommend you do. When I hear from someone who likes my work, gets what I do, or just has a question or some information of their own to share, it lights up my day. I love it! And if you're a writer wondering whether to query my nonfiction agent, Jennie, and/or Pen and Sword, I recommend you do so and wish you the very best of luck.

Appendix 1 – corpse chronology and body details

Many local newspapers printed details of the bodies retrieved from the water or the shoreline following the wreck. This appendix is in no way an exhaustive or complete list, and in order to make it user friendly and not overly long I have edited this information somewhat, removing the entries which only include gender, for example, rather than pocket contents and clothing. This provides a snapshot, albeit partial, of what the less fortunate members of this group of emigrants, travellers, and crew were wearing on that awful day. As such, I hope it proves an interesting resource for social and clothing historians, and also serves to remind readers of the very ordinary humanity of the people who died on the *Ocean Monarch*.

Monday 28 August

'the Liverpool Borough Coroner proceeded to hold an inquest on the bodies of five of the sufferers who were brought to this port on Saturday by the steam tug – namely Mary Tobin, Geoffrey Lynch, Ellen Teirney, Elizabeth Atherton, and a boy name unknown.' (*Hampshire Advertiser*, 2 September 1848)

Sunday 3 September

'as the sloop *Merlin*, Captain Stephen Garratt, of this port, was entering the river Dee, the crew picked up the body of a female, of about fifty years old: hair a little gray. She had on a black satin dress, silk bonnet, covered with crape, cloth boots, and in her pocket were found two purses. In one was found three shillings: the other empty. The body was interred at Bagilt [*sic*] the following day.' (*Albion*, 18 September 1848)

Monday 4 September

'Captain Kainch, of the *Royal Sovereign*, a Dublin trader, picked up the body of a respectably dressed man opposite the River Dee. The deceased had a plain ring on the little finger of the right hand, an eye glass, a watch, No. 1662, a pawn ticket for a watch, pledged for 16*s*. at Coxon and John's, Leeds. The name on the ticket is 'Pawson, St John's-lane.' He appears to be about twenty-five years of age, had on a brown coat, satin vest and tie, and blue trousers. The body was in a far advanced state of decomposition.' (*Liverpool Mercury*, 8 September 1848)

Wednesday 6 September

'inquest held at New Brighton, before Mr Churton, coroner, on the body of a man found drowned, supposed to be from the Ocean Monarch. He was about thirty-five or forty years of age; had on a brown Oxford tweed shooting coat, blue trousers, blue and red plaid waistcoat, and neckerchief supposed to have been red. [Also] … the body of a female was picked up outside the river, by the Vale of Clwyd steamer. She is supposed to have been one of the sufferers from the Ocean Monarch, but the body was not identified. She was about five feet in height, and apparently pregnant. Had on cotton drawers, black petticoat, and black stuff apron, but no outside dress. A plain gold ring was on the wedding finger. Verdict, found drowned.' (*Liverpool Mercury*, 15 September 1848)

'the steamer Orion, on her passage from this port to Carnarvon, picked up two bodies about [unclear] to the eastward of the Ormshead, and took them on with her. These bodies are supposed to be those of Samuel Fielding and William Scambro. Upon the person of one, supposed to be Fielding, was found thirty-nine sovereigns and a half, and some silver coins, also a watch, maker's name Bradford, No. 2,613, having the ticket "Knight, watchmaker, 28, Oldham-street, Manchester." He had also about him three passengers' contract tickets, showing that he (Fielding), together with William Scambro, and several others, were passengers on board the ill-fated vessel, the Ocean Monarch. On the other body were found eleven pounds, with the initials "B.S." on the inner case of his watch which appears to have been made by Glowes [Clowes?] of London, and is numbered 3,001. The money found has been deposited in the hands of Messrs [unclear] bankers, till the friends of the deceased make out a satisfactory claim.' (*Albion*, 18 September 1848)

Friday 8 September

'a number of other bodies were seen floating in with the tide, and the inhabitants generally assembled to secure them and convey them ashore for interment. From the confusion naturally attendant upon such an event, and the discoloration and disfigurement of the several bodies, it is difficult to give a definite description of each. The following particulars, however, collected on the spot, may be relied upon, and will, we hope, be the means of leading to the identification of some of the bodies, and of enabling surviving relatives and friends to pay their last mournful tribute of duty to the deceased. The bodies washed up at Blackpool, including the one on Wednesday evening, were seven in number, viz., four females, and three males.

First Female. – A portly lady, apparently about thirty years of age, of middle stature, with auburn hair. She had on a second mourning large plaid cotton dress, white flannel petticoat, black worsted stockings, and black stuff boots, and round her neck an elastic guard, attached to which is a small camphor bag. She appears to have been a married lady, as there was on the third finger of her left hand a gold wedding ring, also a gold hoop, in which was set a pink coloured stone or glass stamped in the inside with the initials "J. C."

Second Female. – This deceased is of slender make, having on her head a Dunstable bonnet, and a dress of blue hail showered print, blue cotton skirt or top petticoat, and a red flannel under-petticoat, and a red and white woollen plaid shawl. Under her dress she had on a man's waistcoat made of worsted cloth, with a small red flower on a light ground, and small metal buttons. On the wedding finger was a gold ring, marked in the inside with the initials "G. W." Round her neck was a double link of coral neck beads with a gold clasp, and her arms appeared much scorched. This female had been thrown into premature confinement, and was partly delivered of a child. She appears to be about 34 [some papers say 43] years of age.

The third female was tall and slender, having a fine head of auburn coloured hair. Her dress was a dark claret, made of Orleans cloth, fitted up to the neck. Under her dress she wore a white skirt and white flannel petticoat; she had also on a pair of white socks. Round her neck was some black tape, attached to which were two apparently common box keys.

The fourth female was a girl apparently about seven or eight years of age, having on a green plaid overcoat open at the front, light blue socks, and a pair of new ankle strap shoes.

The following are some particulars respecting the males cast ashore:-

First – An aged man with bald head, without upper garments, having on a linen shirt, plain at the breast, with horn buttons at neck and wrists. He had on two pair of woollen cloth trousers made of fine cloth, the colour of the under pair being light blue, and of the top (which buttoned up in front) black; brown knitted worsted stockings, height, 5 feet 8 or 9 inches.

Second Male. – This was evidently the body of a sailor, having on a blue flannel shirt, a pair of blue pilot cloth trousers, and a pair of Wellington sailor's boots. Round his body he wore a leathern [*sic*] belt, in which was a sheath containing a whittle knife. He appears about 30 years of age, and had long black hair. In his pocket was a small box key.

Third Male. – The body of a boy, apparently about seven years of age, having on a jacket and trousers made of drab cotton cord, each knee of which was patched with a dark coloured material of the same description.

In addition to the above seven (two of which were cast up near South Shore), four bodies, all females, were washed up near Norbreck. The following are a few particulars respecting these: - In one of the female's pockets was found a scent bottle, a coloured bead purse containing 16s., one wedding and two ornamental rings; a silver watch, black braid watchguard and ribbon, and small gold watch-key and gold chain: five keys and one lock. On the person of this deceased was a pair of light blue jean stays, a purple silk dress, white petticoat trimmed with lace, and a good pair or cloth boots. In the pocket of another (who was attired in a brown silk dress and appeared about 35 years of age) was found £8 in gold, one shilling, three combs (including one tortoiseshell comb for the back hair), penknife with pearl handle, a purse, and a wrist-cuff. The body of a third seemed to be that of a young person about 14 years of age. Two of the above had on plaid dresses, and one a fine bonnet with veil attached. Three out of the four, we understand, were interred on Friday afternoon at Bispham. The other body was kept as it is expected it would be owned by some of her articles. From the articles found in her pocket, her name is supposed to be Elizabeth Steele.' (*Glasgow Herald*, 15 September 1848)

'five bodies washed ashore at Lytham: the first, that of a stout muscular man, about five feet nine inches high, without a coat, but he had on a dark waistcoat and trousers, and chamois leather braces, and round his neck a string of beads, to which was attached a crucifix. The next was a good-looking female, with auburn hair, about the middle stature; she had on a dark-coloured laced petticoat, and a pair of new stays, black stockings, and black cloth boots, inside of which was marked "H. Murray." Hand on the fourth finger of her right hand a tortoiseshell ring, and on another finger a hoop, in which were set two red stones; round her neck was a string of coral beads to which a cross was attached.- The third was a very stout-made female, supposed to be an Irishwoman. The only clothes she had on were an under petticoat and chemise, and nothing in her pockets except a small wood needle case. The next were two boys, apparently each about sixteen years of age. One of them was dressed in a dark plaid frockcoat and trousers of the same; had nothing in his pocket but a small quantity of worsted. The other had on a dark plaid coat, and dark trousers, but nothing on his person.' (*Albion*, 18 September 1848)

[This account includes the same descriptions as above then this, which adds another person's details] 'Six bodies have been cast upon the Lytham coast – three women, one man, and two boys. In the pocket of one of the women was found a passenger's ticket, issued from the packet-office of Mr Harden and Co., with the name, of James Mantagh, Mrs Mantagh and infant, and Jane Mantagh written on it. In the pocket of another was found a dark rosary of beads and a crucifix. The last named was about 30 of age. There was nothing particular about the dress of the man. The boys, both about the same age, 16, were dressed in plain frockcoats and trousers. Their bodies were interred at Lytham church on Saturday afternoon.

A correspondent, whose letter is dated Heysham Tower, near Lancaster, writes as follows:- "A dead body has been washed up near to my house, perfectly naked. I suspected, from a paragraph in the *Illustrated London*

News of the 2d of September, that it might prove to be that of a young man who was lost from the Ocean Monarch. I have had it examined by the Mayor of Lancaster, a highly respectable medical man, and his opinion is that the marks of violence had been caused after death by the beating of the body upon the rocks. Another body has been picked up clothed in black, and from a letter and book found in one of the pockets it appears to be a person of the name of John Curly, who has a brother and sister named James and Catherine Fallon, Roxbury, Massachusetts, America. There was a card in his pocket, of Michael Ryan, 9, Dublin-court, Carlton-street, Liverpool, apparently a lodging-house. The letter is dated Roxbury, July 14, 1848, and the Liverpool post-mark is August 2, 1848. His clothes are carefully preserved; they are not in good condition. According to the Act of Parliament 48 Geo. III., c. 75, both these bodies will be decently interred in the church-yard of this parish, and the necessary expenses charged to the county.

If you will give publicity to this in your widely extended journal the relations will know that the remains of these poor persons have been properly cared for."' (*The North Wales Chronicle and Advertiser for the Principality*, 19 September 1848)

[same people as above but with different details] 'Description of the body of a girl which was washed ashore at Southport on the morning of the 8th inst.:- About 14 years of age, dressed in brown petticoat next the skin, black stuff over-petticoat, dark-blue or black cotton dress, with small white spots, and has a Catholic Gospel, attached to a piece of blue ribbon, round her neck. In consequence of the state of the body it was deemed advisable to bury it at once. Description of the body of a young man, washed up near Heysham Tower, near Lancaster:- He is 18 or 19 years of age, light brown hair, five feet four inches high; he is perfectly naked, with a black garter round one knee; the garter is a piece of narrow black tape. The nails of his hands are carefully pared, as if not used to hard work. He is of slight figure, and not thick legs.' (*London Evening Standard*, 12 September 1848)

'The bodies of two women and a male child (about 3 years old) were washed up at Silverdale … One of the females was much burnt, and one of her legs was broken by the knee. She appeared about sixty; the other about fifty. She had on a blue worsted stocking, tied round with a hempen string, a few blue glass beads in her pocket, and a common ring, with a piece of glass in it, on her finger. The bodies were in an offensive state of decomposition, and, without any inquest having been held over them, were decently buried, on Saturday evening, at the parish church of Warton.' (*Liverpool Mail*, 16 September 1848)

NB: do NOT read this entry if you are squeamish or prone to bad dreams!

'[letter from Jno. Nicholson, Clifton Arms, Lytham] At six o'clock this (Friday) morning I went on the shore at Blackpool, the tide being at its height at half-past seven, during which time I saw three bodies worked up, all women: one with a silk dress on; the second with a plaid mourning dress on, a wedding ring, and hoop, I should say rather an expensive one; the third was dressed like an Irish reaper girl, with a straw hat and waistcoat, and in this instance the woman seems to have been delivered of a child, either at the time or after the accident took place. For an hour the body might be seen floating, and a bird picking on the top of it, only moving from it when it saw a breaker a-head, and it continued to do so until within a few yards of the beach. The baby seemed to be quite perfect. … One [body] seems to be coming up now as the coach is starting for Lytham (half-past nine). A lady who was with me at the time the woman with the wedding ring and hoop on was taken up says, that from the description given, she will prove to be the woman whose children were saved, and saw their mother drowned and floating amongst the wreck. Being at Lytham now, I hear that there has been two taken up, a man and a woman. The man is now lying in an out-house belonging to the Clifton Arms, and is very much disfigured. More are expected up by the next tide.' (*Bolton Chronicle*, 9 September 1848)

'washed ashore at Formby:

A black man, fifty years of age, five feet nine inches high, dressed in black cloth trousers, blue flannel shirt, blue stockings, and strong shoes.

A male, about thirty years of age, five feet eleven inches high, dressed in a black cloth coat, light brown knee-breeches and leggings, blue and white-striped vest, dark blue stockings, and laced boots, had in his pocket a comb, strap and spur, and a card, with the following address, "James Quail, lodging-house, 69, Dublin-street, near the Clarence Dock, Liverpool."

A male, about twenty-six years of age, five feet ten inches high, dressed in black cloth trousers and vest, and fine linen shirt, has been identified by his father as Joseph Bladen, from Birmingham, engine fitter.

A female, fifteen or sixteen years of age, four feet four inches high, in a state of nudity.

A female, about forty-five years of age, four feet six inches high, dressed in brown merino dress, black stockings, low strong shoes, had in her pocket three shillings and a farthing, and one of Harnden and Co.'s passenger contract tickets,

A} 52} No. 354
13}

Names.	Age.	
Winifred Keegan…	45	Ocean Monarch for Boston.
Rosey Mulrooney…	16'	

(*Liverpool Mercury*, 15 September 1848)

[This seems to refer to the bodies above, with some repetition but additional details too] 'A black man, fifty years of age, five feet nine inches high, dressed in black cloth trousers, blue flannel shirt, blue stockings, and strong shoes. A man about thirty years of age, five feet eleven inches high, dressed in a black cloth coat, light brown kneebreeches and leggings, blue and white striped vest, dark blue stockings and laced boots; had in his pocket a comb, key, strap and spur, and a card with the following address, 'James Quail, lodging-house, 69, Dublin-street, near the Clarence Dock, Liverpool.' A man about twenty-six years of age, five feet ten inches high, dressed in black cloth trousers and vest, and fine linen shirt; has been identified by his father as Joseph Bladen, from Birmingham, engine fitter. A girl about sixteen years of age, four feet four inches high, in a state of nudity. A woman about forty-five years of age, four feet six inches high, dressed in a brown merino dress, black stockings, low strong shoes, had in her pockets 3s., 0 ½ d. and one of Harnden and Co.'s passenger contract tickets, 'A 13 52, No, 354 Winifred Keegan, 45; Rosey Mulrooney, 16; Ocean Monarch for Boston." (*Northern Star and Leeds General Advertiser*, 23 September 1848)

Saturday 9 September

[this may refer to the Mantagh victims previously mentioned] 'the body of a female, supposed to be an Irishwoman, was cast on shore [at Lytham]. In her pocket was found a wedding ring, and in her purse the shipping note, on which was written the names "James Murtorphy, 24; Mrs Ditto, and infant, 20; and Jane Murtorphey, 18, sailed in the Ocean Monarch. £2 paid and £6 to pay".' (*Albion*, 18 September 1848)

'Found, on Saturday morning, at Southport, the bodies of two females, one female child, and one male, supposed to be passengers per Ocean Monarch.

First.- About 30 to 35 years of age; brown worsted dress, with silk flowers; in her pocket a brown silk purse, three shillings in silver, on her finger a gold ring with letters "M.A.A." on a plate, and a gold wedding ring; also a watch (stated to be brass) round her neck, No. 10,6999, maker, O'Reilly, Dublin; in her pocket two shells, one with "Mary Ann" on it. [probably Mary Ann Anderson, 24]

Second.- 45 to 50 years of age, stout made. Brown stuff dress, check gingham petticoats, twilled worsted shawl, with plain centre and blue border. In her pocket a gold locket, with hair, brass wedding ring on finger, and, from a piece of letter found in her pocket, her name is supposed to be Spencer.

Third.- Child about four years of age. Dress, plaid cloak, blue and green, white holland pinafore, one drab cloth boot on.

Fourth Male.- About 30 years of age, 5 feet 6 or 7 inches high, stout made. Dress, black frock coat, black waistcoat, blue cloth trousers, check shirt, Wellington boots. In his pocket a red silk purse, a penknife, with white bone handle, two pocket books, a bunch of keys, and 2*l*. 13s. 7d. in money. Supposed to be Daniel Pollard, Huddersfield, to which place information has been sent.' (*London Evening Standard*, 12 September 1848)

'A body was picked up in the river Lune, near Glasson Dock … a boy about 12 or 14 years of age … from [his] dress, belonging to the working class.' (*Bell's New Weekly Messenger*, 24 September 1848)

Sunday 10 September

'also cast up [on the shore at Lytham] the body of another female, supposed to be an Irishwoman; she had on a light print dress, in chintz pattern, ... linsey petticoat with a plaid binding, no stays, gray stockings, and strong shoes. Had not anything in her pockets but a pair of scissors and the keys of her box. As the particulars of the dresses, &c., may probably catch the eyes of their relatives, they will have the mournful satisfaction of knowing that the bodies of their friends have all been decently interred in the graveyard of the parish church. The various articles found on their persons, with the clothes &c., are in the hands of the police at Lytham, who will give them up to any persons to whom they belong.

...an inquest was held at Llandrillo yn Rhos, before the coroner of the Denbigh district, upon the bodies of three women, one man, and two children picked up by the crew of the sloop Robert, from Liverpool for Rhos. The following is the description taken by the coroner:

A female child, apparently from five to six years, sandy hair and rather stout; had on when found a black Holland dress, black and red petticoat, white flannel ditto, white and red worsted stockings, and a striped black and red waist belt, also two common cotton handkerchiefs, figured.-

A woman, about forty, five feet six inches, in a state of pregnancy, dark brown hair, lusty, front teeth sound and entire, with the exception of two, which were beginning to decay. Had on a second mourning delaine dress, woollen stockings, cloth boots, and dark-coloured undergarments. Upon this body were found four shillings, and a few trifling articles, such as thimbles, needles &c. Her chemise was marked with the letters M.S. with thread.-

A male, to all appearances a sailor, middle-aged, five feet ten inches, long brown hair, stout, and very muscular, and his whiskers appeared to have been recently shaved. Had fastened to his ears a pair of gold ear-rings, and had on a flannel shirt, Guernsey frock, and drawers of good quality.-

A male child, about two or three years; had on a striped dress, a pair of stays with three buttons, and a pair of shoes tied with ribbon.-

A female, from thirty to forty, five feet six inches, good figure, beautiful sound teeth, black hair. Had on a dark Orleans dress, white figured cotton stockings, a very good pair of black cloth boots, nearly new. A purse in her pocket containing seven sovereigns. Two American notes, one for five dollars, and the other for two. Also a receipt from one "David Jones, hosier, &c., bottom of Rigby-street, Liverpool," for either ten shillings or ten pounds. This document was so much tattered as to render it almost illegible. One sovereign, and 12s. 6d. in silver, loose in her pocket, and a light fine watch-guard, of delicate make, to which was attached a small round flat locket, containing a piece of silk, a brooch, set in gold, three American coins, and one British penny piece; also, two large brass keys, of very peculiar make, two gold rings on the second finger of the left hand, and a pair of gold ear rings.-

A female, about thirty, five feet, long dark brown hair, front teeth rather large, regular and entire, had on a red and white print dress and a brown guilt [?] petticoat.

The following is a description of seven bodies picked up at Abergele:-

A female, about thirty, with light auburn hair, about five feet two inches, hair lost, teeth of upper jaw lost. Had on a black merino dress, two gray flannel petticoats, two flannel jackets, black woollen stockings, and drab-coloured cloth boots. Found upon her three letters, two of which were addressed to "Jonathan Lord, North Andover, State of Massachusetts, North America," and the other to "Mr Samuel Kershaw, Captain Horley's Mill, North Andover, Massachusetts;" also, a piece of leather, bearing the following address:- "Mrs Rebecca Hill, passenger to Mr George Hill, with Andrew Hart, Middlesex Factory, Massachusetts, America;" also, a wedding ring and a contract paper for the Ocean Monarch, upon which appeared the name Rebecca Hill, 36, Sophia Hill, 8½, Sarah Anne Hill, 9½; likewise a clasper blue and red bead purse containing 10s. in silver, and a leather purse containing 3s. in silver &c.,

A man, about five feet ten inches, middle-aged, black hair, irregular teeth. Had on a smock frock, a brown frock coat, a corduroy double-breasted vest, and trousers (with a patch on the latter,) blue worsted stockings, and bluchers. Upon him were found a steel tobacco box, (full of the weed,) and 2s 6d. in silver enclosed in it, a penny piece, and a common table knife, two broken clay pipes, and some loose matches.

A man, about five feet seven inches, very small regular front teeth, age about twenty-two, brown hair. Had on a linen smock coat, dark corduroy trousers, (in which was a joiner's rule pocket,) a flannel waistcoat, blue cotton stockings and bluchers. Found the following articles:- A pocket clasp knife, a large horn snuffbox, with the name "Mary Haslam" cut upon it, and two keys.

A woman, about five feet two, and about sixty, very thin and slender. Had on a brown figured Orleans dress, scarlet-coloured petticoat, check apron, and white cotton stockings, no shoes, nor boots. Nothing found.

A woman, five feet two inches, rather slender, aged about thirty, light auburn hair; had on a gingham apron, and a brown dress: no boots or shoes.

A black man, apparently about twenty-five, five feet seven inches, good front teeth, entire; had on a dark green coat, with figured brass buttons, a black satin vest, black cloth trousers, a plaid silk neckerchief, and white worsted stockings. All his clothes were of a good quality and genteelly made. Nothing was found upon this man except a common key: but it may be stated that when first discovered both his waistcoat pockets were turned inside out. He was floating at the time when first seen.

A man, about five feet seven inches, rather slender, front teeth of upper jaw wanting; had on a plaid sporting jacket, and trousers of a smaller plaid, a plaid worsted scarf, and woollen stockings, no boots or shoes. Were found upon him a small cotton bag, containing three half penny pieces, also a contract paper for the Ocean Monarch, upon which were written the names Ann Nesbitt, – Cuddy, – Muldoon. [probably Arthur Muldoon, 24, travelling with his family (all lost) rather than 16yo Acles Cuddy]

A man about six feet, about forty years of age, stout, light hair, teeth in the upper jaw irregular, and the two middle ones rather large. Had on a very good black dress coat, double-breasted black vest, black buckskin trousers, a dark plaid scarf, and white cotton stockings. His shirt was marked with the letters J. S. B. No.6, and on his feet were a pair of bluchers. Upon the body of this man were found the following articles:- A silver hunting watch, with a gold chain, two gold seals, and a gold watch key; also, a common linen purse, containing four sovereigns, four penny pieces, a penknife, a small silver vinaigrette, and a bunch of keys, (eight in number), a pocket book, and amongst other documents, a "warrant, dated October 12th, 1847, under the hand and seal of Thomas James Arnold, Esq., one of the Metropolitan magistrates, for the apprehension of Edward Glass, charged on the oath of Thomas Bennett, constable of the parish of St. Luke, with having deserted his wife, Betsy, whereby he had committed an act of vagrancy." Also, a printed ticket, of which this is a true copy:- "Communist Covenant. We hereby covenant and declare that co-operation and association should succeed competition and private property, and believing that Communion of Goods was an element of the Original Model Christian Church at Jerusalem, we hereby call for its restoration as a religious duty. No. 63, 1848. John Parry, member, Gosdwyn Barny, founder."' [this body was James Smith Bacon] (*Albion*, 18 September 1848)

'three bodies (two women and a boy) were washed ashore at Kunhid, near Milnthorpe, and eight at Hest-bank. They are supposed to be a portion of those who perished in the Ocean Monarch. On the same day, the body of the steward of the ill-fated vessel, a coloured man, named Cummins, was picked up by the Welsh steamer Cambria, near the spot where the catastrophe occurred. … [female body] found on the shore, under or between Meliden and Prestatyn, parish of Meliden, county of Flint; - She is of short stature, hair apparently red; she is of respectable appearance, and has on the fore-finger of left hand a massive embossed diamond ring; she has on drawers, flannel petticoat, white petticoat, no shoes or stockings; from what can be seen she has a night-gown frilled at the hands. The ring is in possession of the parish-clerk.' (*Liverpool Mercury*, 12 September 1848)

Monday 11 September

Bispham South Shore district, woman, washed up, about 40, coloured print dress with one front tooth out and the others not found on the left hand a wedding ring and hoop.

'afternoon, the master of the steam-boat Skerryvore picked up the body of a man unknown near the wreck of the [*Ocean Monarch*]; he appeared to have floated up from the forepart of the ship. The deceased was about 35 years of age, five feet six inches in height, and had on a flannel jacket, calico shirt, corduroy trousers, and flannel socks. A verdict was returned of found drowned.' (*North Wales Chronicle*, 12 September 1848)

Saturday 16 September

'The second [inquest] was on the body of a man unknown, picked up by a boatman, named John Ashbrook, residing at 46, Lumber-street, on Saturday last, about a mile and a half to the northward of the north-west light-ship. On his person was found a silver verge watch, with the makers names, "Stockdale and Stewart, Newcastle, No. 238;" a purse containing 5*s*. 2 ½ *d*., two steel rings, three knives, and a horn pipe. The body was much disfigured and decomposed. A verdict of found drowned was returned.' (*Carnarvon and Denbigh Herald and North and South Wales Independent*, 23 September 1848)

'[this] afternoon the body of a man, name unknown, picked up by a boatman near the Lightship, was also deposited in the [dead-house, at Prince's Pier]. The following description of the unfortunate deceased may aid relatives in their identity:- A man about five feet five inches in height, dressed in a blue cloth frock coat, red plush vests, with white sleeves, dark tweed trousers, black tie round his neck, shoes and dark stockings on. He had in his pockets a silver verge watch, with an India-rubber guard, and a steel chain and key, three knives, a pipe, and 5s. 2d. [Also?] A man, about five feet eight inches in height, dressed in striped plaid trousers, gray worsted stockings, flannel singlet, and blue striped cotton shirt. He had in his pockets 13s. 6 ½ d., a bunch of keys, a letter stamp, and several letters, addressed "John Atkinson, Bradford, Yorkshire." A female dressed in a black stiff petticoat, drab cloth boots, with dark blue cotton stockings, and cotton apron. She had in her pocket a small looking-glass and two keys.' (*Albion*, 18 September 1848)

Sunday 17 September

'A body [was found] on Cockerham Sands, supposed [to] have formed part of the crew of the Ocean Monarch. [He was] a man between 30 and 40, [from his] dress, belonging to the working class.' (*Bell's New Weekly Messenger*, 24 September 1848)

The third [inquest] was on the body of a woman unknown, found by Captain Wm. Roberts, of the steam-tug *Albert*, on Sunday morning last, about eight miles to the westward of the northwest light-ship. On the body was found two keys, a small round looking glass, and a white hand-kerchief. Deceased had on drab cloth boots, blue cotton stockings, black stuff petticoat and apron, a cotton chintz dress, and calico chemise, and was about five feet two inches in height. A verdict of found drowned was returned.

[Of bodies found] those which have been identified, their relatives have had the little property found upon them handed over. Four inquests were held [later in the week] before the borough coroner, P. F. Curry, Esq. The first was on the body of a man, named John Atkinson, a currier, found floating about two miles to the westward of the northwest lightship, on Sunday last, by a boatman, named Henry Wilson, who resides in Marlborough-street. The body was identified by Mr Wm. Atkinson, who resides at Clayton, near Bradford, as being that of his brother, who sailed… The deceased had on his person a bunch of keys, a penknife, a metal stamp, with two stamps on it, the one a lion's claw, and the other a coat of arms, with a sum of 13s. 6½ d. on his person, which were identified by the brother of the deceased. The jury found a verdict of accidentally drowned. (*Carnarvon and Denbigh Herald and North and South Wales Independent*, 23 September 1848)

Monday 18 September

'an inquest was held in the Grand Jury-room, Beaumaris, on view … the bodies of a male and female … who were picked up by the steamer Orion, on her passage from Liverpool to Menai-bridge yesterday week [at around 2pm], about ten miles east of the Ormeshead. Mr Slater, one of the churchwardens, produced the following articles found on the persons of the sufferers:-

On the person of the female were found £35 [£55? Or sovereigns?] in gold, a silver thimble, a brass thimble, a pin-cushion, a leather purse with steel cap, a [long] silk beaded purse, a rosary, a crucifix, an eyeglass in horn frame, two small medals of saints, a heart-shaped pincushion, a coral chain necklace and crucifix.

On the person of the male were found £39 [or sovereigns?] in gold, 1s in silver, two bunches of small keys, a pocket knife, a steel pen and brass holder, a tin inkstand, a piece of lead pencil, a tooth comb, two nutmegs, a few iron nails, an iron box japanned, a short clay pipe about five to six inches in length. … Verdict, found drowned. The bodies were buried in Beaumaris churchyard. The property found remains in the possession of the churchwardens.' (*Albion*, 25 September 1848)

'The fourth [inquest] was on the body of a man unknown, found floating by John Garner, an apprentice on board the *Taliesin* steam-boat, about four miles from the Point of Ayr, on the Welsh coast, on Monday last. Deceased had on a blue cloth coat and vest, corded breeches, and black woollen stockings, was about five feet ten inches in height, and had a sovereign in his pocket. The body was much decomposed, and appeared to have been some time in the water. Verdict, found drowned.' (*Carnarvon and Denbigh Herald and North and South Wales Independent*, 23 September 1848)

Tuesday 19 September

'inquest was held on ... the body of a man unknown, picked up on Saturday week, about a mile and a half to the northward of the Northwest Lightship. On his person were found a silver verge watch, with the makers names, 'Stockdale and Stewart, Newcastle, No. 258', a purse containing 5s. 2½d., two steel rings, three knives and a horn pipe. The body was much disfigured and decomposed.

[Also] On the body of a woman unknown, found yesterday morning week, about eight miles to the westward of the Northwest Lightship. On the body were found two keys, a small round looking glass, and a white handkerchief. Deceased had on drab cloth boots, blue cotton stockings, black stuff petticoat and apron, a cotton chintz dress, and calico chemise, and was about five feet two inches in height.

[Also] On the body of a man unknown, found floating about four miles from the Point of Ayr, on the Welsh coast, on Monday. Deceased had on a blue cloth coat and vest, corded breeches, and black woollen stockings, was about five feet ten inches in height, and had a sovereign in his pocket. The body was much decomposed and appeared to have been some time in the water.' (*Albion*, 25 September 1848)

Friday 22 September

'a man, unknown, was picked up near the spot where the Ocean Monarch was destroyed. He had on a black coat, striped trousers, plaid vest, and boots which laced up the front; height about 5 feet 7 or 8 inches. The body was much disfigured, and no idea could be formed as to the face or complexion. – Verdict, found drowned.' (*Liverpool Mercury*, 26 September 1848) [same man, who was also described as wearing 'pepper and salt trousers'] 'the Skerryvore picked up the body of a respectably-dressed man, about one hundred yards from where the ill-fated ship sank. He was dressed in a fine black frock coat, plaid trousers and vest, and had on Wellington boots. His body was in an advanced state of decomposition.' (*Albion*, 25 September 1848)

5 October

A man's body washed up at Langness, Castletown Bay, Isle of Man. He was 5ft 8, and probably 40–50 years old. Mr James Thomson, coroner, held an inquest then the body was buried in Malew churchyard.

13 October

'THE body of a female was washed ashore on Saturday morning last at Llandudno Bay, supposed to have been one of the ill-fated sufferers on board the Ocean Monarch. The only clothing she had on were a calico chemise, and a coarse black merino gown, which renders it probable that she must have been in bed when the alarm was given. There were no marks whatever on the clothes so as to lead to the discovery of the name. The poor remains were so decomposed and mutilated as to render it impossible even to guess at the age. In the afternoon an inquest was held on the body before Mr Hope Jones, deputy coroner, and the remains were afterwards decently interred in Llandudno churchyard.' (*The Principality*, 20 October 1848)

Appendix 2 – known grave locations and inquests

It should be noted that many of the people listed here have no grave marker, and some are named at inquests but do not have a specific graveyard listed. Additional information is very welcome!

1. **Mary Tobin**, 38, Hoylake Inquest, buried St Anthony's Catholic Church, Liverpool
2. **Geoffrey Lynch**, 58, Hoylake Inquest
3. **Ellen Teirney**, 55, Hoylake Inquest, buried St Mary's, Liverpool, entry 1146 30 August
4. **Elizabeth Atherton**, 15 months, Hoylake Inquest
5. **Mary Jones**, 48, Manchester, Holy Trinity, West Kirby, entry 94 28 August
6. **Margaret Shereane**, 52, Glossop, Holy Trinity, West Kirby, entry 95 28 August
7. **Elizabeth Jackson**, 5, Sheffield, buried Holy Trinity, West Kirby, entry 97 29 August
8. **John Atkinson**, 33, Bradford, found near lightship 16 September, currier, inquest 19 September ID'd by brother William from Clayton near Bradford, buried 20 September St Michael's, Pitt Street, Liverpool, entry 3805
9. **John Ashbrook**, 46 Lumber-street, found near lightship, buried St Mary's, Liverpool, entry1294/5/6 (unsure which)
10. **Samuel Fielding**, 60-70, picked up with William Scambro by Orion steamer east of Ormshead
11. **William Scambro**, 60, picked up with Samuel Fielding by Orion steamer east of Ormshead
12. **James Healy**, 42, West Kirby, Holy Trinity, of 22 Greenough Place, Woodward Street, Manchester

13. **William Pawson**, 19, Leeds, buried in Birkenhead entry 790, picked up opposite river Dee by Royal Sovereign, inquest 7 September then buried
14. **Elizabeth Steele**, washed up near Norbreck, 8 September
15. **John Curly** – or Charles? – washed up at Heysham, near Morecambe, 8 September, buried 10 September Heysham entry 465
16. **Joseph Blaydon**, 25/28, Birmingham, buried 12 September entry 803, St Peter's, Formby
17. **Daniel Pollard**, 30, Huddersfield, found at Southport 9 September buried with eleven others 11 September Christ Church, Southport
18. **? Spencer**, 45-50, found at Southport 9 September, buried with eleven others 11 September Christ Church, Southport
19. **Jane Murtorphey/Mantagh/Mentagh/Murtagh**, 18, Ireland, washed up at Lytham 9 September, buried with eleven others 11 September Christ Church, Southport
20. **Alice Wrigley**, 26, Bolton, buried 9 September, All Hallows, Bispham, entry 503
21. **James Smith Bacon**, recovered at Abergele 10 September and buried there in St Michael's graveyard then reinterred Abney Park Cemetery, London
22. **Richard Cummings**, 38, found floating near North-west lightship 11 September
23. **Samuel Pollard Saile**, 22, buried Southport Christ Church 11 September entry 462
24. **Esther Jackson**, 29/30, Sheffield, buried 14 September, entry 3803 St Michael's, Pitt Street, Liverpool, found 11 September by Vale of Clwyd steamer
25. **Sarah Thompson**, 25, Liverpool, picked up 12 September by schooner George
26. **Jane Roberts**, 36, 13 September found dead on shore opposite Great Crosby and buried St Helen, Sefton, then reinterred with brother at St Mary's, Birkenhead, 18 September
27. **James Ronayne**, 48, from Manchester, buried Llandysillis, Caernarvon, entry 573 14 September
28. **Joseph Shaw**, 30, Glossop, buried Llandysillis, Caernarvon, entry 372[?572?]
29. **Emma Bell**, 40, Walter Street, Manchester, buried 13 Oct entry 3809 St Michael's, Pitt Street, Liverpool

Using the details included in contemporary newspapers, I have tentatively identified the anonymous remains of six individuals but there is no way to prove this conclusively either way after so long.

1. **Mrs Mantagh/Mentagh/Murtagh/Murtorphey**, 20, washed up at Lytham 8 September, buried 9 September probably at St Cuthbert, Lytham
2. **Winifred Keegan**, 45, washed ashore at Formby 8 September, buried 12 September at St Peter's, Formby either entry 806 or 807
3. **Mary Ann Anderson**, 24, found at Southport, buried with eleven others 11 September Christ Church, Southport
4. **Rebecca Hill**, 36, recovered at Abergele 10 September, buried in St Michael's graveyard
5. **Arthur Muldoon**, 24, recovered at Abergele 10 September, buried in St Michael's graveyard
6. **Jane Roper**, 2 or 3, of Bilston, Birmingham, recovered from water and died on boat, buried Llandysillo 28 August

Appendix 3 – medals list

There were a number of medals, honours, and rewards given to rescuers. The accuracy of records available online vary, so this list should be approached with caution and viewed as incomplete. A fellow researcher has raised the possibility that Frederick Jerome did not receive the gold medal many sources claim he was awarded, and instead chose a monetary reward. If anyone has any information regarding the medals or any other aspect of this episode in history I would really appreciate hearing about it at gillhoffs@hotmail.co.uk or via the publisher.

Admiral Grenfell was awarded the Liverpool Shipwreck and Humane Society Marine Medal in gold, inscribed with the words, '[T]o Admiral Grenfell for assisting in saving the People from the conflagration of the Ocean Monarch, 24th March 1848'. Similar gold medals were awarded to **Thomas Littledale** of the *Queen of the Ocean*, **Captain Joaquim Marques Lisboa** of the *Afonso*, **Captain George Dani** of the *Prince of Wales*, and **Frederick Jerome** of the *New World*. **Captain Knight** of the *New World* was offered the gold medal but declined it.

The Liverpool Shipwreck and Humane Society Marine Medal in silver of the first class was awarded to officers of the *Afonso*: **Commander Francisco Xavier d'Alcantia** and **Lieutenants Genuino Auguste de Barros Torrias, Jose da Costa Agevedo, Joaquim Lucio A'Aranjo,** and **Francisco Leopoldo Cabral da Cunto e Teive**; also to **Jotham Bragdon**, chief mate of the *Ocean Monarch*. This medal, in silver of the second class, was awarded to seamen of the *Afonso*: **Francisco da Silva, Joav Candido, Marques Garcia,** and **Justiso Jose**. A silver medal was also awarded to **James Batty**, mate of the *Prince of Wales*.

Seamen from the *Ocean Monarch* who were singled out for particular praise included **William Warwick**, **William Roberts**, **Philander Stewart**, **Robert Gleninning**, **Daniel Wilder**, and **James Stockwell**. The Massachusetts Humane Society awarded each man with a medal worth $10 for their bravery.

Recognition and money were also given, in varying amounts, to other sailors involved with the massive rescue operation, such as Mate **William Edward Baalham** and seamen **William Strand**, **George W. Rossiter**, **William Grove** and **Edward H. Coe/Cox** of the *New World*. They crewed the boat that braved the waters beside the burning ship for seven hours, along with the vessel commanded by boatswain **Thomas Forbes**, which carried seamen **Henry Curtis/Carter**, **Edward Dugdale**, **William Johnson**, and **Frederick Jerome**. There were many presents, dinners, and much deserved celebrations for the people involved in saving so many lives that day. A fraction of the rewards received are listed here, and I should also point out that many of the people involved with the rescue and the aftermath remain unsung heroes and their omission from this book is in no way deliberate. All deserve recognition and to be remembered.

'The Cambridge Conundrum' – **William Edward Baalham** of Liverpool was awarded a silver medal worth $20 by the Massachusetts Humane Society, as was boatswain **Thomas Forbes**. An oval brass medal was also inscribed with the words, 'The Massachusetts Humane Society, to Wm. E. Baalham, Officer of Ship New World who by his gallant efforts was successful in rescuing many persons from the ship Ocean Monarch, burnt at sea, Aug. 24th. 1848.' This replica was apparently found in summer 1926 30ft above the ground, on a ledge on the arch which connects the Old Library and the west block of Third Court at the University of Cambridge. The metal was still bright, suggesting it had not been there long. If anyone can help solve 'the Cambridge Conundrum' please get in touch!

Names list

This list includes names drawn from newspaper accounts, memoirs, and lists published in the press of the time. Where it has been possible to connect alternate spellings or names to one person I have done so, but there are likely to be names here which do not belong to anyone on board because, for example, a friend or relative made the initial booking in their own name rather than that of the party travelling on the *Ocean Monarch* that day. Captain Murdock said there were 338 passengers altogether. There are 436 individuals listed here so approximately a hundred names more than there should be. I have included a '+' sign next to their details if their presence on the ship is corroborated, names in bold indicate survival, and '*Sunbeam*' is included if they took the replacement voyage offered on that ship. Where possible, I have also noted which vessel rescued each person and any other details such as who they were travelling with and where they came from, along with age, job, and marital status. This is the most complete list possible at this moment in time but I hope to hear from more descendants and researchers and continue to amend as necessary.

1. Allen, Margaret – lost
2. Anderson, Mary Ann, 24 – lost
3. **Anderson, Mrs – lady of Dr Anderson, formerly Miss Hardwicke of Wisbech**
4. Anderson, Thomas, 5 – lost
5. Ashbrook, John – 46 Lumber-street, body recovered +
6. Atherton/Hatherton, Elizabeth, 15m, no sign of similarly named family – lost +
7. Atkinson, John, 30/33, Bradford, joiner recently doing business in North-street – lost +
8. **Bannister, Elisha (Elijah?) – rescued with Freckleton & Walker +**
9. **Bannon, Peter, 40, Sunbeam +**

10. Banson/Bansom, William, 20 – lost
11. Baring/Barry, Johanna, 25, Tralee, Ireland – lost
12. Barker, George – lost
13. Bell, Eliza(beth), 20 – lost
14. Bell, Emma, 40 – husband survived, ticket booked with Joseph Kelly, body recovered – lost +
15. **Bell, John, 41 – turner/machine maker, 13 Walker/Walter Street, Manchester, worked at Fairbairn's, lost wife Emma (no kids), going to America in search of work +**
16. **Bell, William**
17. **Blamire, Sarah, 37, widow, sister to Thomas Chadwick, tailor, Bridge- street, Leeds – travelling with 2 nieces and nephew, Edwin Neesom, Sarah Summersgill, and Jane Neesom +**
18. Blyden/Bladon, Joseph, 28, Birmingham – body washed ashore at Formby Point 8-9-48, inquest 12-9-48, buried with 4 others that day in Formby Churchyard – lost +
19. **Booker, Edwin, 18, Sheffield +**
20. **Booker, James, 61, Bent's Green, Ecclesall, Sheffield, farmer, wife stayed home, hands burnt +**
21. **Booker, Mary, 24/27, Sheffield +**
22. Brady, Patrick, 8 – lost
23. Brenihan, Jeremiah (Brenhiam, Hugh – lost) (Brasson, Jeremiah – lost)
24. **Brettall, Jane, 41, Sunbeam +**
25. **Brettall, Thomas, 44, Sunbeam +**
26. **Brisnall, Jeremiah/Jerry/John, 30, Mitchelstown, Ireland, Sunbeam +**
27. Brown, infant? – lost
28. **Brown, Frederick, 4**
29. **Brown, Henry/Mary**
30. **Brown, John, 30**
31. Brown, Leah, 30? – lost
32. Brown, Thomas, 8? – lost
33. Brown, William, 45 – lost
34. **Burns, Dennis, 24**
35. **Burns, Eliza, 22**

36. Burns, Mary – lost
37. Buttan, Mary – lost
38. Butterworth, Joseph, 30 – lost
39. **Callaghan, Abby**
40. **Callaghan, Ann**
41. Callaghan, Dennis, 50, Tralee, Ireland – lost
42. **Callaghan, Ellen**
43. Callaghan, John, 14, Tralee, Ireland – lost
44. Callaghan, Nora/Norry (daughter), Tralee, Ireland – lost
45. Callaghan, Susan, 19 – lost
46. **Carey/Carby, Mary, 14, Sunbeam +**
47. **Carling, Dennis**
48. **Carney/Carey, Johanna/Joanna, 27**
49. **Carney/Carey, Margaret**
50. **Cary, Mary, Thurles, Co Tipperary, Ireland – Queen of the Ocean +**
51. Cashman, Darby, 7 – lost +
52. Cashman, Edmund, 2 – lost +
53. Cashman, Mary, 20 (mum, Mary, 39, saved) – lost +
54. **Cashman, Mary, 39 (5 children lost) +**
55. Cashman, Maurice, 5 – lost +
56. Cashman, Nancy, 10 – lost +
57. Clark, Catherine, 19 – lost
58. Clark, Isabella, 6 – lost
59. Clark, Mary, 23 – lost
60. Coombs/Coombes/Combs/Cambs, John, 20, Liverpool, dad ran a shoe shop there – lost
61. Condon, Eugene, 27, Mitchelstown, Ireland – lost
62. **Connor, James, 20, Sunbeam +**
63. **Constantine, Ann, 47, Sunbeam +**
64. **Constantine, Thomas, 49, Sunbeam +**
65. **Corcoran/Cochrane, Dennis, 21, Sunbeam – Queen of the Ocean +**
66. **Coxe, Mary Anna, 3 – picked up by New World with aunt and taken to New York +**
67. **Coxe, Peter, 25 – +**

68. Coxe, Rachel, 25 – lost with infant, 6m +
69. Coxe, 6m – lost with mother +
70. Coybry/Coyley, Timothy, 40 – lost
71. Coyle, Catherine, 25 – lost
72. **Crawley/Crowley, husband Edward, Killarney, sister lost +**
73. **Crawley/Crowley, wife Ellen, Killarney, sister lost +**
74. **Crook, Mary, 40 – picked up by New World with niece and taken to New York +**
75. Cuddy/Cudy, Acles, 16 – lost
76. **Cullin, Jeffrey**
77. Curley/Curohy, Edward, 30 – lost
78. Curley/Curohy, Ellen, 30 – lost
79. Curley/Curohy, Owen, 21 – lost
80. Curly, John, body washed up – lost
81. **Curran, Dominick, 20/32**
82. **Darwin/Darwen/Durven/Devine, Bridget/Betty, 47, Sunbeam +**
83. **Darwin/Darwen/Durven/Devine, infant girl, Sunbeam +**
84. **Darwin/Darwen/Durven/Devine, James, 47, Sunbeam +**
85. Deacon, Alice, 27 – lost
86. Delanham/Delangham, Patrick, 26 – lost
87. **Denny, Mary**
88. **Dohaghan, Mary (a child, its mother lost) +**
89. **Dolan, John, 18, Sunbeam +**
90. **Dolan/Doran/Deran, Edward, 20, Sunbeam +**
91. **Dolan/Doran/Deran, John, 18, Ireland, Sunbeam +**
92. **Donnelly, Arthur, 60, Loughgall, Co. Armagh, Sunbeam – Prince of Wales +**
93. **Donnelly, Betsy/Betty, 60, Loughgall, Co. Armagh, Sunbeam +**
94. **Donnelly, Catherine 'Kate', 18, Loughgall, Co. Armagh, Sunbeam +**
95. **Donnelly, John, Loughgall, Co. Armagh +**
96. **Donnelly, Patrick, 20, Loughgall, Co. Armagh, Sunbeam +**
97. Donohue/Donoghue, Darby, 20, Tralee, Ireland – lost
98. **Donovan, Betsey**
99. **Donovan, Eliza**

100. Dougherty/Doherty, John, 40 – lost
101. Dougherty/Doherty, Martin, 35 – lost
102. **Druen/Dinan/Durran/Dimeen, Mary, 18, Killarney, Ireland – Prince of Wales +**
103. Drury/Drumry, James, 11, Mitchelstown, Ireland – lost
104. Drury/Drumry, Julia, 48, Mitchelstown, Ireland – lost
105. Duneen/Drinan, Mary, Killarney or Tralee, Ireland – listed as both saved and lost
106. Dunning, Julia, body recovered – lost
107. Durgen, Catherine – could this be the child Mary Dohogan's mum lost? – lost
108. **Dwyer/Davis, William, Mitchelstown, Ireland**
109. **Dwyer/Dwyn, Catherine, 25, Mitchelstown, Cork, Ireland – Prince of Wales +**
110. **Ellis, Mary, 40, Mitchelstown, Ireland**
111. Fanning, Michael, 25 – lost
112. Fielding, Anne/Anna, 60 – lost
113. **Fielding/Fielden, Samuel, Glossop, 60/65/70, fustian weaver, Sunbeam – Prince of Wales – severely burnt hands, last alive off wreck +**
114. Fielding, Samuel, Glossop, 60-70, lost, body recovered +
115. Finan, Bridget, 25 – lost
116. Finan, Mary Ann, 25 – lost
117. Finan, Mary, 4 – lost
118. **Fisher, Henry, 20 +**
119. Fisher, Sarah, 25 – lost
120. **Fleming/Flemming, John, 20, Killarney, Sunbeam – 'lamenting an aged father missing' +**
121. **Fleming/Flemming, Michael, 40, Killarney +**
122. **Flood, Bridget, 12**
123. **Flood, Catherine, 15, Sunbeam +**
124. Flood/Floyd, Margaret, 15 (daughter) – lost
125. Flood/Floyd, Margaret, 45 – lost
126. **Freckleton/Frickleton, John, 22 – rescued with Bannister and Walker +**
127. **Gaffney/Goffney, Bridget, 20, Sunbeam +**

128. Gaffney/Goffney, Mary, 13 – lost
129. **Gallavin/Galvin, Julia/Juliet, 20, Tralee, Ireland, Sunbeam – travelling with Nora/Norry +**
130. Galvin, Nora/Norry, 32, Tralee, Ireland, travelling with Julia Galvin – lost +
131. George, John, 33 – lost
132. **Gibney, Ann(e), 20, Sunbeam +**
133. **Gilliat, Mrs – daughter of late Mrs Morris, Wisbech, 3 children died +**
134. **Gleeson, Catherine, 20, Ireland**
135. **Gleeson, Daniel, 20, Ireland, Sunbeam +**
136. Gleeson, infant – lost
137. Gleeson, infant – lost
138. **Gleeson, John, 40, Mitchelstown, Ireland**
139. Gleeson, Mary Ann, 24 – lost
140. **Gleeson, Michael, 15, Mitchelstown, Ireland, Sunbeam – other injuries plus severe laceration to hand +**
141. Gleeson, Philip, 3 – lost
142. Gleeson/Gleesod, Ann – lost
143. Gleeson/Gleesod, Mary – lost
144. Glyn(ne), Hugh, 30 – lost
145. Gormly, Margaret, 17 – lost
146. Grayson/Grason, Ann, 20 – lost
147. Grayson/Grason, Catherine, 18 – lost
148. Green, Rosanna, 25 – lost
149. **Greenhouse/Greenough, William, 20 – gave evidence at pilot inquiry +**
150. **Grillin/Griffin, Patrick, 20, Sunbeam – Queen of the Ocean +**
151. Guffie, Patrick – lost
152. Hall, Thomas – lost
153. Halloran, Margaret, 12 – lost
154. **Halloran/Holloran, Sarah, 12, Ireland, Sunbeam +**
155. Hamon, John – lost
156. Hanley/Hanly, Murthy, 20 – lost
157. Hanlon, William – lost
158. **Hannah/Hannon/Hamon, John, 24, Sunbeam +**

159. **Harwood, James, 32**
160. **Headley/Hardley/Hurdley, Edward, 20**
161. **Healing/Healy/Healey/Haley/Hally, Thomas, 20, Mitchelstown, Ireland**
162. Hely/Hiley, James, 41 – iron founder, wife and five children residing near Manchester – lost +
163. Henry, James, 20 – lost
164. Hill, Rebecca, 36, Rochdale – lost +
165. **Hill, Sarah Ann, 9, Rochdale – mum, Rebecca Hill, 36, unaccounted for – Prince of Wales +**
166. **Hill, Sophia, 8, Rochdale – mum, Rebecca Hill, 36, unaccounted for – Prince of Wales +**
167. **Hooker, Ellinor/Eleanor**
168. **Hooker, James**
169. **Hooker, Mary**
170. **Horridge, John – Queen of the Ocean +**
171. **Howard, Henry**
172. **Hughes, Edward – lost one child +**
173. **Hughes, Eliza, 26 (wife) +**
174. **Hughes, Emanuel, 27**
175. **Hughes, infant – might be Samuel? +**
176. Hughes, John, 14 – lost
177. Hughes, Mary – lost
178. **Hughes, Samuel, 35 – separate pair**
179. **Hughes, Samuel?**
180. Jackson, Elizabeth, 5, Pinstone Street, Sheffield – body found, back of head damaged – lost +
181. Jackson, Esther/Sarah, 30/29, Pinstone Street, Sheffield – husband survived – body found – lost +
182. Jackson, Richard, 19m, Pinstone Street, Sheffield – lost +
183. Jackson, William 'Willy', 4, Pinstone Street, Sheffield – body found – lost +
184. **Jackson, William, 30, Pinstone Street, Sheffield, pawn broker, family lost, picked up by Sea Queen and taken to New York +**
185. Johnson, Jane – lost
186. Johnson, John, 23 – lost

187. Johnson, Mary – lost
188. Johnson, Thomas – lost
189. **Jones, Edward, 48, Sunbeam – small farmer from Irlam, Manchester, lost wife Mary and £60 +**
190. **Jones, George, from Bilston, Wolverhampton – married 15 August 1848, St Leonards, Bilston, Wolverhampton +**
191. Jones, Jane, 20 – lost
192. **Jones, Leodosia, from Bilston, Wolverhampton– married 15 August 1848, St Leonards, Bilston, Wolverhampton +**
193. Jones, Mary, body recovered (Edward's wife) – lost +
194. Jones, Thomas, 30 – lost
195. Kay(e), Mrs, 26 – lost
196. Kay(e), Thomas, 27 – lost
197. Kealing/Keating, Nora/Norry/Mary, 30, Tralee, Ireland – lost
198. Keegan/Keogan, Winifred, 45 – body recovered, ticket with Rosey Mulrooney, 16, on it too – lost +
199. **Kegan/Kean/Keeghan, Michael, 35/25**
200. **Kelleher/Killeher/Relleher, Ellen, 30, Sunbeam +**
201. **Kelleher/Killeher/Relleher, girl infant, Sunbeam +**
202. Kelly, Edward, 31, Tralee, Ireland – lost
203. **Kelly, Kelley, John, 36, from Tralee or Killarney, Co Kerry, Sunbeam – Queen of the Ocean, travelling with Edward Kelly +**
204. **Kelly, Thomas**
205. **Kelly/Kelley, Johannah, 18, from Killarney, Co Kerry, Sunbeam – Prince of Wales +**
206. **Kershaw, Ann/Emma Ann, 2, Sunbeam +**
207. **Kershaw, infant (duplicate?)**
208. **Kershaw, Margaret, nearly drowned, suffering from immersion in water (actually Martha?) +**
209. **Kershaw, Martha, 38, Sunbeam**
210. **Kershaw, Mary Ann, 2 (duplicate?)**
211. Kilby/Kelly, Catherine, 18, Tralee, Ireland – lost
212. **Kilmartin/Kilmarton, Daniel, 30, Sunbeam +**
213. **Leary, Catherine, 7/8, Tralee, Ireland, Sunbeam – taken naked on board Afonso with brother, aunt Joanna might have been on Sunbeam too +**

214. **Leary, Daniel, 12/11, Tralee, Ireland, Sunbeam – taken naked on board Afonso with sister, aunt Joanna might have been on Sunbeam too +**
215. **Lester/Lister/Leavy, James, 16 – initially reported lost, siblings from Sleaford, Lincolnshire +**
216. **Lester/Lister/Leavy, Mary Ann, 28 – initially reported lost, siblings from Sleaford, Lincolnshire +**
217. **Lester/Lister/Leavy, Thomas, 32, Sunbeam – initially reported lost, siblings from Sleaford, Lincolnshire +**
218. **Lloyd/Loyd, Margaret, 22**
219. **Lloyd/Loyd, William, 25**
220. Lowes, Neville – lost
221. **Lynch, Michael, 21, Sunbeam +**
222. **Maher/Mohan/McMahon, James M., 20, Sunbeam +**
223. **Martin, Peter**
224. **Martin, William**
225. Marvety/Mavity, wife – lost
226. Marvety/Mavity, William, 24 – lost
227. Maxwell, Mary, 20 – lost
228. Maxwell, Robert, 46 – lost
229. **McAdams, Patrick, Ireland, saved – maybe from Co. Armagh area +**
230. **McCartney/McCarthy/McCartley, Ann**
231. **McCartney/McCarthy/McCartley, Daniel, 26**
232. **McClellan(d), Elizabeth, 32**
233. **McClellan(d), James, 16**
234. **McClellan(d), Jane Ann, 19**
235. **McCombs/McCoombs – on board Pilot Queen of Chester +**
236. **McCurran, Daniel**
237. **McDonell, John**
238. **McDonell, Mary, 24, Sunbeam +**
239. McEvoy, Jane, 25 – lost
240. McEvoy, Mary, 4 – lost
241. **McFall, John, 24, Sunbeam +**
242. McGee, Mary/Margaret, 20 – lost
243. **McGuinn/McGuire, Catherine**

244. **McGuinn/McGuire, William, 27, Sunbeam +**
245. **McGuinn/McGuire/Maguire, Mary, 18, Co Cavan, Ireland – Queen of the Ocean +**
246. **McLoughlin, John, 20, Sunbeam +**
247. **McMahon, Patrick – Queen of the Ocean +**
248. **McMahon, James Joseph, 20 – fleeing Ireland with a price on his head +**
249. **McManus, Ann, 20, Sunbeam +**
250. **McManus, Patrick, 20 – Queen of the Ocean +**
251. **Mills, William**
252. **Molan/Molin/Maulin, Davis, 11, Mitchelstown, Cork**
253. **Molan/Molin/Maulin, Ellen, 13, Mitchelstown, Cork**
254. **Molan/Molin/Maulin, Johanna, Mitchelstown, Cork**
255. **Molan/Molin/Maulin, John, 9, Mitchelstown, Cork, Sunbeam +**
256. **Molan/Molin/Maulin, William, 42, Mitchelstown, Cork, Sunbeam – Prince of Wales +**
257. **Monahan/Minnahan/Minihan/Minham/Moynahan, Humphrey, 20, Tralee, Ireland, Sunbeam +**
258. **Monahan/Minnahan/Minihan/Minham/Moynahan, Johanna, 20, Tralee, Ireland, Sunbeam +**
259. **Monahan/Minnahan/Minihan/Minham/Moynahan, Maurice, 20, Sunbeam +**
260. Moyuch/Moynch/Moynah, John, 17 – lost
261. Muldoon, Arthur, 24 – body recovered, lost +
262. Muldoon, child – lost
263. Muldoon, June – lost
264. Muldoon, Margaret, 20
265. **Mullaw, Johanna (duplicate?)**
266. Mullong, Betsey/Betsy – lost
267. Mulvoney/Mulroney/Mulrooney, Rosey, 16 – lost
268. **Murphy, Patrick, 25, Sunbeam +**
269. **Murray/Murry, John, 26**
270. Murtagh, Jane, 18 – body recovered, lost +
271. **Murtagh/Mentagh, James, 24, Sunbeam, wife died, body recovered +**

272. **Murtagh/Mentagh, John, 1, Sunbeam, mum died, body recovered +**
273. Murtagh/Mentagh, Mrs, 20, body recovered – lost +
274. Murty, William – lost
275. **Nangle, James, 25, Sunbeam +**
276. Neelson/Neesom, Mrs Sarah, 44 – lost
277. **Neesom, Edward/Edwin, 19/17, stuff presser, son of Joseph Neesom, press-setter, Marsh-lane, Leeds – travelling with cousins and aunt Mrs Blamire +**
278. Neesom, Jane, 17 – accompanying aunt Mrs Blamire and 2 cousins, all 3 saved, dad Joseph Neesom, press-setter, Marsh-lane, Leeds – lost +
279. **Neesom/Summersgill, Sarah, 16/17, daughter of late Thomas Summersgill, pattern dyer, Sussex-street, Bank, Leeds – travelling with cousins and aunt Mrs Blamire +**
280. Nesbitt/Nesbith/Nesbett, Mary Ann, 20/26 – lost
281. Nolan, James/Jane, 22 – lost
282. Nolan, Margaret, 18 – lost
283. Nolan, Nancy, 17 – lost
284. **O'Brien, James, 15, Sunbeam +**
285. O'Connor, Daniel, 30 – lost
286. O'Connor, Mary, 28, his wife – lost
287. **O'Hara, Bridget (Biddy), 18, Sunbeam, travelling with Catherine O'Hara lost +**
288. O'Hara, Catherine, 20, Bridget (Biddy) O'Hara saved – lost
289. **Orange, John Baptist, 25 +**
290. **Orange, William (?probably misrecorded JBO)**
291. **Oregan, Patrick – Queen of the Ocean +**
292. **Orrell/Owell, Louis/Lewis, 25, Sunbeam +**
293. **Oulton/Outlan/Outlaw, Andrew, 20, Dublin, Sunbeam – possibly Andrew Newton Oulton of 36 Dame Street +**
294. Parker, George, 14 – lost
295. Parkinson, Elizabeth – lost
296. Parkinson, Esther – lost
297. Parkinson, infant – lost
298. Parkinson, William – lost

299. Pawson, William, 19, boot closer, father Joseph Pawson who keeps White Lion Inn, Quarry Hill, Leeds, and wrote about bereavement, sister Jane Roberts lost too – lost +
300. Pollard, Daniel, Huddersfield, about 30, body recovered – lost +
301. **Pollard, Sarah, 20**
302. Pollensale/Pollinseale/Pollinarate, Samuel, 21 – lost
303. Quinn, another son – lost
304. Quinn, Mary – lost
305. Quinn, son – lost
306. **Quirk/Quick, Michael/Patrick, 39, Mitchelstown, Ireland**
307. **Radcliff/Ratcliffe, James (Jim), 22, Salford, Manchester – big brother of Chartist Joe Radcliff/Ratcliffe, earlier hidden in hold then arrested and removed – Prince of Wales +**
308. Regan, Bridget – lost
309. **Regan/Ryan, Catherine, 18, Mitchelstown, Ireland, Sunbeam – in Missouri with PR? +**
310. **Regan/Ryan, Mary, 20, Mitchelstown, Ireland, Sunbeam +**
311. **Regan/Ryan, Michael, 20, Sunbeam +**
312. **Regan/Ryan, Patrick, 23, Mitchelstown, Ireland, Sunbeam – in Missouri with Catherine Ryan? +**
313. **Reynolds, Ann, 20, Sunbeam – Thomas, 20, lost +**
314. **Reynolds, Catherine, 7, Sunbeam +**
315. **Reynolds, James, 12, Sunbeam +**
316. **Reynolds, Thomas, 10, Sunbeam +**
317. Reynolds, Thomas, 20 – rest of family survived – lost +
318. **Reynolds, William, 3, Sunbeam +**
319. Roberts, Jane, 20/25 – married George Roberts, Leeds, 2q 1848, brother William Pawson (also lost) – going to Boston then Staffordtown, New Hampshire, to join husband – body buried – lost +
320. **Rodgers, Edward**
321. Ronayn(e)/Ronan/Rowen/Rooney, Catherine, 11, Manchester – lost +
322. Ronayn(e)/Ronan/Rowen/Rooney, Eliza, 9, Manchester – lost +
323. Ronayn(e)/Ronan/Rowen/Rooney, James, 48, Manchester – lost +
324. Ronayn(e)/Ronan/Rowen/Rooney, Margaret, 48, Manchester – lost +
325. Ronayn(e)/Ronan/Rowen/Rooney, Margaret/Mary/Jane, 17, Manchester – lost +

326. **Rooney/Ronayn(e)/Ronan/Rowen, Joanna/Johanna, 28, Manchester – rest of family lost – Prince of Wales +**
327. **Rourke/Rowk, Michael, 25**
328. **Routh/Ruth, Ellen, 26, Sunbeam +**
329. **Routh/Ruth, Michael, 26, Ireland, Sunbeam – ?farmer in Marengo, Illinois +**
330. **Ryder, Daniel/Samuel, 27, Sunbeam – Jane lost? +**
331. Ryder, Jane, 27 – lost
332. Sale(s)/Sail(e), Samuel Pollard, 22 – brother of James Sale(s)/Sail – lost +
333. Sale/Sales/Sail(e), James, 24 – lost? +
334. **Sale/Sales/Sail(e), Mrs Mary, 24 – much contused +**
335. Sale/Sales/Sail(e), Sarah, only child of James and Mary, lost? +
336. **Sanders, William, 26, Sunbeam +**
337. **Savage, Frederick**
338. **Sayers, Jeremiah – poem to raise money for them**
339. **Sayers, Jerome – poem to raise money for them**
340. **Sayers, Thomas – poem to raise money for them**
341. Scambro/Scamborough/Scanlon/Scanlan/Scanlore, William, 60 – body washed up – lost +
342. Shaw, Joseph, 30, Glossop, buried Llandysillis, Caernarvon – lost +
343. **Sheard/Shread/Surr/Shurr, Joseph, 22/24, Huddersfield, handloom weaver – alleged murder victim +**
344. **Shearon/Sheene/Sherwen/Sherne, Edward, 50, Glossop – wife (Margaret?) also passenger, unsure if lost, gave evidence at inquest: slid down a rope from poop to rope, Batty threw rope, put him on board Prince of Wales +**
345. Shearon/Sheene/Sherwen/Sherne, Margaret, 50, wife of Edward, from Glossop – lost +
346. Shore, Edwin/Edward, 4 – mum Emma lived, dad in USA – lost +
347. **Shore, Emma, 37, Glossop – lost two children before leaving to join husband in USA and two in wreck +**
348. Shore, Sarah Ann, 9 – mum Emma lived, dad in USA – lost +
349. Smith, Ann, 18 – lost
350. Smith, Ellen, 14 – lost
351. Smith, infant – lost

352. Smith, Margaret, 15 – lost
353. **Smith, Mary, 10 – Sunbeam +**
354. **Smith, Peter, 18, Sunbeam – Queen of the Ocean +**
355. Smith, Peter, 19 – lost
356. Smith, Thomas, 8 – lost
357. **Smith/Smyth, Mary Ann, 20 – sought by Harnden & Co. in NY, taken with Jackson +**
358. **Somerville, Sarah**
359. Spencer, Frances/Francis, 24 – lost
360. body recovered of married female Spencer 45-50 – lost +
361. Spencer, William, 22 – lost
362. Steele, Elizabeth – body washed up – lost +
363. Sullivan, Catherine – lost – probably the Irish speaking Kate age 3? Prince of Wales +
364. Sullivan, Darnby/Darby, 16, Mitchelstown, Ireland – lost
365. Sullivan, Ellen, 2 – lost
366. Sullivan, Geoffrey, 20, Mitchelstown, Ireland – lost
367. Sullivan, Johanna, 4 – lost
368. Sullivan, Nancy, 20, Mitchelstown, Ireland – lost
369. **Summersgill, John**
370. **Swallow, Elizabeth (Betty), 39, Huddersfield – probably a baker +**
371. **Swallow, Sarah +**
372. Taylor, George, 1y 10m – mum Mrs Ann Taylor, Number 1, Victoria Place, Leeds – lost +
373. **Taylor, Mary Ann, 25 – lost Sarah, 3y 9m, and George, 1y 10m, in wreck – of Number 1, Victoria Place, Buslingthorpe-lane, Leeds – children tied to waist. Drowned on way to see husband James in Oxford, Mass. +**
374. Taylor, Sarah, 3y 9m – mum Mrs Ann Taylor, Number 1, Victoria Place, Leeds – see her info – lost +
375. **Thompson, Charles, 32 – young seaman from Liverpool, travelling with wife and little girl, niece Alice Morris, 8, tied child to waist, died after ½ hour, wife too +**
376. **Thompson, Elizabeth, 45 +**
377. **Thompson, Henry, 12, Sunbeam +**

378. Thomson/Thompson, Alice, 8 – actually Alice Morris, niece of Charles? – lost +
379. Thomson/Thompson, Sarah, 25 – wife of Charles – lost +
380. Tierney, Bridget, 23, Omagh, Ireland – lost +
381. Tierney, Ellen, 55, Omagh, Ireland – son James is a labourer in Liverpool – inquest on body – lost +
382. **Tobin, Honora, 34**
383. **Tobin, Johanna, 26 – single, heading for Boston, evidence at inquest, sister Mary died +**
384. Tobin, Mary, 38 – going to Boston with sister Johanna, inquest on body – lost +
385. **Tomlinson, George, 25 – moulder from 11 Chatham-street, Leeds, naked in sea ½ hour +**
386. Towns/Towers, William, 33 – lost
387. **Walker, James, 22 – rescued with Bannister and Freckleton +**
388. **Warburton, Elizabeth, 20 +**
389. Warburton, George, 18 – lost +
390. Warburton, infant (with Mary) – lost +
391. **Warburton, John, 50 – (children?) George, Mary, and infant lost +**
392. Warburton, Mary, 21 – lost +
393. **Warburton, Mary, 46, Bury – rescued from the mast, stayed with bereaved Mary Ann Taylor at Mr Whalley's Three Legs of Man Inn, Red Cross Street +**
394. Ward, Edward, 8 – lost +
395. Ward, Eliza(beth), 24 – Sarah Anne and Edward lost +
396. Ward, Sarah Ann(e), 9 – lost +
397. **Welch/Walsh, Richard**
398. **Wells/Wills, William**
399. **White, Henry, 21, Sunbeam +**
400. Willis/Wills, wife, 30 – lost
401. Willis/Wills, William, 48 – lost
402. Wilson, Catherine – Joshua's wife? – lost +
403. Wilson, infant – could it belong to Joshua W that survived? – lost +
404. Wilson, James, 26 – lost
405. **Wilson, Joshua – Berkeley Street, Strangeways, Manchester – printer who tied wife and child together but lost both when he lost hold of the rope +**

406. Winstanley, James, 27 – lost
407. **Woods, Catherine, 17, Sunbeam +**
408. **Woods, Frances, 18, Sunbeam +**
409. **Wrigglesworth, Peter, 25/6, Leeds – heckler, Bank, Leeds +**
410. Wrigley/Winsley, Alice, 26, Bolton/Bury, originally Gigg, Scotland, wife of James Winsley, grave – lost +
411. Wynn(e), Mary, 24 – lost

The stewards and stewardesses and other non-crew staff included:

1. Brown, David – cook – lost
2. Cumming, Richard, 38 – steward, body identified by wife Charlotte – lost
3. Cummings, Elizabeth – stewardess – lost
4. Douran, Joseph – second steward – lost

Cabin passengers: there were thirty-one 1st and 2nd cabin passengers altogether according to Captain Murdock, twenty-seven of whom are listed here so another four are probably not included in the correct section but to be found listed among the steerage passengers.

First class cabin passengers

1. **Dow, Alexander B., Glasgow – Afonso +**
2. **Dow, Jane Crawford, Glasgow – Afonso +**
3. **Ellis, William, Belfast – ship surgeon, MRCS – Pilot Queen +**
4. **Fellowes, James Knowlton, Lowell, Massachusetts – jeweller/watchmaker/philanthropist, Afonso +**
5. Graham, daughter, 9, Manchester – lost, AKA 'Andrews' – Walter, Mary, 9 +
6. Graham, Mr, Manchester – lost, AKA 'Andrews' – Bacon, James Smith, London +
7. Graham, Mrs, Manchester – lost, AKA 'Andrews' – Walter, Mary Ann nee Gudgeon, +
8. **Gregg, George, Salem +**
9. **McHenry, Thomas, Mobile, Alabama or Orleans, Ma. +**
10. **Southworth, Nathaniel, Boston – artist, d 23 April 1858 +**

Second class cabin passengers

1. **Bristow, Whiston Henry – formerly a clerk to Wm. Anderson, Sen., and Co., London – Queen of the Ocean +**
2. Bunning/Banning, Maria, Miss +
3. Howard, child, England +
4. Howard, Mrs, England +
5. Lynch, Geoffry/Jeffrey, 58, formerly of Drumon, Kerry, from Killarney, Ireland, lost – travelling with Murphy women, David Murphy (not travelling)'s mother and 3 sisters, mother and 1 sister lost – inquest on body +
6. Murphy, Ann, 30?, sister of David Murphy, Killarney – lost +
7. Murphy, Eliza(beth?) – b1806 if RC, Killarney, family of David Murphy? +
8. Murphy, Jane – family of David Murphy, Killarney? +
9. Murphy, mother or sister of David Murphy, Killarney, lost +
10. **Powell, J. Henry, 26, 52 Portman Place, Madianhill, London, merchant, wife lost? – Pilot Queen, Sunbeam +**
11. Powell, Mrs, 28 (lost?), 52 Portman Place, Madianhill, London +
12. Reynolds, Mrs +
13. Roper, Jane, 2/3, retrieved from water alive then died? – Prince of Wales +
14. **Roper, Lissy, 3/4 – Prince of Wales +**
15. **Roper, Hannah/Anna, Bilston, Birmingham – two children travelling with her – Queen of the Ocean – ill in hospital, 3yo returned to her after wreck +**
16. Shaw, Mrs – notice in paper, looking for her +
17. Siddall/Liddall, James, Maine +

Captain and crew (saved) forty-two crew including captain, according to Captain Murdock, so three remain unnamed here. NB, there is no sign of Richard Mattaign of mermaid-rescue fame online

1. Armand, Hugh, Liverpool – Prince of Wales – may have been a passenger rather than a crewman
2. Austin, Christopher J. – Queen of the Ocean

3. Bassett, Henry
4. Blodgett, William – Queen of the Ocean
5. Bragdon, Jotham, first officer
6. Bramen, Frederick
7. Brannon, Richard – Queen of the Ocean
8. Buckley, S., 2nd carpenter
9. Chiene/Cheyn, James
10. Christian, Christian – Queen of the Ocean
11. Colver, Henry – Queen of the Ocean
12. Gibb(s), William Perry, second officer
13. Gleninning/Glindining, Robert
14. Green, William
15. Gulliver, William
16. Hiller, Thomas – Queen of the Ocean
17. Jenkins, Edward E.
18. Jones, Adam AKA Woodman, Richard – Queen of the Ocean
19. Jones, Henry – Queen of the Ocean
20. Keeler, John – Queen of the Ocean
21. Locke, Charles Daniel, American – Queen of the Ocean
22. McLaughlin, John – Queen of the Ocean
23. Moody/Moray, Samuel – Queen of the Ocean
24. Moore, William James, carpenter – Queen of the Ocean
25. Murdock, James, Captain – Queen of the Ocean
26. Nason, Charles – Queen of the Ocean
27. Neland/Nelund, William R. – Queen of the Ocean
28. Ormrod, Henry
29. Pratt, W.H. – Queen of the Ocean
30. Quimby, Edward
31. Roberts, William – statement at inquest
32. Rogers, Edward
33. Stewart, Philander
34. Stockwell, Isaac – Queen of the Ocean
35. Stockwell, James
36. Sweet, Jonathan – Queen of the Ocean
37. Vain/Vane, George – Queen of the Ocean
38. Walker, William

39. Wallace, William
40. Warwick, William
41. Wilder, Daniel
42. Wilson, James

Select Bibliography

Newspapers

Anti-Slavery Bugle, 6 October 1848

Armagh Guardian, 4 September 1848

Belfast Commercial Chronicle, 30 August 1848

Belfast News-Letter, 29 August 1848

Belfast Protestant Journal, 8 July 1848

Bell's Life In London And Sporting Chronicle, 24 September 1848

Bell's New Weekly Messenger, 24 September 1848

Bolton Chronicle, 2 September, 9 September, 28 October, 25 November, 9 December 1848

Boston Post, 14 June 1847

Bristol Mercury, 30 September 1848

Cambridge Chronicle and Journal, 9 September 1848, 6 February 1904

Carnarvon and Denbigh Herald and North and South Wales Independent, 2 September 1848, 17 November 1849

Chester Chronicle, 8 September 1848

Cincinnati Enquirer, 10 July 1888

Coleraine Chronicle, 27 October 1849

Cork Examiner, 14 June, 28 June 1848

Derbyshire Advertiser and Journal, 2 April 1847

Dublin Evening Packet and Correspondent, 19 August 1848

Dublin Weekly Nation, 17 June 1848

Dumfries and Galloway Standard, 30 August 1848

Examiner, 16 September 1848

Freeman's Journal, 27 September 1847, 31 August 1848

Galway Vindicator, and Connaught Advertiser, 23 February 1848

Glasgow Herald, 28 August, 15 September, 10 November 1848, 23 April 1855

Gore's Liverpool General Advertiser, 31 August 1848

Halifax Guardian, 13 September 1848

Hampshire Advertiser, 9 September 1848
Hampshire Telegraph and Sussex Chronicle, 8 June 1899
Hull Advertiser and Exchange Gazette, 25 August 1848
Illustrated London News, 23 September 1848
John O'Groats Journal, 1 September, 29 September 1848
Kentish Gazette, 31 October 1848
Kentish Mercury, 29 January 1848
Lancaster Gazette, 2 September 1848
Leeds Intelligencer, 2 September, 9 September 1848
Leeds Mercury, 2 September 1848
Limerick Reporter, 5 September 1848
Liverpool Journal, 16 September 1848
Liverpool Mail, 29 August, 2 September 1848
Liverpool Mercury, 3 April 1846, 29 August, 2 September, 12 September 1848, 24 July 1849
London Daily News, 1 September 1848, 16 October 1849
London Evening Standard, 26 August 1848
Manchester Courier and Lancashire General Advertiser, 26 August, 23 September 1848, 27 January 1849
Manchester Times, 26 August 1848
Morning Advertiser, 2 February, 9 June, 1 September, 2 September 1848
Morning Chronicle, 4 September 1848
Morning Post, 28 August, 8 September, 18 November 1848
Newcastle Courant, 8 September 1848
North Wales Chronicle and Advertiser for the Principality, 29 August, 5 September 1848
Northampton Mercury, 8 February 1817, 28 October 1848
Northern Whig, 2 September 1848
Nottingham Review and General Advertiser for the Midland Counties, 8 September 1848
Preston Chronicle, 30 September 1848
Reading Mercury, 26 August 1848
Roscommon Messenger, 6 September 1848
Royal Cornwall Gazette, 8 September 1848
San Francisco Call, 16 August 1895
Sheffield Independent, 16 September, 21 October 1848

Southern Reporter and Cork Commercial Courier, 5 September 1848
Southport Visitor, 22 May 1851
Staffordshire Advertiser, 12 August 1848
Stamford Mercury, 6 June 1848
The Albion, 4 September 1848
The Crayon, 1 June 1858
The Dublin Evening Post, 8 February 1848
The Pilot, 19 June 1848
The Principality, 8 September, 20 October 1848
The Sailor's Magazine and Naval Journal (1848)
The Southern Reporter and Cork Commercial Courier, 5 September 1848
The Spectator, 26 August 1848
The Sumter Banner, 20 September 1848
The Tablet, 2 September 1848
The Times, 26 July 1848
The Welshman, 1 September, 15 September, 3 November 1848
Tuam Herald, 22 April 1848
United Service Gazette, 26 August 1848
Vermont Phoenix, 22 September 1848
Westmorland Gazette, 26 August 1848

Additional resources

Letter from Sir Charles Trevelyan to Lord Monteagle, 9 October 1846
St Luke's workhouse records, London (with thanks to researcher Maureen Thomas)
Andover workhouse inquiry, 1846
American Passenger Act of 1848, HC Deb 11 February 1848, Vol 96, cc536–41
The Transactions of the Provincial Medical and Surgical Association, Volume 18
Friends' Review, Vol. 1
The Burning of the ship Ocean Monarch, with a full account of Frederick Jerome, the noble-hearted sailor (etc.), G.E. and C.W. Kenworthy, New-York, 1848
Clyne, A., *Centenary of the Burning of the 'Ocean Monarch'*, Nautical Magazine v160 1948
Ellis, Len, *St Michael's Church, Abergele, A Guide to Early Gravestones circa 1667 to 1894*, 2016

Houston, F. and J., *Ships Afire at Sea*, Sea History 150, Spring 2015

Rowlands, T., *Atgofion am Llandudno (Recollections of Llandudno)* (pamphlet translated by T. Parry, 1893).

Houston, H. and A.F., *Mr Webster's Greatest Painter* (Historical New Hampshire, Spring/Summer 2001)

Coney, Helena, *Joseph Bladon and the Ocean Monarch Disaster* (self-published, CreateSpace, 2016)

Books

Aughton, P., *Liverpool: A people's history* (third edition, Carnegie Publishing Ltd., Lancaster, England, 2008).

Bolster, W. J., *Black Jacks: African American Seamen in the Age of Sail* (Harvard University Press, Cambridge, Massachusetts, London, England, 1997).

Chief Justice Cushing Chapter, D.A.R., *Old Scituate* (Earnshaw Press Corporation, Boston, Massachusetts, 1921).

Coleman, T., *Passage to America* (Hutchinson, 1972).

Coogan, T. P., *The Famine Plot* (Palgrave Macmillan, Hampshire, 2012).

Dean, G. & Evans, K., *Nelson's Heroes* (The Nelson Society, England, 1994).

Derby, J. C., *Fifty Years Among Authors, Books and Publishers* (Winter and Hatch, Connecticut, 1884).

Emerson, R. W., *The Letters of Ralph Waldo Emerson*, Volume 7 (edited by Tilton, E.M., Columbia University Press, New York, 1939).

Fellows, J. K., *Letters to the Press: For the Home Circle* (Vox Populi Press, Lowell, Massachusetts, 1885).

Fitzgerald, P., and Lambkin, B., *Migration in Irish History, 1607–2007* (Palgrave Macmillan, Hampshire, 2008).

Gamlin, H., *Twixt Mersey and Dee* (D. Marples & Co., Liverpool, 1897).

Green, Martin, *The Problem of Boston* (Longmans, London, 1966).

Handlin, Oscar, *Boston's Immigrants* (Belknap Press, USA, 1979 edition).

Hibbert, C., *The Illustrated London News: Social History of Victorian Britain* (Angus and Robertson, London, 1975).

Laxton, Edward, *The Famine Ships* (Bloomsbury Publishing, Great Britain, 1997).

Mangan, J. J. (ed), *Robert Whyte's 1847 Famine Ship Diary: The Journey of an Irish Coffin Ship* (Mercier Press, Ireland, 1994).

Morrison, Andrew, *The Industries of Cincinnati: Her Relations as a Centre of Trade; Manufacturing Establishments and Business Houses* (Metropolitan Publishing Company, Ohio, 1886).

Percival, J., *The Great Famine: Ireland's Potato Famine 1845-51* (BCA, London, 1995).

Pictorial Liverpool, (fourth edition, Liverpool, 1848)

Webber, S. G., *A Genealogy of the Southworths (Southards)* (The Fort Hill Press, Boston, Massachusetts, 1905).

Recommended sites

I couldn't have researched the people involved with any of the shipwrecks I write about without sites such as Ancestry, FindMyPast, British Newspaper Archive, Peter Higginbotham's Workhouses site and FindAGrave. Apart from the latter two, these are all pay-for-use sites but completely invaluable to any researcher. I am so glad – for many reasons – to live in the Age of the Internet.

Index